FROM
BOOM
TO
BUST

AND BEYOND

FROM
BOOM
TO
BUST
AND BEYOND

JERRY TUMA

EXcel
BOOKS
A STRANG COMPANY

Most STRANG COMMUNICATIONS BOOK GROUP products are available at special quantity discounts for bulk purchase for sales promotions, premiums, fund-raising, and educational needs. For details, write Strang Communications Book Group, 600 Rinehart Road, Lake Mary, Florida 32746, or telephone (407) 333-0600.

FROM BOOM TO BUST AND BEYOND by Jerry Tuma
Published by Excel Books
A Strang Company
600 Rinehart Road
Lake Mary, Florida 32746
www.strangbookgroup.com

Unless otherwise noted, all Scripture quotations are from the Holy Bible, New International Version of the Bible. Copyright © 1973, 1978, 1984, International Bible Society. Used by permission.

Scripture quotations marked CEV are from the Contemporary English Version, copyright © 1995 by the American Bible Society. Used by permission.

Scripture quotations marked KJV are from the King James Version of the Bible.

Scripture quotations marked NKJV are from the New King James Version of the Bible. Copyright © 1979, 1980, 1982 by Thomas Nelson, Inc., publishers. Used by permission.

Design Director: Bill Johnson
Cover design by Justin Evans

Library of Congress Cataloging-in-Publication Data:
An application to register this book for cataloging has been submitted to the Library of Congress.
International Standard Book Number: 978-1-59979-917-9

First Edition

09 10 11 12 13 — 9 8 7 6 5 4 3 2 1
Printed in Canada

TRIBUTE TO JAMES MCKEEVER

Though not widely known outside of investment newsletters and conference circles, James was the number one rated investment newsletter writer of all time, racking up average annual returns in excess of 60 percent per year for over a decade on his high-risk model portfolio. James went to be with the Lord in 1994, but not before passing on a great deal of wisdom, for which I am eternally grateful. I am, indeed, honored to have called him my mentor.

In addition to his award-winning newsletter, James spoke at numerous investment conferences, sharing the speaking platform with such notables as Ronald Reagan (just prior to becoming president) and Alan Greenspan. James was also a prolific author of books, authoring more than thirty titles, many of which were award winners. Thank you, James, for your investment into my life. Thank you, Jeanni (James's widow) and Mike (his son). I was privileged to know this man.

DEDICATION

I'd like to dedicate this book, which represents the culmination of fifteen years of work, to my family. To my wonderful wife, Ramona, who's never given up on me despite whatever obstacles we've faced, you're my soul mate, best friend, and life partner.

To my son, Sam Tuma, his wife, Angie, and their clan, Noah and Jacob. Also my daughter, Hannah Gigley, her husband, Aaron, and the rest of the Gigley clan, Aaron Jr., Alyssa, Alaina, and Isaac. This book is purposed to do our part to preserve your legacy, heritage, and future.

CONTENTS

LIST OF CHARTS

ACKNOWLEDGMENTS

I'D LIKE TO thank all of the Excel Books staff for their input and hard work, but especially Barbara Dycus, our editor, who has contributed greatly to this project.

Also, without the Cornerstone staff this book would never have been possible. Thanks to David McCord and his incredible research; Allan Jordheim, the chartmeister; and Debbie Bashaw's typing and input has been invaluable. Thanks to Jenny Swanwick, Liz Chapa, Vicki Ingrassia, Jody Wood and all of her intercessor team, Joe Askins, Anne Tate, and Alisa Jordheim for your prayers, and those of countless others. Thanks to Doris Moses and Beth Cassidy for holding down the company fort; Sherman Hohenberger and Steve August for their work with our clients. Also, to our Baton Rouge branch, Darrell Delphen and Donna Gregory, you have given valuable insight and inspiration. Thanks as well to Kent Kirkman for his help on charts and data.

Also, a big thank you to Mike and Cindy Jacobs, who have simultaneously encouraged, prodded, and cajoled me into doing this project.

Above all, thank you, Lord!

INTRODUCTION

THE MATERIAL YOU are about to read will be considered controversial by some but is based upon intense research involving the last fifteen years of my life. Ever since I entered the financial resources industry in 1980, I've had a sense that America would someday go through an intense financial struggle, very difficult times. Yet I always wondered about the timing.

In the early- to mid-1990s I discovered a book by Harry S. Dent Jr. entitled *The Great Boom Ahead*, which not only differed with much of the prevailing wisdom of the day but actually predicted that the greatest economic/market boom in history was just around the corner.[1] Keep in mind, it was written in 1993, not long after the crash of 1987 and the Persian Gulf War recession, and stood almost alone in predicting that the greatest boom in history was dead ahead.

Immediately upon reading this book, I had a deep sense that it was largely correct and began to incorporate demographics into our investment planning.

While I haven't always agreed with Harry, his basic premise has proven correct, and many of his predictions in *The Great Boom Ahead* were astoundingly accurate and relevant even today.

An old saying about demographics is that demographics are destiny. We know precisely how many people were born in the United States every year, plus we know how and when most people spend their money. Hence, we can easily extrapolate the big-picture trends.

In fact, the major megatrends are, in my opinion, much easier to discern than short-term trends, which can be affected either positively or negatively by innumerable factors, many of which could be categorized as surprises or shocks. But, the big-picture trends, the really, really big-picture trends—trends that last decades, not days, weeks, or months—march along through time with almost robotic precision. Like a giant cruise ship moving toward a port, the big-picture megatrends remain in place until they reach their destinations.

In other words, shorter-term trends are sort of like the passengers on the ship. They can play shuffleboard, relax while reading a book, or gorge themselves on shrimp cocktail. Short-term trends are very unpredictable. The major megatrends are like the ship on its course. It won't change until the captain changes destinations. Megatrends are slow moving, long-term, and relentless; they get where they are going regardless of short-term, cyclical changes.

So, as you read this book, keep in mind that lots of things will change over short-term periods—one reason I've tried not to be too predictive about shorter-term events. All the while, the bigger picture trends are relentlessly moving toward completion as the baby boomers move one step nearer to retirement. I would also like to recognize Ed Yardeni and Ken Dychtwald for their contributions toward the study of demographics.

In addition to the U.S.-based trends, we'll also incorporate global trends, as China, India, and an assortment of Asian tigers move toward freedom and free enterprise. Mostly, they have not arrived but are certainly moving in the right direction.

Finally, we'll look at preparation. If we're correct in our summation that a long-term demographic winter has just started, you'll need to know how to prepare and to know how to prosper. Different strategies will be needed for different times, and these are certainly different times.

We hope you enjoy this endeavor, which is the result of several decades' worth of research and of courses I've taught, stemming from our radio broadcasts.

New times require new strategies. Please take a moment to recognize that we're headed into uncharted waters, areas of the ocean most of us who are living have never been in before. But again, demographics are destiny. The course of this demographic/economic ship relentlessly travels on.

PART 1

GETTING READY FOR THE DEMOGRAPHIC WINTER

CHAPTER ONE

PARADIGM SHIFT IN REAL TIME

OVER THE LAST thirty years, the long-term economic prosperity of the United States has been nothing short of fantastic. In just over two hundred years, our country has progressed from a fledgling group of colonies to the greatest country on the planet—the greatest in the *history of our world*. Our economy and our military are second to none. Yet a rising peril exists, a peril so great that it threatens all of our lives, our futures, and our destinies.

In recent decades, we have gone from a hardy, self-sufficient, honest nation that needed no help from abroad but was always ready to help others to a nation now dependent on other countries to fund our debts, supply our goods, and finance our government.

We've gone from honesty and truth to situational ethics, where it might be OK to lie, steal, or cheat as long as one doesn't get caught.

We've gone from self-reliance and hard work toward government dependency, from equal opportunity toward equalized outcomes, from saving and investing to debt dependency and consumer addiction, from valuing life to cheapening it. In just about every area, America has moved toward the moral gutter.

Yes, I know good, honest, hard-working, God-fearing people still inhabit the good ol' U.S. of A. That's what keeps me going and gives me hope for the future.

Yet to be blind to the moral decay we've allowed is to live in a state of denial. America, come back to your roots.

Yes, there's hope! Yes, there's room for optimism! But first comes reality—and the reality is that America now faces both economic and political challenges that are unprecedented in our lifetimes. America is at war with itself.

Just after 9/11, the greatest tragedy for modern times, for a short flicker, a momentary snapshot in history, our country stood together in common grief and bond. For a short flash of time, our leaders stood and wept, prayed, and planned together. Yet this time of unity passed through our nation's psyche like a bolt of lightning in the night. One moment it was there; the next...gone.

Divisiveness returned, as did vicious, personal attacks, and self-centered agendas. One group rose up against another; ideologies clashed once again. Without rhyme or reason, one brief moment after uniting against our common enemy, our war with ourselves returned.

Given the changes that have taken place over the last generation, it might be useful to look at just what happened. What caused this great moral divide? What tectonic shift has taken place to move this great nation away from the roots, values, and morals that made America the greatest country in world history?

We're a nation divided, of two minds now, and how better can this be depicted than by the red states versus the blues. In the last three presidential elections, the nation has been divided against itself—sharply divided along ideological and geographic lines. Where did this divide start? How did we become liberal or conservative—so widely divided?

Let's start at the beginning. Any study of our nation's history will prove that our nation was founded by God-fearing people. From the pilgrims seeking refuge against religious persecution to the founding fathers at the Constitutional Convention, through Lincoln and all the way to Reagan, America has godly roots. Our government and our laws were established upon the principles of the Bible.

Yet sometime back, a portion of our nation took a different fork in the road. Some chose to look at life differently. To view the origins of this divergence, let's look at a few principles taken from a different perspective by viewing a document known as the *Humanist Manifesto*.

THE *HUMANIST MANIFESTO*

The *Humanist Manifesto I* was written in 1933, and the *Humanist Manifesto II* was written in 1973. It's noteworthy that both documents were written at times of great economic turmoil: 1933, just after the worst of the Great Depression, and in 1973, during the worst recession (at that time) since the Depression.

I am listing below some of the main humanist beliefs that are found in these two documents.

Humanist Manifesto I (1933)[1]

- The universe is self-existing and was not created.

- Man, as a part of nature, has emerged through a continuous process.

- Man's religious culture and civilization are the products of a gradual development due to his interaction with his natural environment and his social heritage.

- The nature of the universe as depicted by modern science makes unacceptable any supernatural or cosmic guarantees of human values.

- The complete realization of human personality is in the here and now.

- The humanist finds his religious emotions expressed in a heightened sense of personal life and in cooperative effort to promote social well-being.

- The goal of humanism is a free and universal society in which people voluntarily and intelligently cooperate for the common good.

- Man is at last becoming aware that he alone is responsible for the realization of the world of his dreams, that he has within himself the power for its achievement.

Humanist Manifesto II (1973)[2]

- Humanists still believe that traditional theism is an unproved and outmoded faith, salvationism still appears to be "harmful," and reasonable minds look to other means for survival.

- Humanity, to survive, requires bold and daring measures.

- Only a shared world and global measures will suffice.

- We find insufficient evidence for belief in the existence of a supernatural; as non-theists, we begin with humans not God, nature not deity.

- We can discover no divine purpose or providence for the human species. No deity will save us; we must save ourselves.

- Promises of immortal salvation or fear of eternal damnation are both illusory and harmful.

- Moral values derive their source from human experience. Ethics is autonomous and situational, needing no theological or ideological sanction.

- In the area of sexuality, we believe that intolerant attitudes, often cultivated by orthodox religious and puritanical cultures, unduly repress sexual conduct. The right to birth control, abortion, and divorce should be recognized.

- The separation of church and state and the separation of ideology and state are imperatives.

- If unable, then society should provide means to satisfy their basic economic, health, and cultural needs, including, wherever resources make possible, a minimum guaranteed annual income.

- We look to the development of a system of "world law" and a world order based upon transnational federal government.

- We believe in the peaceful adjudication of differences by international courts and by the development of the arts of negotiation and compromise. War is obsolete. So is the use of nuclear, biological, and chemical weapons. It is a planetary imperative to reduce the level of military expenditures and turn these savings to peaceful and people-oriented uses.

- The world community must engage in cooperative planning concerning the use of rapidly depleting resources.

- The problems of economic growth and development can no longer be resolved by one nation alone; they are worldwide in scope.

- What more daring a goal for humankind than for each person to become, in ideal as well as practices, a citizen of a world community.

I don't want to leave the impression that I think all card-carrying humanists are vampire-like, blood-sucking, evil people. No, in reality I believe that most are kind, caring individuals who truly *do* want to improve the world and reduce or eliminate human suffering as much as possible. They believe in their ideals.

If you read the documents from front to back, you'll see that they do want to improve man's lot in life. It's just that their methodology and belief systems are so different and antithetical to what most of us believe and hold true, and, I might add, to what made our country great to begin with. I believe that, if unchecked and left to their own devices and agendas, they would lead not only the United States but also the world in a direction that will ultimately result in much harm, not good—unintentionally, of course.

Their economic theories are not only flawed but also have been tried again and again with the same result—failure. While capitalism is not perfect and will not produce fairness or equal distribution of income, it has proven, without question, to be the best economic system man has devised. We'll go into detail on this issue later, but for now, isn't it obvious that with the fall of the Soviet Union and the complete makeover of both China and India, Communism and Socialism do not work? Let's be honest and look at the hard facts!

The pages of these manifestos absolutely declare:

1. We believe in no God.

2. We must save ourselves.

3. We are a product of evolution.

4. We believe in controlling our "limited" environmental resources.

5. We are a product of the culture that surrounds us.

6. There are no moral absolutes.

7. Profit motivation and acquisition is either evil or morally flawed.

8. Sharing (Socialism) is morally right.

9. Mankind *alone* is responsible for the fulfillment of his dreams.

10. We must control our environment.

11. We believe the world is overpopulated.

12. We believe in a shared world and global controls (world government plus Socialism).

13. We believe in government on a planetary scale.

14. Ethics are situational. Right and wrong can change depending upon the circumstances.

15. We must be tolerant of all other sexualities.

16. Church and anything resembling Christianity must be altogether removed from all facets of government influence.

17. There should be a minimum guaranteed annual income.

18. A world law system should be instituted, as well as a transnational government.

19. Peaceful negotiation means the appeasement of tyrants.

20. Excessive population growth must be stopped; thus, we must encourage birth control, abortion, and euthanasia.

21. Extreme disproportions of wealth must be reduced on a worldwide basis.

There you have it! In two different treaties, humanism—a self-described religion dedicated to man's own power and ingenuity—has set the agenda for our country and our world.

If humanists have their way, gone will be much of America's independence, many of our freedoms, liberties, abundance, and opportunity. In its place will be controls, excessive taxation and regulations, equalization (not of opportunity but of results), and lost national sovereignty. We are at war—divided into two camps. "America! America! God shed His grace on thee!"[3]

"Why," you ask, "spend all this time explaining what humanists believe? Just who are these people?" To start with, both John Dewey, the father of modern education, and the educator Horace Mann were avowed humanists. Dewey was a signer of the 1933 *Manifesto*, and if you'll look at their influence, you'll find that most of America, despite a proclaimed belief in God and the Bible, has been largely influenced by their thinking. It has helped formulate most Americans' worldview or paradigm.

Their values largely reflect the values of liberal or left-leaning individuals and have been widely disseminated throughout the textbooks and curriculum of public education, journalism, and the media. Most Americans believe in God but behave like humanists in many ways. (Pollster George Barna's 2009 survey revealed that 90 percent of Americans say they believe in God or a universal being, and 50 percent believe in the Bible.)[4]

KEYNESIAN REVOLUTION

No discussion of the role of government and the economy would be complete without the inclusion of John Maynard Keynes (1883–1946). Keynes was an agnostic (or atheist, depending upon the source cited) and early on was a part of a group of Fabian socialists at Cambridge. Keynes (pronounced "canes," like a walking cane) was the first to advocate government intervention into the marketplace.

Prior to Keynes, most primarily followed the lead of classic economists such as Adam Smith, who believed in God and held that if the markets and economy were allowed to function on their own, they would do just fine. Smith referred to the "invisible hand" that guided both markets and the economy within proper boundaries of supply and demand without ongoing human intervention.

Keynes, on the other hand, advocated direct intervention by the government, especially when economic times grew difficult. Initiatives such as public works and other infrastructure projects could stimulate the economy when businesses either would not or could not expand and grow. His primary contributions to economics and politics revolve around these facets:

1. When the economy is in a slump (recession or depression) the government should temporarily go into debt and spend money to stimulate the economy. Once the economy begins to grow again, the government should then repay the debts incurred during the slump. In other words, Keynes still believed in a balanced budget over the long run, but not necessarily in the short run. Had this remained the philosophy and practice of western governments, then this might have worked out. But, as we shall see later, once the politicians learned that deficit spending could be *good* for the economy, Pandora's box was opened and, once opened, could not be shut.

2. Keynes believed that full employment in the economy (the textbook definition is 4 percent unemployed) could not be achieved without government intervention. In no way, shape, or form do I believe this to be true. Normally, by the time the political process has time to work and intervene in the economy, whatever measures are instituted are either too late, not enough, or no longer necessary. By that time the economy has already adjusted. This is not always the case, especially when *extreme* economic duress is occurring, such as what we are facing now.

3. Keynes called for global economic structures, removal of the gold standard, and a global currency.

Keynes partially got his way during the 1944 Bretton Woods Agreement, as he advocated the creation of a world central bank, a global currency (the Bancor), and a global clearinghouse for the management of currencies and trade imbalances.

The United States had the upper hand in the negotiations and designed most of the plan, but part of Keynes's plan was adopted in the creation of the International Monetary Fund and the World Bank.

The U.S. dollar became the reserve currency of the world (convertible into gold for foreign countries), and fixed exchange rates were adopted.

Keynes's primary contributions to our current status economically as a nation has been enabling politicians to spend all the money they want (not what Keynes advocated, but ultimately what occurred); direct government intervention in the economy; and a global financial system, not yet fully implemented but being advocated currently.

Without Keynes, endless government budget deficits would not have been possible. Our government would not be sitting on an $11 trillion (and counting) national debt, with a looming budget crisis once Social Security and Medicare begin to unravel.

Keynes's ideals also empowered liberals and advocates of big government to mandate government controls of private enterprise. Keynes believed that it was not possible to trust a free market and capitalist system and that it must be highly regulated in order to promote the common good.

While some government controls are both necessary and good, an overdependence upon government controls, regulations, and the taxation necessary to pay for all of the new programs produces economic stagnation. Plus, it retards freedom and wealth creation, as we will show in subsequent chapters.

Finally, globalists, who believe in a one-world socialist government with its attendant controls, have been empowered by Keynes and those of his ilk. While, in fairness to Keynes, others have since taken many of his principles far further than he advocated at the time, the Keynesian Revolution, which occurred between 1936 and 1970, has provided the intellectual framework for liberal economic and financial belief systems and provided a global socialistic paradigm for hard-core leftists to hang their hats on. By the 1950s and 1960s most economists were Keynesians.

Starting in the 1970s, Milton Friedman, who started the monetarist movement, and Austrian economists Ludwig Von Mises and Friedrich Hayek began winning converts after we'd seen the result of two decades of Keynesianism in action—ultimately resulting in the 1970s stagflation.

Ronald Reagan and Margaret Thatcher were both supply-side, free-market advocates and reversed decades of policy in their respective countries, resulting (along with demographics) in the most enormous economic boom the world has ever seen.

Now the current economic crisis—as seen with Fannie Mae and Freddie Mac's refinancing plans, posted Friday, March 13, of this year—is reincarnating

Keynesianism.[5] Bailouts, government interventions, and control of private industry are making enormous comebacks.

In the coming pages of this book, I will attempt—as best I can—to describe what events have taken us morally and economically down our present path. Morals, economics, and worldview are inextricably linked. Morals and spiritual behavior have actually *created* our present economic environment and crisis. We are, in many ways, beginning to reap what we've sown as a nation. These moral and economic choices have been based upon what we believe, or what we've chosen to believe.

You may remember the old computer term, "Garbage in; garbage out." In early computer programming, we learned that if you programmed the hard drive with bad data, the computer merely regenerated bad results. Bad data input; bad data output. Garbage in; garbage out.

Our nation's present psyche is much the same today. We've filled our minds, created our worldview, and based our paradigms upon what in my opinion is faulty data. Armed with studies of world deprivation and poverty, we've believed a lie.

In the upcoming chapter about our demographic winter, I'll show how this came about, first focusing on the results of the bad data. Our current economic crisis has at its roots bad data based upon faulty assumptions. Yet, many in the worlds of academia, media, and politics have based their entire careers upon these false assumptions. As a result, we are a nation divided. We are of two minds.

I'm reminded of a passage in the Book of James: "That man should not think he will receive anything from the Lord; he is a double-minded man, unstable in all he does" (James 1:7–8). Another passage from the Old Testament comes to mind. In 1 Kings, Elijah challenges the nation of Israel about its beliefs: "How long will you waver between two opinions?" (1 Kings 18:21).

How long, America? How long will you waver between two paradigms, two worldviews? How long will you say with your mouth that you believe in God and the Bible while behaving as if there are no moral absolutes?

The moral norms of man, absent of God's eternal principles, come and go. Paradigms shift over time depending upon the latest fads or conventional wisdom. In the 1970s the media was focused upon the next ice age (see *Time* magazine, "Another Ice Age," June 27, 1974). Today it's global warming, world deprivation, starvation, and overpopulation. Humanists believe that we must control our environment, plan our futures. "There is no God to save us. We must save ourselves," to quote the *Humanist Manifesto*. Everything that liberals believe emanates from these basic premises, and many—repeat, many of them—are based upon faulty data and assumptions as a result of what just a few men believed in the late sixties and seventies, which has since been disproven and completely discredited. Don't believe me? Read on! The data doesn't lie.

In subsequent pages we will attempt to show first the root causes of this faulty thinking. What drove us to these assumptions and behaviors in the first place, and what data needs revising? Next we will attempt to prove how our current economic crisis rises from this baseline of faulty thinking. Next are solutions, both national and individual. There is a way out of this mess, but not until we recognize and change the false beliefs and behaviors that created the problems in the first place.

America has entered a period unlike any in its history. We've faced economic meltdowns before, and conflicts on a grand scale. But never have we faced these types of issues with the moral and intellectual divide that we now have.

The nation was divided regarding slavery and states' rights during the Civil War, yet both sides still prayed to the same God and read from the same Bible. Now, half our country believes one thing; half, another. There is a moral divide!

We see it even in the court system. Half the Supreme Court comes from one perspective; half, from another. One justice swings back and forth—an almost perfect picture of where our nation is today.

So, as we move into the later chapters of this book, I'll do my best to lay out a blueprint, an economic blueprint. Planning for your future is not so difficult if you can see the blueprint unfolding before you. We don't have to be taken by surprise, shocked, and disillusioned. Thus far, no one has batted a thousand, perfectly predicting every economic twist and turn. But you don't have to. Economically, if you get the major trends right—if you're 80 percent accurate about the big picture—over time you'll do very well. We'll also lay out the future as we see it. We will deal with our current economic reality, as brutal as it may be, then with the hope and long-term potential.

As you read these pages, please keep in mind that nothing is impossible. No matter how challenging the next ten to fifteen years become, we can come out on top in ultimate victory.

I'm reminded of a cycle. It's a cycle of liberty and abundance, selfishness and complacency, freedom and bondage that has recurred, in one form or another, throughout history. I call it the Cycle of Liberty, or the Liberty Clock.

Alexander Fraser Tytler, a Scottish history professor at the University of Edinburgh around the time the U.S. Constitution was drafted, has been credited with writing the following concerning democracies:

> A democracy cannot exist as a permanent form of government. It can only exist until the voters discover that they can vote themselves largesse

[generous gifts] from the public treasury. From that moment on, the majority always votes for the candidates promising the most benefits from the public treasury, with the result that a democracy always collapses over loose fiscal policy, always followed by a dictatorship.

The average of the world's great civilizations before they decline has been two hundred years. These nations have progressed in this sequence:

> From bondage to spiritual faith;
> From faith to great courage;
> From courage to liberty;
> From liberty to abundance;
> From abundance to selfishness;
> From selfishness to complacency;
> From complacency to apathy;
> From apathy to dependency;
> From dependency back again to bondage.[6]

This was later modified by Henning Prentis Jr. to include a fear phase, which I believe is more accurate. Fear creates the incentive to receive solutions designed to fix the crisis, thus creating dependency and bondage. Chart 1-A below shows the Tytler Cycle with the addition of the fear stage, as modified by Prentis.

Cycle of Liberty

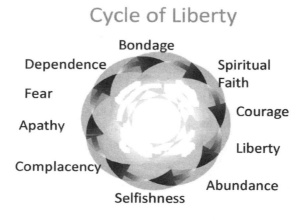

Chart 1-A[7]

Looking at this through the lenses of the current economic and political circumstances, the cycle, I must admit, is a bit chilling.

Where are we as a nation on this cycle? Does the cycle have to repeat itself?

Is it inevitable? What lessons should we learn, and how do we move to the next phase? Can we move to the next phase?

We will attempt within the pages of this book to answer, to the best of our knowledge, these questions.

Where do you suppose we are on this cycle? It appears to me that we are currently in the fear cycle, moving from fear to dependency and on toward bondage.

If this cycle is recurring again in human history, as it appears to have done time after time due to human nature, we must first recognize where we are now and how we got here. Then and only then will we be able to set a course to successfully navigate our futures.

We know from the study of secular history (Greece, Rome, Great Britain, etc.) that great empires tend to come and go. We can study biblical history (read the Book of Judges) and see this same cycle as well.

I don't believe for one minute that this means we are doomed to repeat the past or that America's future is one of past glory. But I do believe that without great spiritual faith and courage, this cycle will come to its natural conclusion.

America is not necessarily fated to become the next Greece, the next Roman Empire, the next great civilization to fall, but it must reform. Without reformation, I believe America will go by the way of the great empires. But, reformation is within our power if, and only if, we rely upon God.

The principles that brought America to this place, the principles that made America great, the principles to which our founding fathers ascribed were not principles of democracy—*they were principles of faith.* At the conclusion of the Constitutional Convention, after the drafting of our nation's foundational document, a reporter asked Benjamin Franklin what form of government the founders had given us. His response: "A Republic, if you can keep it."[8] His response was telling.

The founders knew the cycles of history. They knew what had been the downfall of the great empires. They knew human nature. They also knew it would be difficult to keep the republic.

This brings us back to our present time. Will we, as the present-day people of the United States of America, keep the republic—or will we let it fall?

Forces will attempt to move us into a global financial and economic system that has socialist, godless roots at its core. These forces will be powerful and difficult to deal with, especially because of the current economic crisis, which is about to get worse, not better. Years, even decades, of planning have gone into the blueprints that are designed to be implemented during the present crisis. Yet, all is not lost.

This cycle, while challenging and, I believe, especially painful over the next ten to fifteen years, also provides great hope, great potential for long-term optimism if we will heed the call. That is why the last chapter of the book is titled "The Call."

So our nation is truly at a crossroads, a crossroads, I believe, as great and as potentially dangerous as any we have been through in our entire history. That statement says a lot. Will we, as a nation, make the right decisions? Will we heed the call? Will we turn our country around, even at the potential peril of our "lives, liberty and sacred honor," as did our founding fathers, or will we quit?

It is always easier to back down from a fight. Easier to acquiesce rather than confront. Easier to lie down and give up rather than pick up and start over.

It is my belief that God is not finished with this great country. I believe He desires to use her as He has in the past, even to greater measure. But, a crucible lies before us.

In the pages of the book I will do my best to lay out not only the financial challenges we face, plus possible national and international solutions, but also to offer personal financial strategies for the future.

I believe we face a ten-to-fifteen-year period that could be as challenging as any time in our history, which truly says a lot. We have entered a period of *demographic winter.*

Think of the winter season. It's cold. The trees lose their leaves. Insects die. We experience challenging freezes, snowstorms, blizzards, and ice storms. Winter is never pleasant to live in (unless you're on the ski slopes). But live we must.

We have entered a demographic and economic winter. Economic cycles last longer than the seasons of weather, generally a decade or more. I believe that this demographic/economic winter will last until approximately 2023 (for reasons we will explain later). It will be very hard, potentially some of our most difficult economic times ever, but we must, during this crisis, remember that it is a season! It is not permanent. It may seem like the world is ending at times; indeed, it will likely feel that way.

But we must—while enduring, growing, and hopefully prospering during this season—remember that it is a season! Springtime will again occur. Though this winter is long and hard, that is not the end of the story.

Throughout this book I will refer to a principle that I think we must follow, known as the Stockdale Paradox. It is found in the national bestseller, *Good to Great.*[9] Named after Admiral James Stockdale, the highest-ranking U.S. prisoner of war during Vietnam. This paradox encapsulates one of the most important principles of *Good to Great.*

"This is a very important lesson. You must never confuse faith that you will prevail in the end—which you can never afford to lose—with the discipline to confront the most brutal facts of your current reality, whatever they might be."

—James Stockdale

I'll refer to this principle throughout the book, as I feel that this approach is what we must have to survive, hopefully prosper, and come out of this crucible on the other side. I want to be a contributor, not a casualty of war, during the winter.

Additionally, I believe this same pattern to be biblical. A famous passage Christians often quote to each other, which I refer to as a "refrigerator verse" (people sometimes put verses on a sticker on their refrigerator to remind them of God's promises), is Jeremiah 29:11:

"For I know the plans that I have for you," declares the LORD, "plans to prosper you and not to harm you, plans to give you hope and a future."

People tend to forget the context of this passage. The prophet Jeremiah gave the Hebrews this message of a future, hope, plans, and prosperity in the midst of their worst nightmare. The people of Israel had been taken captive by the Babylonians due to the people's disobedience and were in the midst of captivity (or bondage, to quote Alexander Fraser Tytler)! God said to them, "I know the plans I have for you—plans for hope and a future."

In this book, it is with this mandate that we will pursue hope for a future—a good future, a prosperous one—yet at the same time, not failing to recognize and deal with the most challenging elements of our current reality. It's a twofold sword of Hope + Reality = Destiny, and I believe America still has one.

So, as we explore our past, present, and future financially, economically, and politically in these pages, it is my hope to challenge you to have the courage to look at the difficulties ahead with unwavering faith in the future. Do we not owe this to our children and grandchildren? Let's get started!

CHAPTER TWO
FALLACIES THAT RULE THE WORLD

I MAGINE THE WORLD WITHOUT CHILDREN. Hard to imagine, isn't it? No playgrounds filled with joy and laughter, children running about, being watched by teachers and parents. Doesn't sound much like a fun place does it? The world certainly is not in a situation where there are no children. However, western societies, as well as places like China and the rest of the developing world that have developed a worldview toward global overpopulation concerns, have increasingly begun to look upon children as a burden, rather than the traditional viewpoint, which affirms that children are a blessing and that the more children you have, the more blessing they tend to produce.

Armed with studies of world deprivation, starvation, and shortage and lack, philosophers, academics, and media moguls altered our view of society and of the world, beginning in the late 1960s. This was due, in part, to what proved to be temporary shortages caused by the largest generation in the history of the United States—76 million baby boomers (born between 1946 and 1964)—who began to enter the economy and workforce.

Viewed through lenses of permanent shortage and lack, these later proved to be temporary shortages caused by an enormous bulge of people entering our society all at one time. Yet these shortages drew doom-and-gloom prognoses from a wide variety of sources and began capturing the minds of many of the elite academics and media in the U.S. and throughout the rest of the world.

MALTHUSIAN THINKING

This type of thinking actually began more than a century earlier, led by an economist and demographer named Thomas Robert Malthus (1766–1834). (For additional information about Thomas Robert Malthus, see the resource box at the end of this chapter.) Malthus was an English political economist and demographer. He expressed views on population growth and noted the potential for populations to increase rapidly, often faster than the food supply available to them—a phenomenon known as a *Malthusian catastrophe*, described fully in his *Essay on the Principle of Population*.[1]

Malthus believed that the world's food supplies would only increase arithmetically (1, 2, 3, 4, 5), while population would grow geometrically (1, 2, 4, 8, 16, 32). He felt this would doom large portions of mankind to lives of suffering, deprivation, death, and disease, and that a lack of resources (including food) would always imperil mankind.

Malthus obviously underestimated society's ability to grow without limits. Thus far his theory, if you want to call it that, has proven unfounded. Massive global food shortages and starvation on a grand scale have not occurred. The starvation periods of recent years in sub-Saharan Africa were largely the result of poor economic planning, drought, corruption, and purposeful genocide. The world can certainly support its present population with adequate food, given adequate economic resources.

As proof of this, consider that today food is cheaper and more abundant than ever, even if many still go hungry. Indeed, according to the World Bank, the price of food, adjusted for inflation, declined by 53 percent between 1980 and 2001. The amount of food calories available per person has increased some 20 percent since the 1960s, even as fewer and fewer people still work as farmers. The United Nations reports that "the most rapid increase has been in the developing countries where population more than doubled and daily food calories available per person rose from roughly 1,900 to 2,600 calories."[2]

Food shortage issues have been cropping up globally for the last year or two. More Malthusian catastrophe? Mankind outgrowing its limits again? Or, the result of *human* behavior? In my opinion, it's the latter.

Millions of acres of land are now being converted to grow corn or sugarcane for ethanol production. In 2007, corn was planted on an additional 14 million acres.[3] According to a February 11, 2008, article in *Science Daily,* "Such conversions for corn or sugarcane (ethanol)...release 17 to 420 times more carbon than the annual savings from replacing fossil fuels."[4]

Over the past few years we've seen the conversion of millions of tons of corn into gasoline—*enough to feed millions people*—despite the fact that you need 1.5 gallons of ethanol to drive the same distance you go on a gallon of gasoline.[5]

In addition, corn uses more fertilizers and pesticides per unit of land than any other biofuel feedstock. Until the carbon debt is repaid, biofuels produced on converted lands actually emit more carbon than the fossil fuels they replace.[6] Researchers at Princeton University have estimated that it will take roughly 167 years to work off the carbon load placed into the atmosphere, given off due to chemical pesticides used in the production of the corn used to produce the ethanol—in order to "save the planet."[7] This boondoggle belongs in the law of unintended consequences Hall of Fame.

Second, China and India's emergence as first-world economies (China in particular, as India is about 15 years behind them) has radically altered the food supply balance. Here's how: For over the last two decades, China has seen millions of rural workers move to the cities. These migrant workers are no longer available to farm in rural areas but now work in factories. It is estimated that the floating population of migrant workers has increased at a speed of 5 million a year, reaching 160 million by 2010 and continuing to grow from there.[8]

So, first they don't produce food anymore. Second, as city dwellers they must buy their food. Five or ten million people per year converting from farming to food-buying makes a big difference in the global food supply balance over a decade or more. In addition, as people become more affluent, they tend to consume more meat. Along with rising incomes, the average Chinese citizen has seen his or her meat consumption, primarily pork, rise 45 percent between 1993–2005.[9]

What does this have to do with food shortages? On average it takes five times more grain in terms of calories consumed to feed a pig than to consume the grain ourselves.[10] Thus, the more meat people eat, the less efficiently we're using our resources. (Estimates run as high as ten times the caloric consumption for grain-fed U.S. beef.) A similar situation is developing in India, only on a smaller scale, as they've just begun their globalization process.[11]

So does this mean that the world is running out of its scarce resources again? No, it means that humans have changed their behavior on a grand scale and farming has yet to catch up. But catch up it will. These things are cyclical.

Despite the fact that a lot of hand-wringing is going on concerning global food supplies—and it's a lot more than just hand-wringing to the poorest of the poor—the resultant food issues are primarily driven by human behavior, not any type of Malthusian absolute limitations.

Food shortages, as they appear in the near future, will not be the result of mankind being unable to feed and keep up with its population, but rather of poor economic and political planning, combined with natural events and/or war. A state of permanent food deprivation due to overpopulation cannot be supported by data, only by opinion.

Malthusian-type projections and studies by such notable groups as the Club of Rome projected that by 2000 the world would enter a period of massive starvation, where as much as a third of the world would die from malnutrition, starvation, or disease. These projections were widely disseminated through the media and began to dominate the thinking processes of many Americans.

The Club of Rome is a global think tank that deals with a variety of international political issues. (For more information about the Club of Rome, see the resource box at the end of this chapter.) It was founded in April 1968 and quickly gained public attention with its report *Limits to Growth*. Since its publication in 1972 it has sold thirty million copies in more than thirty translations, making it the world's best-selling environmental book.[12]

To this day, Malthusian thinking suffuses the environmental movement and casually informs most people's thoughts about the future. But if Malthus was right about the factors that limited human population growth before his time, he was exactly wrong about what the next two centuries would bring. Since he wrote his book, human population has increased more than six-fold, and the amount each person consumes has increased at an even more rapid pace.

Instead of widespread famine came a still-expanding system of mass production and mass consumption. Within the United States, the population was 3.6 times greater at the end of the twentieth century than at the beginning, but living standards, meanwhile, are variously estimated to have increased by between 14 and 25 times.[13]

PAUL EHRLICH

Next came Paul Ehrlich's bestseller, *Population Bomb*, which not only misled an entire generation, but also now carries on in the form of extreme environmentalism.[14] The book is primarily a repetition of the Malthusian catastrophe argument that population growth will rise exponentially but the available resources, in particular food, are already at their limits.

Ehrlich, a biology professor with a background in insect biology, is hardly an expert in demography or population trends. His work has been completely discredited in my opinion (see chapter end), yet dominates the thinking of most in the environmental movement, as well as much of the rest of the "liberal" agendas. For example: Erlich predicted the U.S. population would fall to only 22 million by the year 2000 due to famine and mass starvation. He only mised the mark by some 270 million!

While I'm certainly not in favor of pollution, we must *steward* the world's resources while focusing on long-term growth and prosperity. We must not become myopic about one particular facet of economic development.

To ignore or retard longer-term trends of human progress and advancement in order to micromanage environmental issues is a losing cause. We must take care of the planet (it's the only one we have) but do so with prudence and factual data, not wild conjecture and projections of imminent disaster based upon faulty thinking and research.

Ehrlich's *Population Bomb* (along with other parallel thinking) convinced many in this country, especially those of the intellectual community, academics, and the media, that the world was facing a certain future of starvation and deprivation. Thus, in order to survive, we had to control our populations and work to reduce the number of people in the world or at least slow the rate of growth.

Shortage and permanent "lack" thinking proved fleeting in terms of its economic impact in the eighties and nineties. We did see shortage after shortage in the 1970s. But again, these were not due to permanent lack of resources but were temporary shortages caused by a society that failed to anticipate just how immensely the enormous wave of children born after World War II would impact the various elements of society and our economy.

Shortages began as early as the late 1950s, starting with shortages of diapers, baby food, and elementary schools. One demographer, David Cork, refers to this as the "pig in the python" bulge of baby boomers that began moving through every element of society.[15]

All of this affected radical change. Every place the boomers landed, they created shortages, simply because no one had anticipated that many people of that particular age living in the country at the same time.

1970s Stagflation

Thus, shortages did abound, but they were not signs of permanent limits on resources. Rather, these were temporary shortages created by the lack of capacity to sustain the enormous bulge of the boomers' needs.

By the 1980s, most of corporate America had caught on to the fact that this enormous group of people now known as the baby boomers was affecting every element of American life. Rather than creating world deprivation, lack, disease, and famine, this baby boom generation launched an unprecedented period of economic growth and prosperity.

As an example of this, in 1980 the Dow Jones Industrial Average was under 1,000, where it had languished for almost fourteen years due to stagflation caused largely by poor demographics and Keynesian economic policies of excessive government control, regulation, and taxation. (See Chart 2-A.)

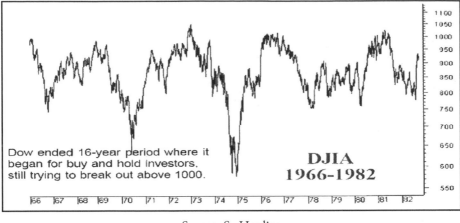

Dow ended 16-year period where it began for buy and hold investors, still trying to break out above 1000.

DJIA
1966–1982

Source: Sy Harding
Chart 2-A

This period of stagflation (economic stagnation plus inflation) was largely the result of two economic forces. The first was demographics. As we shall elaborate upon in subsequent pages, economic growth is dependent upon consumer spending. The more consumers you have entering their peak-spending mode (ages 45–50), the stronger the economy will be, as we'll see later.

In the 1970s we experienced a drop in consumer spending due to the fact that the Depression-era birth rate had plummeted. Births dropped radically during the Great Depression, which made sense because people were depressed![16]

Thus, a very small group of Americans were propelling the economy at that time.

If you take the year 1930, then add 45 years to it to project peak family spending for that age group, you get 1975 (1930 plus 45 for peak family spending age equals 1975). Thus, part of the '70s' economic malaise was resultant from low birth rates during the Depression. We'll discuss consumer spending, birth rates, and ages more in a moment.

The second factor that increased the misery of the 1970s was political and economic in origin. LBJ's guns-and-butter Vietnam acceleration, plus social spending (the Great Society), in which ever more was added to FDR's programs from the 1930s, led to unprecedented rates of inflation as government spending ratcheted out of control.[17] Added to this were the Carter years, where micromanaging the economy was taken to an all-new level.

During the 1970s, terms such as *stagflation* and the *misery index* (inflation plus unemployment) were created. All in all, the '70s was largely a miserable decade.

REAGAN PLUS BOOMERS EQUALS PROSPERITY

But starting around the time of Reagan, the unprecedented baby boom generation began graduating from school and entering the workforce. Starting with minimal impact at first, boomers began having families, buying houses, and pushing both the economy and the stock market higher.

Before the final wave of economic boomer influence reached its apex in 2007, the Dow hit 14,000. (See the next chart.) That's an increase of 1,727 percent in the most widely watched stock index in the world.

Massive fortunes were made over that time. As a matter of fact, prior to the late eighties, the term *billionaire* was almost unheard of. Thirteen billionaires existed in the United States prior to 1985, with only a few being especially noteworthy, like Warren Buffett and Bill Gates. By the time we got into the late 1990s, there were over a thousand billionaires worldwide and dozens of multibillionaires throughout the world.[18]

DOW JONES INDUSTRIAL AVERAGE 1980–2008

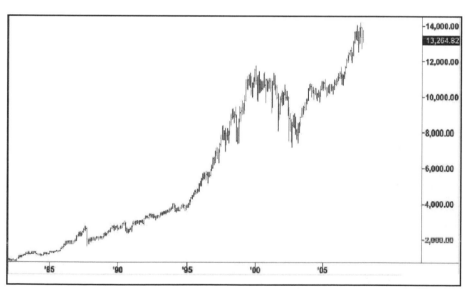

Source: Cornerstone Financial Services

Chart 2-B

The period of prosperity launched in the early 1980s is literally unparalleled in world history. Stop for a moment and ask yourself, What caused this unparalleled growth and unmatched wave of prosperity?

More people bought homes, cars, and clothing during this time than at any other time in world history. As a result, more wealth was created than at any other time in world history. There were new companies, new technologies. The Internet and the telecommunications/technology revolution took over.

All of these innovations and growth came about largely as the result of one thing—the growth and subsequent prosperity of an enormous group of people, indeed a population boom.

As a matter of fact, if you trace world history, even with sketchy statistics prior to this century, you will find that there is an immutable link in societies that have dominated throughout world history. For the most part, for advanced countries, the larger the population group becomes, the larger the number of people there are to fill the society and the economy, and the more financially blessed the society tends to be.

Obvious modern exceptions would be 1950–1980 Communist China under Mao and Socialist India from 1950–1991. The reason these societies experienced poverty was not due to their massive populations but rather to their political and economic systems. Communism and Socialism do not work. Now that free-market reforms have been instituted and are taking hold, both of these countries are creating their own economic prosperity.

We believe there is irrefutable proof over the long run, as we will demonstrate, that prosperity generally comes to societies that have free trade and large numbers of offspring. This has been the view throughout history until recent years.

Think about it for a moment. When seventy-six million people got out of high school and college and first moved into the workforce, what did they want to do? They started by living in apartments. Then they moved into starter homes. They began buying cars, having kids, and taking those kids to McDonalds. An unprecedented wave of consumer spending and prosperity was launched and has stayed with us for almost three decades.

Like a Hawaiian surfer riding a gigantic fifty-foot wave, a veritable tidal wave of consumer spending from boomers engulfed the entire U.S. and world economy. American investments, stocks, bonds, real estate, every element that we use to measure financial wealth and health in this country, have been carried along on this *gigantic* wave—all the way to the beach. It has been a truly wonderful and phenomenal period of growth.

Current-Dollar and "Real" Gross Domestic Product[19]	
Annual GDP in billions of current dollars	
1980	2,789.5
1981	3,128.4
1982	3,255.0

Current-Dollar and "Real" Gross Domestic Product	
1983	3,536.7
1984	3,933.2
1985	4,220.3
1986	4,462.8
1987	4,739.5
1988	5,103.8
1989	5,484.4
1990	5,803.1
1991	5,995.9
1992	6,337.7
1993	6,657.4
1994	7,072.2
1995	7,397.7
1996	7,816.9
1997	8,304.3
1998	8,747.0
1999	9,268.4
2000	9,817.0
2001	10,128.0
2002	10,469.6
2003	10,960.8
2004	11,685.9
2005	12,421.9
2006	13,178.4
2007	13,807.5
2008	14,264.6

Note that the GDP (before inflation adjustment) rose from 2.7 trillion to 14 trillion as 76 million boomers moved into the work force and began their consumer spending splurge.

BOOMER WAVE HITS THE BEACH

Unfortunately the tide has now shifted. The boomer wave has now hit the beach. The monstrous consumer spending and economic growth wave created by seventy-six million baby boomers, the largest consumer group in the history of the world, had to hit the rocky shores—and the first wave to hit the beach is the U.S. housing market.

I strongly believe, and I have been researching this topic for more than fifteen years without finding an easy or painless solution to this problem, that we have now entered an unprecedented demographic winter, something unknown to the modern world.

This demographic winter is not affecting only the United States. Western societies in Europe, Japan, and other parts of the world have decided that birth control, abortion, and other methods of population reduction have been needed. These have become the preferred methods for dealing with and attempting to centrally manage human population needs. This stems from the humanistic-type thinking I outlined in the first chapter. (For historical reference, Margaret Sanger and Katherine McCormick submitted the first birth control pill to the FDA in 1956.[20] The Supreme Court trial of *Roe v. Wade* legalized abortion in 1973.[21])

If there is one lesson that we need to learn from this, it's that central planning by large government institutions has historically not been effective and often creates unintended pain, usually caused by well-meaning politicians.

As a free-market economist, I would submit that the vast majority of the time, the marketplace is much better at determining what products or services need to be produced, not some government attempting to control from the top down. The same would be true of "population control." Usually when the government intervenes, it tends to mess things up further; hence, the term *unintended consequences.*

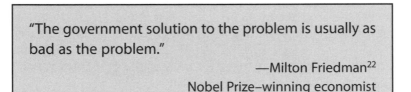

"The government solution to the problem is usually as bad as the problem."

—Milton Friedman[22]
Nobel Prize–winning economist

The point is this—there is no way to alter the number of people born between 1961 and 1974, at which point we saw an enormous drop in birth rates due to a variety of factors, including the sexual revolution, women going to work, abortion, and birth control.

My concern is that we have now entered a demographic winter, which over the next several decades will have enormous ramifications and repercussions, not only upon the people in the United States but on literally the entire world.

Economically, the United States still dominates the world. While other countries may resent this fact, the United States, without question, is still the dominant economy of the world. With less than 5 percent of the world's population and less than 5 percent of the world's land mass, the United States produced nearly one-third of the world's GDP (gross domestic product) in the year 2000. This means that nearly one-third of the goods and services produced in the entire world are produced in the United States.[23]

Whether others like it or not, the U.S. remains the world's proverbial eight-hundred-pound gorilla, although China is working hard to catch up. Hence, the old saying, "The rest of the world sneezes when America catches a cold."

Yet this book is written not only to people in the United States (English-speaking and otherwise) but to those all over the world for this simple reason: the direction that the U.S. economy heads over the next ten to fifteen years will have *massive ramifications* on the entire world economy, affecting both eastern nations as well as Europe and the Middle East.

As U.S. boomers continue to age and move farther and farther away from their peak spending years, this massive population tsunami will literally affect every aspect of American society; and this, in turn, will ripple throughout the rest of the world.

When baby boomers hit the Social Security and Medicare systems en masse, enormous strains will be placed upon our entitlement and retirement systems. Based upon the latest statistics, Social Security's revenue (from taxes) will just *barely* cover its outgo *next year* in 2010.[24]

Much like the massive hit we've just taken in the U.S. housing market (and the banking system because of the housing market), America is about to embark upon a journey it has never been on before.

We have never seen seventy-six million people, who up until this point have been spending, spending, and spending even more, thus driving the economy to ever higher heights, begin to regress in terms of spending, as boomers will as they continue to age and move toward retirement.

Bill Gross, managing director at the giant bond investment firm PIMCO, used his own colorful language to describe the recent past—and provide a vision of the future: "U.S. and many global consumers gorged themselves on Big Macs of all varieties: burgers to be sure, but also McHouses, McHummers, and McFlatscreens, all financed with excessive amounts of McCredit created under the mistaken assumption that the asset prices securitizing them could never go down. What a colossal McStake that turned out to be."[25]

The hit the economy has started to experience in terms of consumer spending will be like nothing we've seen before. By 2007 we received all of the benefit of the upside to this trend. Like the surfer on the fifty-foot wave, we've ridden it all the way to the beach—but the wave is now crashing, and it is going to affect every aspect of our society and the world. My concern, and the main reason for writing this book, is to prepare others financially and otherwise.

Not everyone will listen. Most people react, in terms of their finances, like ladies following fashion—copying others around them. Tuned into consumer magazines, Madison Avenue, and the media, most Americans have been spending with little thought for tomorrow—assuming that the future will be brighter than it is today. For almost thirty years, this type of thinking has paid off, as we have ridden wave after wave of prosperity. Yes, we have had downturns, bear markets, and recessions, but since the early 1980s, every recession has been fairly shallow and short. The market drops, crashes, and bear markets (with the exception of the 2000–2003 drop for NASDAQ and the dot-coms) have been mostly short and shallow.

However, we are now facing something completely unprecedented. We must understand that these mostly short, shallow downturns have occurred during the context of a thirty-year boomer *boom*. In other words, the longer-term megatrend of boomer spending has kept the *busts* short and shallow, with each slowdown followed by another, even bigger wave of consumer spending and prosperity. But now, this trend has started reversing.

THE JAPANESE EXAMPLE

We will never have a perfect economic road map to follow. We will not know for certain exactly how this plays out, but the evidence that we have about previous societies that have gone through anything similar is not encouraging.

Probably the best illustration that we have from modern history would be that of Japan. Japan is a highly mechanized and technologically sophisticated economy. Yet if you look at Japanese society, you'll find that they are much older than we are. Unlike the United States, Japan did not experience a *baby boom* following World War II. Following World War II, Japan was a defeated nation. The Japanese, with Shintoism as the dominant religion of their society, had been trained from birth that their emperor *was God*. (This explains why kamikaze pilots were so dedicated to their cause.)

Believing that their emperor was God and that Japan was destined for world domination, Japan's military defeat left a despondent and depressed nation. Not only were they completely disillusioned by the discovery that their emperor was not God, but they also had two cities lying in nuclear waste. Unlike American GIs after World War II, the Japanese soldiers did not go home and celebrate.

The understanding that everything they had been trained to believe to that point was a lie had begun setting in. Slowly, they began to pick up the pieces and rebuild, reassembling their lives. And rebuild they did, remarkably so.

Thus, even though Japan rebuilt phenomenally and became—until the last decade or so—the second-largest economy in the world (recently surpassed by China), the Japanese population curve looks like ours is about to look, only twenty years in advance. Let me explain.

Because they did not have a baby boom after World War II, the Japanese are, as we said, a much older society than the U.S. If you look at their spending curve you will find out that the Japanese as a society topped out in consumer spending in 1989, *precisely* when both the Japanese stock and real estate markets topped.[26]

You may remember the Japanese buying Pebble Beach golf course, Rockefeller Center in New York, and other notable real estate trophy "assets" in the United States. In fact, by 1989, many were concerned that the Japanese were going to economically take over the world. (You might remember that in one of the movies in the *Back to the Future* trilogy, Michael J. Fox's future boss was Japanese. They had taken over!)

The Japanese real estate market created such an extreme bubble that the Emperor's Palace in Japan and the surrounding land was reportedly valued at a price exceeding the value of all real estate in the entire state of California![27] We now know this to be absolutely absurd, but it demonstrates the height of what we know as an *investment mania*, which we'll cover in the next chapter. The Japanese stock market topped out, with the Nikkei hitting almost 40,000 in early 1990.[28] At that time the average price/earnings ratio of Japanese stock was at 80 (roughly three times more expensive than comparable major tops in the U.S. market). It was truly a mania—right at the top of their demographic curve. Sound familiar? It should!

Unfortunately once the balloon had been expanded to a certain level and burst, there was no way to reinflate their asset values. Japanese stock and real estate could only go one way—down.

After the Japanese demographic wave topped in 1989 and 1990, they experienced a 14-year bear market, culminating in 2002 with the Nikkei (which at its high had been near 40,000) bottoming at 7,800. This represented an 80 percent decline for the average Japanese stock.

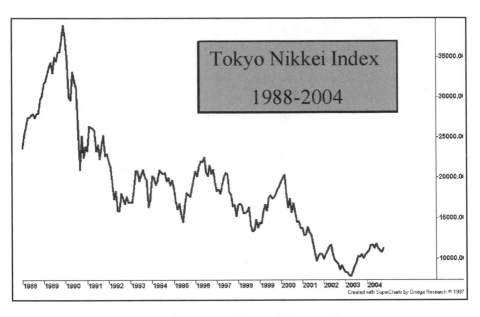

Source: Cornerstone Financial Services, Inc.
Chart 2-C

Believe me, I am not attempting to alarm anyone. Fear-based decisions, as well as greed-based decisions, tend to lead to big problems. But, forewarned is fore-armed. We need to make rational, intelligent, well-informed, well-thought-out decisions, not panicky decisions. We must come to terms with the brutal facts of our current economic reality, which come as a result of being hit broadside unexpectedly by Wall Street's shenanigans, plus a megatop in U.S. housing.

We have no guarantees that the United States will follow the pattern of Japan. Yet, every economic study that we can find demonstrates that there is an extremely close parallel between consumer spending patterns and the overall prosperity or lack thereof economically.

FAMILY SPENDING AND THE STOCK MARKET

In this section, we want to demonstrate that there is a very strong correla-tion between the number of people that hit their *peak* family spending years and the stock market. Peak spending for the average family typically occurs between the ages of forty-five and fifty. Since consumer spending drives the economy, it makes logical sense that the larger the number of people that you have hitting peak family spending, the stronger the economy will be. In turn, the stronger the economy, the more corporate earnings will rise, and the stronger the stock market will ultimately be.

The baby boom generation makes up almost 80 million people, two-thirds of our nation's workforce, and is generally defined as births between 1945 and 1965. As you can see by looking at Chart 2-D, in the late '60s abortion, birth control, and other actions brought the birth rate in our country way, way down, resulting in a much smaller group of people following the boomers—only forty-one million baby busters.

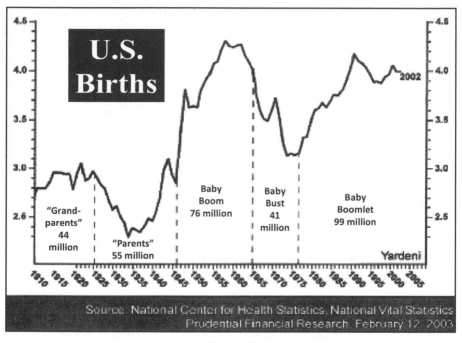

Chart 2-D

Chart 2-E shows the strong relation between the number of people hitting peak spending (births lagged to peak family spending) and the stock market. Note the strong correlation between the number of people hitting their spending peak and the stock market adjusted for inflation. The final wave of boomers will hit their peak spending years between 2003 and 2010, as shown in the chart. Thus, boomers put strong upward momentum behind the economy during this decade. Afterwards the economy should weaken radically.

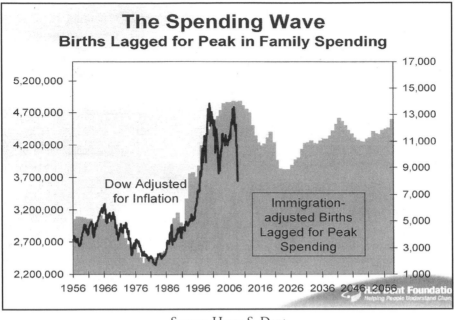

Source: Harry S. Dent
Chart 2-E

But if you look at the very long-term history for the market, you will see something similar to the old real estate saying "Location, location, location." Obviously, location is not the only factor that makes a real estate property successful or not, but it *can be the single most important factor.* The same is true of the stock market regarding earnings. To me it is almost undeniable that the single most important factor over time is corporate earnings, and there tends to be a very strong correlation between the health of American corporations, as reflected in corporate earnings (or profits), and the number of people that are hitting their peak in spending. Notice the long-term correlation between corporate earnings and the S&P 500 in the 1990s in the chart below.

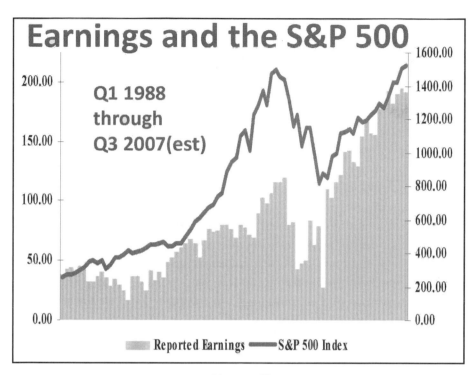

Chart 2-F[29]

Now, look again at the birthrate curves (Chart 2-D). Then compare it to the next chart (Chart 2-E). The second chart simply pushes forward (or lags) the population curve out to *peak family spending*. The baby boomer cycle (which topped in 1961) will hit its final peak for consumer spending in late 2009, when the median boomer family hits its overall spending peak.

Just as the average person peaks in consumer spending for housing at around age forty-four, the average individual peaks in consumer spending for most other items around forty-eight years old. Take this a step further, and this would project the top of the megatrend for baby boomers positively affecting our economy to top out around 2009. Thus, it is our assertion that housing spending tops first (median age, forty-four) and all other spending tops later (median age, forty-eight), as we can see in our current crisis.

A question then presents itself: if the economic wave that is likely to be produced from China, India, and other developing countries (we will discuss this in detail in chapter 8) is such a mammoth wave, how can you be sure that it will not completely offset the decline in spending power and economic thrust of the baby boom generation? Here's why.

In 2006, the average per capita income of a Chinese citizen was $2,010 per year. The U.S. equivalent per capita income for wage earners in the United States was $44,970 per year.[30] Regardless of how many Chinese you have spending, they simply can't offset the boomer spending decrease. It just won't happen fast enough.

Prior to the 2008 meltdown, the world was beginning to see shortages cropping up almost everywhere, most noticeably in petroleum, steel, concrete, food, and other commodities. At the same time, China is experiencing their version of the Industrial and Technological Revolutions *combined*.

To those Malthusians out there, this (again) is not the end of the world. This is not a sign that permanent deprivation is here and that there are not enough resources to go around in the world. This is a *utilization* problem. The world is simply not finding enough of these particular products fast enough to keep pace with the stunning economic growth that has been occurring in these countries and other developing countries around the world.

On the one hand we are seeing the U.S. baby boom generation consumer-spending trend ride off into the sunset; on the other hand we are seeing the economic sun rising in the Far East, which will indeed have a phenomenal impact over the long run.

In terms of shortages of raw materials and commodities, what we are seeing is very similar to what was seen in the U.S. in the 1970s, similar to when 76 million boomers created shortages of all of our own supplies within our country, only on a much bigger scale.

Thus, it is going to take a period of dislocation and problem-solving to navigate the world through this. Until we have the capability of getting enough oil, mining, steel, and other raw commodities to supply these enormous economic giants developing in the Far East, more inflationary pressure, in terms of commodities and energy, from China and India is coming down the road. While in the short term, the boomers moving toward retirement will create deflationary pressures (think California and Florida real estate), in the very long run, inflation could be our worst enemy.

Thus, I am reminded of the old Chinese proverb "May you live in interesting times." The Chinese character for *crisis* represents both *opportunity* and *danger*. The coming time in America and for the world over the next ten to fifteen years, in my view, represents both. On the one hand, many of the greatest potential opportunities of your investment and financial lifetime will likely present themselves during this time. Simultaneously, those years also represent our greatest danger.

> Remember, wealth is not lost; it changes owners. It goes from the hands of the unprepared to the hands of the prepared.

Like the old football saying "Luck is when preparation meets opportunity," there will be unprecedented potential for opportunity for both economic and financial gain. On the other hand, there will be extreme danger as well. Looking at the history of major economic challenges throughout recorded history, challenging times also present great opportunities, and extremely challenging times present the most rewarding opportunities.

The worst recorded economic scenario of modern history was the Great Depression of the 1930s. Even in that environment, the worst economic depression in world history, with unemployment skyrocketing to 25 percent, *there were more millionaires created per capita than in any other time in U.S. history!*[31]

Those that were unprepared, indeed, in essence, lost their assets to others that were either prepared or adapted. I believe that the coming times we face over the next fifteen years could represent equal opportunity and/or danger to this most amazing period of U.S. history.

I am not predicting an economic depression or anything of the sort. As an investment advisor, I strive diligently not to make predictions, because once you've made a prediction, your ego gets involved and you start focusing on being right rather than being flexible enough to change as the situation changes. So, keep in mind that I am not making predictions. What I am saying is that according to everything that I can see on a macroeconomic level, the perfect economic storm has just begun in our country, and I believe that you need to be prepared.

In this chapter we have looked at some of the fallacies and misunderstandings that played a major part in bringing us to this moment in our nation's economic history. In the next chapter, we see more specific causes and consequences of this economic meltdown our nation is facing—and will face for several years to come.

THOMAS ROBERT MALTHUS[32]

Thomas Robert Malthus FRS (13 February 1766–23 December 1834) was an English political economist and demographer. He expressed views on population growth and noted the potential for populations to increase rapidly, and often faster than the food supply available to them. This scenario, outlined in his treatise *An Essay on the Principle of Population*, is known as a Malthusian catastrophe.

Malthus regarded ideals of future improvement in the lot of humanity with skepticism, considering that throughout history a segment of every human population seemed relegated to poverty. He explained this phenomenon by pointing out that population growth generally preceded expansion of the population's resources, in particular the primary resource of food:

"…in all societies, there is a constant effort towards an increase of population. This tends to subject the lower classes of the society to distress and to prevent any great permanent amelioration of their condition."

Malthus also saw that societies through history had experienced at one time or another epidemics, famines, or wars: events that masked the fundamental problem of populations overstretching their resource limitations:

"The power of population is so superior to the power of the earth to produce subsistence for man, that premature death must in some shape or other visit the human race. The vices of mankind are active and able ministers of depopulation. They are the precursors in the great army of destruction, and often finish the dreadful work themselves.

Malthusian theory has had great influence on evolutionary theory, both in biology and in the social sciences. Malthus's population theory has also profoundly affected the modern-day ecological-evolutionary social theory.

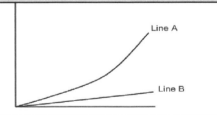

Malthus assumed that population would grow geometrically as illustrated by Line A, while food supplies would only increase arithmetically, as illustrated by Line B.

Malthus obviously underestimated the potential for technology as food supplies fell in cost by approximately 70% over the 20th century while the population of the planet roughly quadrupled.

PAUL EHRLICH, THE POPULATION BOMB[33]

The Population Bomb (1968) is a book written by Paul R. Ehrlich. A best-selling work, it predicted disaster for humanity due to over-population and the "population explosion." The book predicted that "in the 1970s and 1980s hundreds of millions of people will starve to death," that nothing can be done to avoid mass famine greater than any in the history, and radical action is needed to limit the over-population. History proved Ehrlich wrong, as the mass starvations predicted for the 1970s and 1980s never occurred.

GENERAL

The book is primarily a repetition of the Malthusian catastrophe argument that population growth will outpace agricultural growth unless controlled. Ehrlich assumes that the population is going to rise exponentially, but that the available resources, in particular food, are already at their limits. Whereas Thomas Malthus did not make a firm prediction of imminent catastrophe, Ehrlich warned of a potential massive disaster in the subsequent few years. Unlike Malthus, Ehrlich did not see any means of avoiding the disaster entirely. The solutions for limiting its scope that he proposed, including starving whole countries that refused to implement population control measures, were much more radical than those postulated by Malthus.

Reality is, the world food production grew exponentially at a rate much higher than the population growth, in both developed and developing countries, partially due to the efforts of Norman Borlaug's "Green Revolution" of the 1960s, and the food per capita level is the highest in history. On the other hand population growth rates significantly slowed down, especially in the developed world. Famine has not been eliminated, but its root cause is political instability, not global food shortage.

The Population Bomb was written at the suggestion of David Brower, at the time the executive director of the environmentalist Sierra Club, following an article Ehrlich wrote for the *New Scientist* magazine in December 1967.

The Club of Rome[34]

The Club of Rome is a global think tank that deals with a variety of international political issues. It was founded in April 1968 and raised considerable public attention in 1972 with its report *Limits to Growth* which has sold 30 million copies in more than 30 translations, making it the best selling environmental book in world history.

The Club of Rome further publicized the "deprivation" mindset, by predicting that economic growth could not be sustained indefinitely because of the limited availability of natural resources.

To get at the truth we must recognize that cycles of growth tend to wax and wane over long periods, temporary downturns, economic recessions and depressions merely serve historically to "purge the system" of excess debt and speculation, thus creating the foundations for and enabling the next growth boom.

Booms and busts are cyclical in nature and have existed throughout recorded history and will continue long after purveyors of doom have met their final reward.

CHAPTER THREE

BUBBLE, BUBBLE, TOIL, AND TROUBLE

THE GREAT MELTDOWN of 2008 was a demographic wake-up call for Americans. Some lessons from the great meltdown of 2008 are these:

1. There is no free lunch. When mortgage lenders, like carnival barkers, are peddling, "Get your free money; buy the house of your dreams," we need to pay attention that something is indeed wrong.

2. When Wall Street and bankers take extreme risks with what ultimately ends up being taxpayers' money (due to bailouts), we know that something indeed is wrong.

3. When government, in the guise of helping the common man, begins taking over large sectors of the economy (auto, banking, brokerage) while instituting great controls in order to "help the common man," we know that something is indeed wrong.

> "I believe that banking institutions are more dangerous to our liberties than standing armies..."
>
> —Thomas Jefferson[1]

Lehman Brothers, AIG, Fannie Mae (FNMA), Freddie Mac (FHLMC)... Twelve trillion dollars in losses later, the American people (and multiplied millions around the globe) are wondering, What happened? Why did my 401(k) become a 201(k), seemingly overnight? How could such bright, intelligent people make such tragic mistakes, literally collapsing markets around the world and affecting enormous devastation on investment assets worldwide? Was this just a gigantic miscalculation? Too much leverage and greed? Failure to see the forest for the trees? The answer—all of the above.

Certainly greed and leverage came into play here. Short-term Wall Street thinking, driven by an obsession for quarter-by-quarter profits, played a major role. Excess leverage nearly blew up the entire system.

Let's look at the recent history of how this has played out.

MELTDOWN 2008[2]	
September 7	The U.S. government seized Fannie Mae and Freddie Mac.
September 14	Merrill Lynch announced its sale to Bank of America.
September 15	Lehman Brothers, once the fourth largest investment bank, filed for bankruptcy.
September 16	The U.S. government announced an $85 billion emergency loan to rescue insurer AIG, and we began to hear reports of money markets "breaking the buck."
September 19	Treasury Secretary Paulson began drafting his $700 billion Troubled Asset Relief Program.
September 21	The Federal Reserve approved the transformation of Goldman Sachs and Morgan Stanley into bank-holding companies.
September 26	Washington Mutual became the largest thrift failure in U.S. history.
September 29	The FDIC brokered a deal that allows Citigroup to purchase Wachovia's banking operations; the House of Representatives voted down the TARP.
September 30	The Irish government began guaranteeing retail deposits for two years.
October 1	Warren Buffett invested $3 billion in General Electric as part of a $15 billion fundraising plan; Fortis was unable to raise $3 billion in a stock sale due to lack of interest; the U.S. Senate voted in favor of an expanded TARP; European leaders began considering their own bailout.
October 3	The House of Representatives passed their version of TARP, and President Bush signed it into law; Wells Fargo trumped Citigroup's bid for Wachovia.
October 5	Germany and Denmark insured bank deposits; BNP Paribas agreed to take over Fortis for $14.5 billion.
October 6	The Federal Reserve began providing $900 billion in short-term cash loans to banks; Iceland passed legislation that allows the government to nationalize, merge, or force ailing banks into bankruptcy.

MELTDOWN 2008	
October 7	The Federal Reserve made a $1.3 trillion emergency loan directly to companies.
October 8	Central banks in the United States, England, Canada, Sweden, Switzerland, and the European Central Bank all cut half a point off their key interest rates in the first unscheduled rate moves since the aftermath of 9/11; the Federal Reserve agreed to provide AIG with a loan of up to $37.8 billion on top of the $85 billion loan it received in September.
October 10	Wells Fargo won the battle for Wachovia.
October 11	The G7 met in Washington, D.C., to discuss the global economic crisis.
October 13	The Federal Reserve said the European Central Bank, others, to offer unlimited dollar funds.
October 15	The fifteen members of the Euro Zone, led by Germany and France, unveiled large coordinated plans along British lines to provide their banks with capital funding.

THE ROOT OF THE PROBLEM

But the bigger oversight is actually what created the problem in the first place. Greed and excessive risk-taking have always been a part of Wall Street to one degree or another. What makes this time different?

Let's start with leverage. The average Wall Street investment bank, which was 15-to-1 leveraged in 2003, moved to between 30/40-to-1 leveraged near the top of the cycle. But what's truly different this time, and ultimately a much bigger problem, lies at the root of our current crisis, and no amount of government bailout, printing press output by the Fed, or stimulus bailout can fix the root cause. This appeared hidden, at least hidden to Wall Street bankers (hidden in plain sight, that is). The root cause of the meltdown revolves around one word—*demographics*. Wall Street, like much of corporate America (and most international companies), tends to look primarily at short-term results. Big-picture stuff—really big-picture megatrends—tend to escape their attention in the wild pursuit of short-term gains.

Short-term profit maximization is the name of the game. Why? It is due partly to compensation structures that encourage the same. Unlike our academic friends, tenure does not exist in the corporate world. Results are expected *now*! What incentive is there for a CEO at the top of the corporate ladder, whose time in office might last two or three years (maybe ten if he or she is exceptional), to put the long-term shareholders' interests ahead of everything else? If he or she does not perform *now*, he or she won't be there to direct the company for shareholders in the future.

Thus, shorter-term priorities prevail. The problem with this is that by definition megatrends, those lasting a decade or longer, tend to get lost in the shuffle. Corporate CEOs, managers, and other leaders get too busy examining the trees while working feverishly to maximize short-term gains, all the while failing to notice the gigantic forest fire rushing toward them just over the hill.

Explanation of leverage

Frequently in seminars a person will come up to me and ask me to explain the concept of leverage. Let's give it a try. Suppose you bought a commodity futures contract, which allows you to invest $50,000 to control $1,000,000 worth of that commodity.

If the commodity in question were to rise 10 percent in price (from $1,000,000 to $1,100,000), you've more than doubled your initial investment. You invested only $50,000 and made $100,000 profit. Sounds wonderful.

However, leverage works both ways. Suppose instead the $1,000,000 in commodities fell by 10 percent. In this case you lost $100,000, even though you only invested $50,000. Thus, you lost your original $50,000 plus another $50,000.

If the investment fell 20 percent, you'd lose $200,000, and 30 percent would be a loss of $300,000, even though you had only put $50,000 in to start with.

Leverage can produce *extreme* results in either direction. That's why gimmicky mortgages in San Diego (no money down, interest-only, teaser rates, negative amortization mortgages) were a ticking time bomb.

Once housing prices started to fall, no money down on a $1,000,000 home loan produced a loss of $500,000 at current prices in many areas of California.

But even more extreme would be the banks and investment banks. Going from a 15-to-1 leverage, which is high enough, to between 30/40-to-1 leverage at the top of the cycle has produced unmitigated disaster.

Demographics are destiny

Demographics lie at the heart of the problem. How so? First, remember that this all started with the housing market: subprimes, Alt-As, option ARMs—you name it. There was a laundry list of financing options available for a housing market that seemed destined to rise forever, don't you think? (More on these exotic mortgages later.)

Nevertheless, home prices, like all other commodities, will rise as long as there is more demand available than supply. The housing bubble created a huge oversupply of housing, and home prices, like all other commodities, will have to fall in price and keep on falling until prices are cheap enough to entice enough buyers into the market to soak up the available inventory. Estimates vary that there are between 2–5 million surplus homes in America today, in early 2009.[3]

So, in many ways, this housing bust is much like every other real estate bust. There was too much crazy money chasing housing prices ever higher in certain parts of the country, until the market topped out and a vast over-supply developed. Ultimately, all bubbles pop. But in many other ways, this real estate bust is very different, atypical if you will. The difference between this bust and most other real estate busts is the *d* word—*demographics*.

We have already discussed the fact that the baby boom generation—those born after World War II (between 1946 and 1964)—represent the largest popu-lation group in our nation's history. It is a group so large, in fact, that boomers have dwarfed any previous generation. What is not widely known, however, is that the housing market actually topped almost precisely when one would have expected it to top based upon demographics. What do I mean? Census bureau data, taken from extremely large samples of people, can pinpoint with near precision when most people spend their money, depending upon their age.

PEAK SPENDING[4]

Item	Age
Breakfast Cereal	33
Potato Chips	42
Housing	44
Apparel, transportion	48
Roof Repair	70

Data taken from extensive government surveys demonstrate fairly conclu-sively when the average family tends to peak in spending for various items. Looking at the table above, you can see clearly when the average (or median) family peaks in terms of spending for various consumer purchases according to their age.

You can see that the average family peaks in terms of purchasing breakfast cereal at age thirty-three, potato chips at age forty-two, housing at forty-four, most other items at age forty-eight, and roof repair at age seventy. These are average or median numbers, so obviously some people will peak earlier, some later, but this is the norm. In terms of the economy, we are most interested in how this affects the supply-and-demand curve for a variety of products and services.

Laws of supply and demand govern the pricing of any product. So obviously, the best time to come to market with your product (or service) is when there is not enough of your product (or service) to go around. This induces a shortage, thus pushing both the price and profit margin up. Conversely, a surplus of any product will cause the price of that product to go down and force competitors to cut their prices and profit margins in order to compete.

> "The future has already been written. Demographic statistics reliably speak volumes about the shape of things to come. After all, the current supply of 20-year olds is both a known and a relatively fixed quantity. A country can change finance ministers, adjust its money supply, and alter its tax rate, but it can't do anything about the number of people that were born in 1950, 1960, 1970, 1980, and 1990."
>
> —Jim Rogers,
> "Gramps Inherits the Earth," March 1998

Note again that the average family's spending peaks in terms of housing at age forty-four. Next, look at Chart 3-A, showing the birthrate curve for recent generations of people living in the United States. Economic trends are never perfect, nor can anyone perfectly predict every twist and turn of the economy or the markets with absolute precision. Yet, there is one thing that remains very, very constant, and that is demographics—which is one reason demographics are referred to as the "future that has already been written."

There are many things about our future that can be changed; one of the things that cannot be changed is the number of people born in each particular year.

We don't know for certain who will be the next president of the United States or the next chairman of the Fed or the Treasury. We have no idea which political party will be in office years down the road or what the policies of that party might be. Nevertheless, there is one thing we can count on with certainty. We know how many people were born every year based upon census data, and we also know approximately how they will spend their money based on their age.

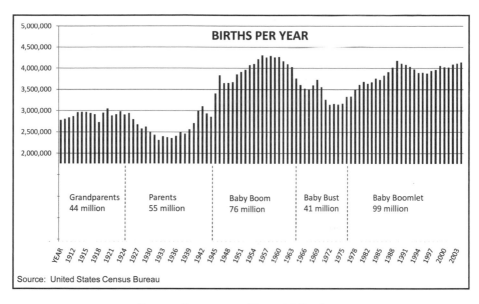

Source: United States Census Bureau

Source: Cornerstone Financial Services
Chart 3-A

Chart 3-A shows the number of births per year. Note that the baby boomer generation topped out in births between 1958 and 1961. If you adjust for immigration, the top was right at 1961 (the largest number of people born in any single year during the previous century). After that, birth rates plummeted sharply due to factors previously discussed—birth control, abortion, and so on. (Remember, we thought the world was overpopulated and headed for mass famine and starvation, don't you know.)

Now do the math. Add 1961 (the year the boomers topped out) plus forty-four (the age when the median family peaks in terms of spending or housing). That would give you a projected top for the U.S. housing market of 2005, almost precisely when the United States housing market topped out in late 2005, early 2006!

Boomers and Housing	
1961	Peak of baby boom births
+44	Peak of spending age for housing
2005	Housing market tops out

This is no coincidence; it did not occur through happenstance. In most areas of the country, housing experienced an unprecedented boom from the late 1980s until 2005, as ever-larger numbers of people bought bigger and better houses—buying second homes, vacation homes, adding granite countertops, and home media centers. The housing market topped out almost exactly when it was projected to top based upon demographics. That's why we often say demographics are destiny.

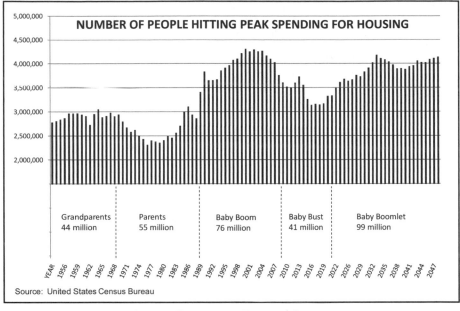

Source: Cornerstone Financial Services
Chart 3-B

Chart 3-B shows birth rates lagged for peak housing spending. Thus, those born in 1961 peaked in spending for housing in 2005, based upon a median spending age for housing of forty-four years of age. The supply-and-demand numbers don't lie. Housing will not likely see a big turnaround (upswing in prices) until around 2016, when the baby boomers' children (*boomlets*) begin approaching their peak spending age for housing.

Thus, the home purchase process nationwide could bottom by around 2012 or 2013 but will not likely begin moving back up strongly until at least 2016.

Home Buying Mania

Exactly at the time when the largest generation in American history hit its peak spending for housing, mania-like investing conditions took over.

Bubble or Mania—When an asset is perceived or its psychological value *greatly* exceeds its real economic value.

What is a mania? A mania, otherwise known as *a bubble,* is when investing emotions get out of hand. During a mania, greed, get-rich-quick thinking, and a sense of missing out pervade most investors' or buyers' thinking, leading them to make what often ends up, in hindsight, looking like a very dumb decision.

Manias have existed throughout recorded history, starting with the Dutch tulip bulb mania in the 1600s all the way through the dot-coms and now the 2000s housing bubble. The characteristics are all the same.

> That which has been is what will be, That which is done is what will be done, And there is nothing new under the sun.
>
> —Ecclesiastes 1:9, NKJV

Below you see a list of typical steps leading to both the boom (or build-up phase of the bubble), then the bust. These conditions haven't changed over the centuries, simply because human nature never changes. This explanation of how bubbles develop is taken from Martin Pring's excellent book *Investment Psychology Explained.*[5]

THE BUBBLE INFLATES

1. A believable concept offers a revolutionary and unlimited path to growth riches.

2. A surplus of funds exists alongside a shortage of opportunities. This channels the attention of a sufficient number of people with money to trigger the immediate and attention-getting rise in price. These are germs that spread the contagion.

3. The idea cannot be irrefutably disproved by the facts but is sufficiently complex that it is necessary for the average person to ask the opinions of others to justify its validity.

4. Once the mania gets underway, the idea has sufficient power and compelling belief to spread from a minority to the majority as the crowd seeks to imitate its leaders.

5. The price fluctuates from traditional levels of overvaluation to entirely new ground.

6. The new price levels are sanctioned by individuals considered by society to be leaders or experts, thereby giving the bubble an official imprimatur.

7. There is a fear of missing out. The flagship or centerpiece of the bubble is copied or cloned as new schemes and projects attempt to ride on the coattails of the original. They are readily embraced, especially by those who have not yet participated.

8. Lending practices by banks and other financial institutions deteriorate as loans are made indiscriminately. Collateral is valued at inflated and unsustainably high values. A vulnerable debt pyramid is a necessary catalyst for the bust when it eventually begins.

9. A cult figure emerges, symbolic of the bubble.

10. The bubble lasts longer than the expectations of virtually everyone.

11. An atmosphere of fast, easy gains almost invariably results in shady business practices and fraud being practiced by the perpetrators of the original scheme.

12. At the height of the bubble, the possibility exists that even the objective person can come up with a simple but eye-catching statistic proving the madness is unsustainable. (In our time [1989–1990], we note that the value of the land encompassing the Emperor's Palace in Tokyo was equivalent to the total value of all [the real estate in] California.)

Virtually all of these ingredients fed the housing mania in housing bubble states like California, Florida, Nevada, and Arizona.

Manias and the Media

In order for a delusion to be disseminated widely enough to engulf an entire culture, the media ultimately moves to center stage, with massive coverage of whatever the predominate thinking is regarding the latest investment craze.

In fact, one analyst, Paul Montgomery, has done extensive research on *Time* magazine covers all the way back to 1924. His findings are that when a financial event appears on the cover of *Time* magazine, the prevailing market trend that is featured on the cover (whether good or bad) will reverse over 80 percent of the time—shockingly at times within thirty days![6] In other words, over 80 percent of the time, *Time*'s cover tells you exactly what not to do. Do the opposite.

This is not to be construed as an indictment of the media. What is happening here is that the media is *extremely* adept at discovering whatever is foremost on the minds of millions of Americans at that particular time. Once an economic or market event is large enough to capture the minds and hearts of millions of Americans to the extent that it seems to be on everyone's mind at the same time, that means that, whatever the trend, it is over! Supply and demand still rules. By the time a trend reaches *Time*'s cover, that trend is normally hitting its peak.

HOUSING PRICES EXPLODED

Armed with "free money" (no money down, no documentation) and the ability to finance the "home of your dreams" with extreme leverage, buyers—like piranha on a bleeding cow in the Amazon River—went stir-crazy buying homes in bubble areas of the country. All this money chased the home purchase process to extreme, unsustainable levels as the Great Mortgage Mania marched on.

DOW JONES HOME CONSTRUCTION INDEX

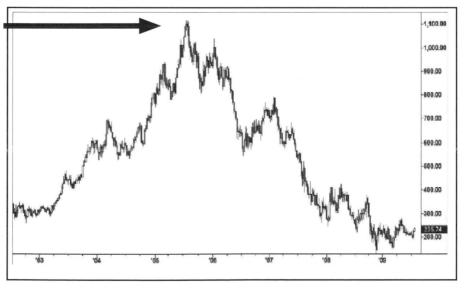

Source: Cornerstone Financial Services
Chart 3-C

Chart 3-C shows the Dow Jones Home Construction Index. The arrow at the top of the chart shows precisely when *Time's* article came out.

Similar findings would also be likely for *U.S. News and World Report* and *Newsweek* (other current-event magazines), but Paul's research was based upon *Time's* covers. Covers of financial magazines also tend to mark major turning points for the market in contrary fashion, yet are less reliable, as these magazines always have financial events on their covers. Current-event magazines like *Time, Newsweek,* and *U.S. News* give better signals, if you will, of when a major market trend has run its course.

All—repeat, all—financial decisions have an emotional component to them. Sometimes it's fear, sometimes greed or get-rich-quick thinking, pride, or ego. Any number of motivators can affect our decision making, but in the case of bubbles, it's almost always greed or get-rich-quick, combined with a sense of being left behind.

Many homebuyers in California, I'm sure, felt they'd never be able to own a home if they didn't get in *now*, despite the fact that home prices in California had long since left their moorings, much like the tech stocks of 1999, and shot into the stratosphere.

Unable to buy the home of their dreams (in some cases, almost any home due to extremely overvalued prices), buyers resorted to a wide variety of gimmicky mortgages designed to just "get in."

Alt-As, subprimes, option ARMs—mortgage lenders' creativity knew no bounds when it came to financing techniques. One lender stated, "If you had a pulse, we gave you a loan."[7] In Bakersfield, California, a Mexican strawberry picker with an income of $14,000 and no English was lent every penny he needed to buy a house for $720,000.[8]

The companies making crazy loans didn't care very much if the homeowner ended up defaulting, for two reasons:

1. Either they didn't plan to hold the loan but instead intended to pass it along to Wall Street, which would bundle, slice-and-dice it, and sell it (along with any subsequent losses) to investors around the world;

2. Or, if they did plan to hold the loan, they assumed home prices would keep rising, such that homeowners could either refinance before loans reset or, if the homeowner defaulted, the losses (i.e., severity) would be minimal.[9]

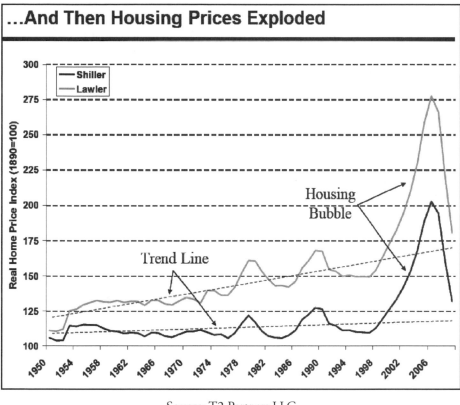

Source: T2 Partners LLC
Chart 3-D

A bubble of the magnitude that developed with the exploding housing prices brought these consequences:

- The entire system—real estate agents, appraisers, mortgage lenders, banks, Wall Street firms, and ratings agencies—became corrupted by the vast amounts of quick money to be made.

- Debt became increasingly available and acceptable in our culture.

- Millions of Americans became greedy speculators and/or took on too much debt.

- Greenspan kept interest rates too low for too long.

- Institutional investors stretched for yield, didn't ask many questions, and took on too much leverage.

- In general, everyone was suffering from irrational exuberance.[10]

Wall Street, eager for another round of profits after the tech boom burst, developed an insatiable appetite for these type of loans, "securitizing" them, which means packaging them together, slicing/dicing, and selling them off to investors literally all over the globe.

Wall Street's demand for loan "product" was a major driver of the decline in lending standards.

- The Asset-Backed Securities (ABSs) and Collateralized Debt Obligation (CDO) businesses were enormously profitable for Wall Street firms.

- To produce ABSs and CDOs, Wall Street needed a lot of loan "product."

- Mortgages were a quick, easy, big source.

- It is easy to generate higher and higher volumes of mortgage loans: simply lend at higher loan-to-value ratios, with ultra-low teaser rates, to uncredit-worthy borrowers, and don't bother to verify their income and assets (thereby inviting fraud).

- There's only one problem: DON'T EXPECT TO BE REPAID![11]

Now all of this nonsense has come back to haunt us. A once-in-a-generation housing boom has now become an unprecedented bust and has taken significant portions of our market and financial system with it.

THE BUBBLE BURSTS

In his book *Investment Psychology Explained*, Martin Pring gives further explanation about the bubble-turned-bust. He gives the following reasons:

1. There is a rise in prices sufficient to encourage an influx of new supply. In the case of the stock market, new issues are offered to investors at an increasing rate. If viable companies cannot be found, money is raised for concepts. In effect, it is possible to lower investment standards because an increasingly gullible public is demanding new vehicles for instant wealth.

2. Another cause (of the bubble's burst) comes from a rise in the cost of interest, either as a result of the increasing demand for credit, a skeptical government, or both.

3. Prices do not just fall; they collapse. The "concept" stocks are exposed for what they are—concepts. Collateral for loans evaporates overnight. Bankers not only are reluctant to expand credit for new ventures but also try to protect themselves by calling existing loans. The result is a self-feeding downward price spiral as everyone heads for the exit at the same time.

4. Inevitably fraud and other shady dealings are exposed. These sometimes represent a cornerstone of the debt pyramid, the removal of which is the primary cause of the price collapse. At other times, they are ancillary or contributing factors that adversely affect the general level of confidence.

5. The government or other quasi-governmental agencies occasionally intervene or try to shore up confidence. Such activity merely gives cooler heads the chance to unload before the real price decline sets in.[12]

Virtually all of these ingredients popped the housing credit bubble. To get a better understanding of exactly how all of this started in the first place, let's look at the chronology of the meltdown and how bubbles burst.

CHRONOLOGY OF THE MELTDOWN

1. Federal agencies are encouraged to lend to poor credit risks. Starting in 1999–2000, Fannie Mae and Freddie Mac are "encouraged" by politicians to give loans to poor credit risks to "encourage" better citizenship.

   This is also an example of attempting to equalize outcomes and is a perfect example of the law of unintended consequences. There is no question that homeowners make better citizens, every socio-economic study around would reach this conclusion! However by "encouraging" (forcing?) more loans to poor credit risks, we inevitably sowed the seeds, if you will, for our own destruction. Congress planted the seeds, then Wall Street watered and grew the destructive crop by going off the deep end with loans and leverage.

2. Boomers decide their homes are their best investments. This perfect storm developed as 76 million people, the largest generation in our country's history, approached peak spending age

for housing and went overboard with upgrades, improvements, and more expensive houses. This massive generation goes gaga over housing.

3. Home prices skyrocket as lenders, eager to get in while the getting's good, create all sorts of gimmick mortgages, allowing Americans to borrow far more than ever before for housing. These gimmick mortgages appear exactly at the top of the boomer demographic housing wave.

4. Armed with more money to spend on housing than ever before (by a factor of three to one), the real estate prices soar as way too much money chases the supply of houses even higher. The average home price in America rises from $151,000 to $250,000 in five years.

    The table below shows just how crazy lending standards got. For example, in 1995 a borrower with an average income of $30,000 could borrow $90,000 on a home loan after putting 15–20 percent down. Thus, his or her debt-to-income ratio was 33 percent.

    By 2007, lending standards had deteriorated to the point that the average wage earner (now making over $40,000 per year) could borrow up to $359,000, allowing 60 percent of his or her income to go to debt service, and could finance the home by paying interest only.

Home Loans	1995	2007[13]
Pre-Tax Income	$30,000	$40,403
Debt/Income	33 percent	60 percent
Borrowing Power	$90,000	$359,000
Payment Type	Full	Interest only

5. Wall Street—eager for a new round of profits after the dot-com bust—invents a new method of earning fees. While mortgages have been "securitized" for years (sold to investors in pools), securitization takes on an all-new meaning during the biggest housing boom in world history. Commercial banks and mortgage firms join the party (i.e., IndyMac, Countrywide, etc.).

6. Consumers join the easy-money party using home equity lines of credit (HELOCs), effectively using their homes as an

ATM. Most of this money was spent (not invested) with a high percentage going toward buying new cars in the bubble states. What a great use of their "investment" dollars!

7. Consumers feel wealthier (rising stock and housing prices); they spend even more money—the so-called "wealth" effect. Debts ratcheted ever higher.

8. Mortgage companies invent creative ways to allow even more debt through creative mortgages, such as subprimes (poor credit risk), Alt-As (low or no documentation—so-called "liar loans"), and option ARMs (low teaser rates that add principal to the end of the loan every year, also known as a negative amortization loan). Creative financing allows the debt pyramids to go up and up—even more money chasing home prices higher.

9. Wall Street hires math and science professors (I'm not making this up) to create inventive new mortgage investments. They divide subprime loans (poor credit risk loans) into five different tranches. Rating agencies then rate many of these subprime tranches as AAA-risk, the highest credit rating available. Triple-A rated subprimes? The ultimate financial oxymoron. (I'm not making this up, either!) These highly leveraged investments become what one author described as a *doomsday machine.*

10. Leverage proliferates. Wall Street then invents a new form of "insurance" known as a credit default swap (CDS). AIG becomes one of the largest purveyors of CDSes. Default swaps are designed to pay back an investor if the underlying mortgages in his or her portfolio go bad (default). By calling them swaps, Wall Street does not have to set aside any loss reserves (for defaults), nor be regulated as true insurance would be.

11. Systemic risk has now multiplied beyond comprehension. Literally no one at this point knows just how much risk is embedded within the system.

12. Losses proliferate as subprime loans begin to go bad. Foreclosures and loan losses pile up.

13. Due to extreme leverage (going from 15-to-1 to 30/40-to-1 leverage), financial firms begin to fail. Bear Stearns starts the bailout parade.

14. Lehman fails. In the midst of the fall 2008 financial debacle, Lehman Brothers is allowed (forced?) into chapter 7 liquidation bankruptcy.

15. This sets off a chain reaction throughout the world as leveraged investments fall in price—creating margin calls and more forced selling. This cascades into the world's markets simultaneously.

16. Credit flows, already slowed by previous events, virtually cease and bank-lending rates soar, deleveraging accelerates.

17. Congress, steadfastly behind the curve, fails to pass a bailout bill before outright panic sets in.

18. Deleveraging goes into high gear as hedge funds, short sellers, and institutions panic.

19. Once the deleveraging process gains momentum, it becomes ongoing and irreversible. Leveraged selling collapses the market until it finally puts in a temporary bottom on November 20, 2008.

Just how did this perfect storm come to be in the first place? How did seemingly rational homebuyers turn into wild speculators? How could august Wall Street investment bankers very nearly blow up the entire financial world?

In a word, *greed*. Greed is addictive. Seemingly rational people, when under its spell, can make simply idiotic decisions. A classic book on this type of behavior is Charles Mackay's *Extraordinary Popular Delusions and the Madness of Crowds*, written in the 1890s.[14] Despite the passing of time, it is still relevant because human nature never changes.

MOB BEHAVIOR

All of us have seen some version of the following classic Western movie. An innocent man is unjustly arrested for a crime he didn't commit and placed in jail by the sheriff. Local hooligans or, more likely, the real criminals begin stirring up trouble, inciting the townsfolk to anger, then rage over the crimes supposedly perpetrated. Soon a lynch mob appears. The sheriff, bound to uphold his duty, threatens to shoot the first one to move in an attempt to control the crowd.

We've all seen this scene at the movies, but reality is that mob behavior often permeates the markets and can greatly affect investment decisions. Mob behavior definitely ruled both in home-buying decisions in bubble housing areas of the country as well as in Wall Street, plus in a number of banks and investment firms.

Part I of the housing bubble fiasco, which nearly blew up Wall Street, revolved around subprime lending and losses from these mortgages defaulting, plus unprecedented leverage associated with these assets-gone-bad.

As you can see in Chart 3-E, loan delinquencies led by subprimes are surging.

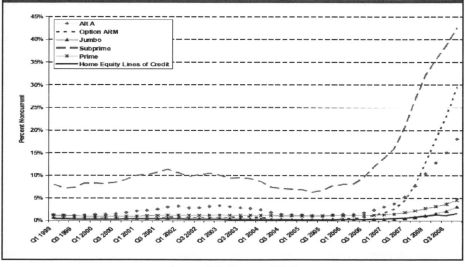

Source: T2 Partners LLC
Chart 3-E

Now we're left with the aftermath. The question becomes, Has the problem been fixed? Has the burst housing bubble, with its attendant financial and market blowups, been repaired or taken care of? Or, have we just seen the first round; could there be more to come? Unfortunately, there is much more to come. The bust from this unprecedented building boom, as 76 million Americans approached peak spending for housing, appears to have several more innings left to run. We're probably only about halfway through the crisis.

CHAPTER FOUR

BRACING FOR THE BIG CHILL

A s MUCH AS I'd like to tell you the financial crisis that began in 2008 is over, I can't. It's far from over! Below is a list of just a few reasons why the bottom appears to be several years away.

1. *Excess inventory of homes*—Current estimates run between 1.5 million and 5 million excess houses on the market due to "euphoric" investment-oriented housing decisions and foreclosures.

   Never before the bubble had Americans considered their homes as their best investment. Unfortunately, millions around the country are now finding out indeed how poor of an investment housing can be when the timing and debt create problems.

   Before the housing market can bottom nationwide, all—repeat, all—of this excess housing inventory must be soaked up, bought out of foreclosure or through distress sales. Housing prices cannot finally bottom out until supply no longer exceeds demand.

> During the housing bubble we created an enormous excess supply of houses due to mania-like "investing" conditions. Foreclosures now add to the supply daily.

2. *Alt-As just starting to reset*—As seen in the following charts, Alt-A mortgages, often euphemistically called "liar loans," are just starting to reset and push payments for homeowners significantly higher.

   As we've seen in round one of the housing bubble, once the subprime interest rate resets began to hit, defaults began to skyrocket.

Alt-As are just beginning to reset, likely leading to even more defaults on Alt-A mortgages between 2010 and 2013. Alt-As were bought by homeowners in all states but were heaviest in the bubble states.

3. *Option ARMs*—Option ARMs are ticking time bombs. Despite the fact that this subset of creative mortgages is numerically smaller than Alt-As, their resets are more devastating, with the average reset going from $1,672 per month to $2,725 per month—*up* 63 percent!

4. *HELOCs (home equity line of credit) and second mortgages*—Home equity lines of credit and second mortgages are 100 percent exposed to loss, as only the primary mortgage holder has rights to foreclose in order to recover some of the losses.

   Estimates are more than $1 trillion in loss exposure to our banking system on these loans, which were issued predominately near the top of the bubble.

5. *Foreclosures/pressure prices*—Home prices continue to fall as foreclosures rise. As home prices fall, it makes it even more difficult for a struggling homeowner, who may have seen his mortgage payment rise dramatically due to the gimmicky mortgage resetting (subprimes, Alt-As, option ARMs). Will he continue to justify this albatross around his neck? Skyrocketing mortgage payments combined with crashing home prices do not make for a quick turnaround or even a short-term bottom.

6. *Strategic defaults.* Many homeowners in bubble areas of the country have strategically decided to default on their home mortgages, despite being capable of making the payments. Strategic default refers to making a decision to walk away from a home that has fallen sharply in value. A 10 percent decline won't do it, but many homeowners are 30 percent or more underwater and are simply walking away. Research shows that people are more likely to walk away if they either know someone else who has done it or it has occurred in their neighborhood, despite the fact that most consider it morally wrong.[1] (I guess it's OK if everyone else is doing it, right?)

7. *Job losses in the hardest-hit areas create more downward pressure on home prices*—Job losses continue as rising unemployment forces more foreclosures. Most consumers have lived paycheck-to-paycheck for much of their lives; thus, when one spouse loses a job, foreclosure often is the consequence.

8. *The "worst" mortgages are heavily underwater*—The most egregious mortgages are primarily grouped in the bubble states, where home prices have fallen the hardest. These bad mortgage types put even more pressure on home prices as default piles upon default.

9. *Expected losses are only half realized*—Thus far, projected losses are less than one-half realized, regardless of which source you use to estimate expected losses. The charts that follow make it obvious that the mortgage fiasco's effect upon our economy and its financial system are hardly over.

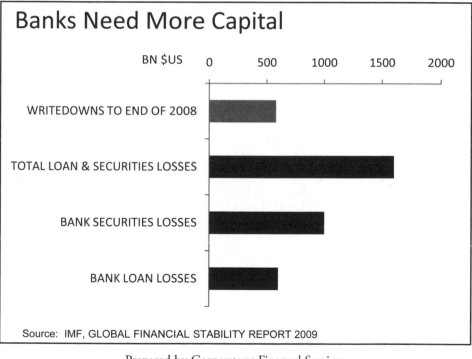

Prepared by Cornerstone Financal Services
Chart 4-A

What's not widely known is that while the subprime fiasco still has time to run and defaults continue to climb, Parts II and III of the debacle are actually bigger in terms of dollar-loan amounts than subprimes ever thought about being. Subprime defaults continue to rise and home prices fall, but one good thing is that at least the vast majority of the subprime interest rate resets are behind us. (See Chart 4-B.)

> "Reinforced by many years of experience, both lenders and borrowers assumed that home prices would keep rising and easy credit would keep flowing, allowing borrowers to refinance before the reset."[2]

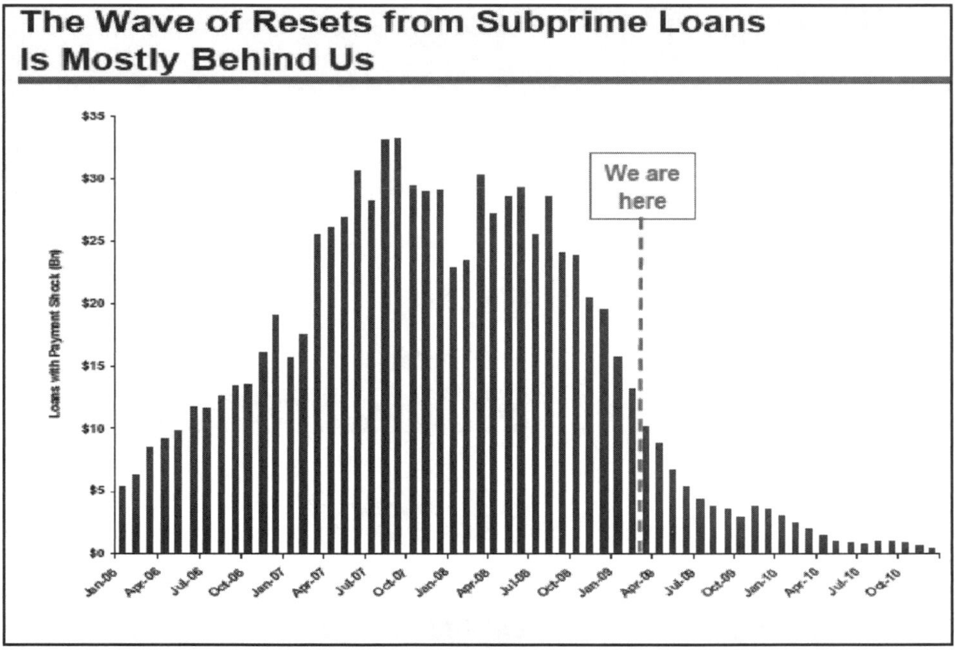

The Wave of Resets from Subprime Loans Is Mostly Behind Us

Source: T2 Partners LLC
Chart 4-B

Alt-A and option ARM mortgage resets, on the other hand, are still mostly ahead of us, and they represent billions more in losses for financial firms. So, as I'm writing this in summer 2009, it appears that round one of the "Great Mortgage Rip-off" is drawing to a close. All of us, myself included, would like nothing better than to hope that all of this is over and behind us. But the reality is, potentially bigger issues lie just ahead. (See Chart 4-C.)

As you can see, most of the subprime resets (upward interest rate adjustments) are behind us. Most Alt-As are ahead of us, not to mention option ARMs. Both of these recently created mortgages have yet to extract their measure of pain upon either homeowners or the financial system.

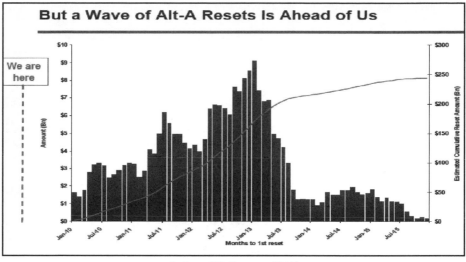

Source: T2 Partners LLC
Chart 4-C

A Primer on Option ARMs

1. An option ARM is an adjustable-rate mortgage typically made to a prime borrower.

2. Banks typically relied on the appraised value of the home and the borrower's high FICO score, so 83 percent of the option ARMs written in 2004–2007 were low or no document loans ("liar loans").

3. Each month the borrower can choose to pay: 1–the fully amortizing interest and principal; 2–full interest; or 3–an ultra-low teaser interest-only rate (typically 2–3 percent), in which case the unpaid interest is added to the balance of the mortgage (meaning it is negatively amortizing). Approximately 80 percent of option ARMs are negatively amortizing. Lenders,

however, booked earnings as if the borrowers were making full-interest payments.

4. A typical option ARM is a 30- or 40-year mortgage that resets (*recasts*) after 5 years when it becomes fully amortized. If an option ARM negatively amortizes to 110–125 percent of the original balance (depending on the terms of the loan), this triggers a reset, even if 5 years have not elapsed.

5. Upon reset, the average monthly payment jumps 63 percent from $1,672 to $2,725 ($32,700 annually).[3]

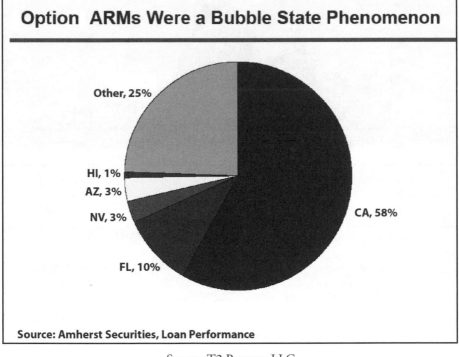

Source: T2 Partners LLC
Chart 4-D

HOUSING FACTS

The following facts about the housing market provide further clarification about our current condition:

- Mortgage-lending standards became progressively worse starting in 2000 but really went off a cliff beginning in early 2005.

- It takes an average of fifteen months from the date of the first missed payment by a homeowner to liquidation of the home (generally a sale via auction).

- There's too much inventory to work off quickly, especially in light of the millions of foreclosures over the next few years.

- While foreclosure sales are booming in many areas, regular sales by homeowners have plunged, in part because people usually can't sell when they're under water on their mortgage and in part due to human psychology. People naturally anchor on the price they paid or what something was worth in the past and are reluctant to sell below this level. In 2005, 29 percent of new mortgages were interest-only—or less, in the case of option ARMs—versus the 1 percent level in 2001.

- The sale of new homes costing $750,000 or more quadrupled from 2002 to 2006.

- In the 2004–2006 time period, between 18–20 percent of all home sales were subprime.

- In January 2009, distressed sales accounted for 45 percent of all existing home sales nationwide—and more than 60 percent in California. In addition, the *shadow* inventory of foreclosed homes already likely exceeds one year, and there will be millions more foreclosures over the next few years, creating a large over- hang of excess supply that will likely cause prices to overshoot on the downside, as they are already doing in California.

- We are also quite certain that wherever prices bottom, there will be no quick rebound.

- Given that lending standards got much worse in late 2005 through 2006 and into the first half of 2007, and that the many other types of loans with longer reset dates are now starting to default at catastrophic rates, there are sobering implications for expected defaults, foreclosures, and auctions in 2009 and beyond, which promise to drive home prices down further.

- More mortgage meltdown:

  » 10 percent of homes built this decade are vacant, and

  » 29 percent of loans in the last five years are underwater.[4]

Hopefully, these issues will be handled better next time, but forewarned is forearmed; and, personally, I'd rather be safe than sorry at this point. So, while defaults on subprimes are still escalating, clearly the reset trend—which is ultimately the primary reason for the defaults anyway—is mostly behind us. Alt-As and option ARM resets are just starting to happen. Most of these resets are dead ahead, taking place primarily in 2010–2012.

Historically, bubbles of this type have taken about six years to unwind for housing, as opposed to around three years for stock bubbles. Because stocks are more liquid and easily traded, their bubbles unwind much faster than less liquid real estate, which takes much longer to go through the foreclosure/sales process.

Aftermath of a "Typical" Financial Crisis

The aftermath of a financial crisis usually includes the following factors:

- *Housing*—six-year adjustment (2006–2012)

- *Unemployment*—rises 7 percent (11–12 percent)

- *Stocks*—3.5-year bear market

- *Real GDP*—down 9 or more percent[5]

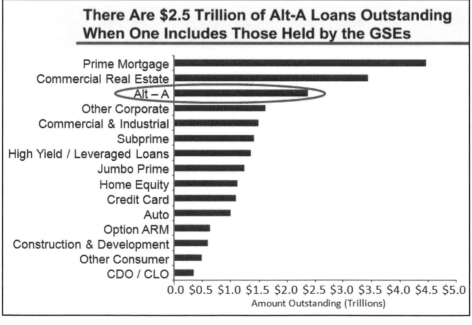

Source: T2 Partners LLC
Chart 4-E[6]

With more than $3 trillion worth of potential losses in Alt-As and option ARMs at risk, falling real estate prices plus rapidly escalating mortgage payments virtually guarantee more pain to come. In spite of authorities' best efforts, more real estate and economic pain lies ahead.

How, you ask, might this affect others not in the bubble states, as well as other financial assets, like stocks?

First, non-bubble states will obviously still be affected, likely to a lesser degree but, in some cases, to a much less degree. It is reminiscent of the dot-com era, when the average dot-com fell 90 percent and the average tech stock fell 80 percent (the NASDAQ fell 78 percent from top to bottom), but the Dow Jones Industrial Average—full of mostly the blue-chip stocks—fell just 37 percent. A 37 percent drop still hurts but is not an irreversible, catastrophic loss (like the dot-coms).

Percent of Last 5 Years—Purchasers Who Are Under Water[6]	
Metro Area	
Los Angeles	54.6
Washington	50.4
Miami	65.1
San Francisco	51.2
San Diego	63.9
Phoenix	36.4
Las Vegas	61.4

Bubble real estate is not likely to fall 90 percent, as the dot-coms were mostly just hype and hope—a lot of hot air waiting to burst. Real estate in San Diego or Las Vegas, while it certainly has tangible value (unlike most dot-coms), still became tremendously overvalued. A 70 percent drop or more is entirely possible, given the fact that many of these areas are already down 50 percent or so, with more mortgage problems on the way.

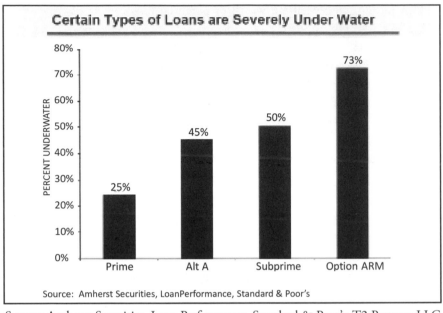

Source: Amherst Securities, Loan Performance, Standard & Poor's; T2 Partners LLC
Chart 4-F

Thus, the greatest mortgage fiasco in our country's history, brought on by the largest population group in our country's history, is definitely not over.

From Wall Street to Main Street

Once the housing debacle hit Wall Street, it then spread to Main Street as consumers, panicked at seeing their 401(k)s plummet while large numbers of major financial institutions went bankrupt almost on a moment-by-moment basis, immediately clamped down on their purse strings.

Remember that consumer spending is what drives the economy, and consumer spending went from high gear into reverse in a matter of sixty days. This, combined with the freezing-up of the credit markets, had a domino effect that spread worldwide.

In Chart 4-G, you can see that global shipping literally fell almost to zero in a matter of less than 6 months. The cost of renting one of the world's largest freight ships dropped from $132,000 per day *to $2,700 a day* in less than 6 months, representing an *unprecedented 94 percent decline* in shipping costs virtually overnight!

Note: This index shows the incredible drop in global shipping, which has recovered
(according to this shipping cost index) approximately one-third from the high.
Chart 4-G

This was such a blind side to the economy, but the magnitude of these losses
in the financial system was completely hidden from consumers; all the while,
authorities continued to reassure us that all was well. As a result, corporations
were totally unprepared for the incredible drop in sales. Unsold inventories
surged, and the only way to get rid of these inventories was to slash prices, as
shown in Chart 4-H.

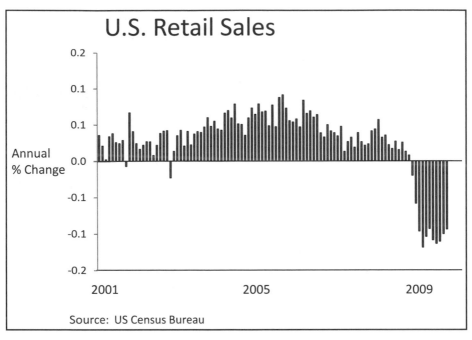

Prepared by Cornerstone Financial Services
Chart 4-H

With U.S. retail prices slashed throughout America, we entered into the world of a central banker's worst nightmare: a *deflationary* environment.

In a deflationary environment, prices fall due to lack of orders. But that's not the worst of it. The problem is that deflationary behavior tends to reinforce itself, thus becoming a *self-reinforcing process*. What do I mean by this?

In deflation, prices begin falling and consumers learn to anticipate that prices will be lower next year—or a few months down the road. They decide to hold off on new purchases. When a large group of consumers decides to hold off on buying things, that creates additional excess inventories for the businesses to have to liquidate. Again, the only way to liquidate inventories is to reduce the prices. Consumers then say, "Aha, I knew if I waited longer the price would go down." This reinforces their beliefs, causing them to hold off on buying even more, thus exacerbating the problem. The cycle repeats itself. The longer this process is allowed to run, the more difficult it is to break.

We've seen two cases of deflation within the last hundred years. The first was in the 1930s, when the U.S. faced a *severe* deflation, which bottomed out in three and one-half years, and the second was Japan's deflationary spiral, beginning in 1990. It appeared to have bottomed out after twelve years (1990–2002) but, in reality, may not yet be over.

In our current crisis, the problem we have is that at the precise top of the demographic megatrend, Wall Street, the banks, and investment bankers all went on a wild mortgage-lending spree. Like a bunch of drunken sailors with pockets full of money, they nearly blew up the system, almost exactly at the top of our demographic curve.

Thus, what we are facing now is not an ordinary, garden-variety recession. It will play out nothing like the recessions we have seen in recent years. Recent recessions have occurred in the context of a thirty-year baby boomer-induced boom. Now we are in the beginning phase of a ten- or fifteen-year *baby boomer bust*. This recession will cut deeper and last longer than any in recent history and has the potential to become a depression before it is over.

During the boom, the banks grossly overlent, and now that the horse is out of the barn, they have shut the door. Although consumers went on a borrowing binge like none in history, they are now feeling a lot less rich than they were before. Making it worse, the biggest wave of boomers is not far from retirement, with a whole lot smaller asset base than before.

Thus, we are in a classic scenario economists refer to as "pushing on a string." The twenty-five-year borrowing binge is over. Banks don't want to lend, consumers don't want to borrow, and until this has time to wash through the system, it won't turn around quickly.

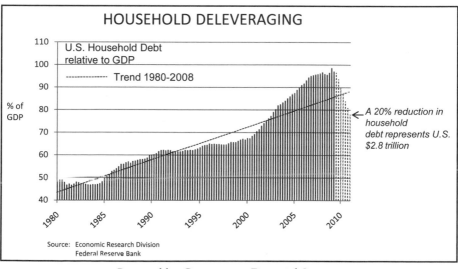

Prepared by Cornerstone Financial Services
Chart 4-I

Chart 4-I shows projected household deleveraging. The dashed line represents the median of what consumers would be expected to borrow based upon normal times. As you can see, during the housing bubble the average U.S. household went much deeper into debt than ever before. Thus, we not only had a housing bubble but a credit bubble as well.

The problem with this picture is that historically the pendulum of change never stops in the middle; it goes from one extreme to the other. In this case, household borrowing, which ran up to extreme levels during the bubble, is unlikely to stop dropping at the trend line but will likely overshoot on the downside as well. This means we have several years of painful deleveraging as consumers reduce borrowing and pay down debt, as well as increase their savings.

So, you might ask, what's so bad about that? Consumers increasing their savings and paying down debt would normally be viewed as a positive and will eventually be necessary to get us out of this morass. The problem is with *when* it's occurring—just after the 2008 meltdown, while unemployment is still skyrocketing, corporations are being hit hard, and bankruptcies are on the rise. It means that this will not be over quickly. When we do finally bottom, it is unlikely that we will have a vigorous bounce off of the low.

Like partygoers on a drunken binge, the hangover for this megatop of consumer spending and borrowing will stay with us for a while.

Unemployment is climbing at the fastest rate since the 1930s. (See Chart 4-J.) This puts ongoing pressure on the housing market. As more people lose their jobs, the mortgage difficulties increase. Clearly neither unemployment nor housing foreclosures have topped out as of August 2009.

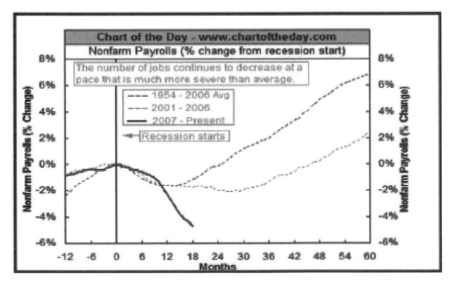

Chart 4-J[8]

MELTDOWN AND THE STOCK MARKET

How will it likely affect stocks and the stock market? In and of itself, a real estate debacle does not necessarily have a devastating effect on the stock market. The 1980s saw a real estate debacle (with a small *d*) during the savings and loan crisis. At one point, 85 percent of the S&Ls in the country were losing money. Most were liquidated or merged out of existence.[9] In fact, the number of banks involved back then was much larger, but the real estate losses were smaller, more contained. Yet the 1980s real estate turmoil barely affected the stock market.

What makes this time different and, indeed, unique is the *magnitude* of losses and the number of people involved, plus the degree of speculation, overvaluation, and leverage.

Remembering that this was the bubble to end all bubbles for U.S. real estate (76 million boomers involved) should create a lasting image. Nevertheless, if—and I repeat, if—authorities had handled things differently, financial catastrophe might have been averted. So while it's possible that the next round of foreclosures won't create a huge negative for stocks, it's highly unlikely.

DERIVATIVE NIGHTMARE

The real problem is not just the real estate, *it's the entire financial system*. Leverage was piled on top of leverage. In the next exhibit, Chart 4-K shows what Warren Buffett has referred to as "financial weapons of mass destruction," also known as derivatives.

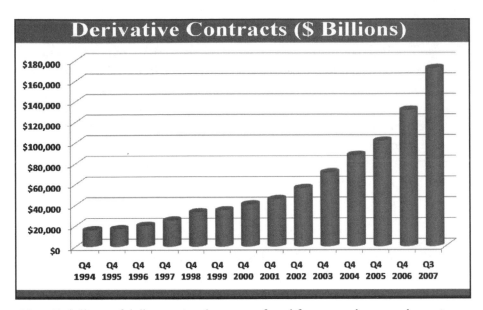

Note: In billions of dollars, national amount of total futures, exchange trader options, over-the-counter options, forwards, and swaps. Data after 1994 does not include spot fix in the total national amount of derivatives.
Source: Cornerstone Financial Services, Comptroller of Currency; Call Reports
Chart 4-K

Chart 4-K shows the dollar amount of derivative contracts held by what *were* the five largest U.S. banks at the end of 2007. It shows $172 trillion worth of derivatives versus a total U.S. economy of $14 trillion—more than *ten times the entire U.S. economy* in just the five largest banks! Note: The estimate is $202 trillion as of summer 2009![10]

What are derivatives? To use an analogy—if you had a bunch of grapes and squeezed them, you'd produce either grape juice or wine. Grapes being the underlying product, the wine or the grape juice would be the derivative.

In financial terms, the S&P 500 is an index of five hundred stocks. If you create an option or futures contract from the S&P—the options or futures contract would be a derivative of the original index.

Derivatives are typically entered into by two parties, ostensibly to mitigate or reduce risk. However, risk cannot be eliminated from the entire *system*. For example, certain types of contracts between AIG and our banks were designed to reduce risk. Known as *credit default swaps*, these contracts would pay the banks back in the event that their subprime mortgages defaulted. While this would reduce risks to the individual banks when the subprimes began going bad, from the standpoint of the *system*, the risk was just transferred from one party to another. When large enough amounts of leverage are involved, risk to the *system* remains paramount.

BAILOUTS, BAILOUTS, BAILOUTS

In response to all of this, authorities have resorted to the use of the printing press like never before in history. Next, in Chart 4-L you see the Fed's expansion reserves—a complete vertical climb.

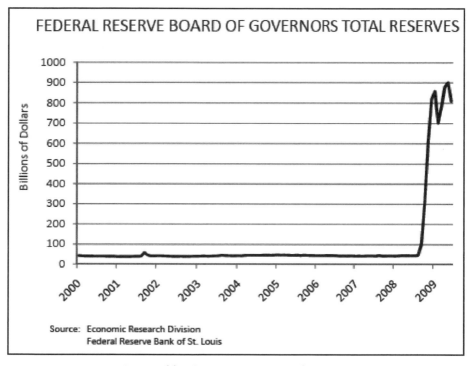

Prepared by Cornerstone Financial Services
Chart 4-L

Prior to the meltdown, the Fed's balance sheet (assets they owned) was under $1 trillion. By sometime next year, if things proceed as announced, the Fed's balance sheet will rise to almost $4 trillion. That means they will have bought $3 trillion worth of *assets* (call it *bailout*) with money they have simply *printed* out of thin air (computer bookkeeping entries).

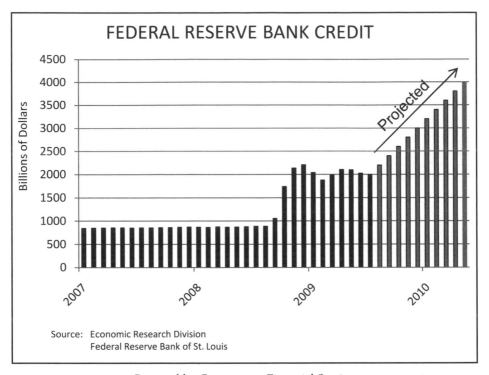

FEDERAL RESERVE BANK CREDIT

Source: Economic Research Division
Federal Reserve Bank of St. Louis

Prepared by Cornerstone Financial Services
Chart 4-M

In the short run, these bailouts are *not* inflationary. With banks not lending and consumers not borrowing or spending, the Fed can pump almost unlimited amounts into the system without setting off inflation.

To use a technical term, the *velocity* of money has plummeted (how fast the money turns over within the system). As long as spending and borrowing remain subdued, there will be no inflation problems to deal with. This is depicted in Chart 4-N—the money multiplier, a component of velocity, has plunged. Thus, consumers and businesses are spending less money *and* at a slower pace, which will keep inflation out of the picture for now.

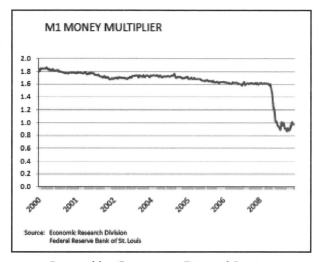

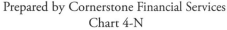

Prepared by Cornerstone Financial Services
Chart 4-N

For at least the next two to three years, deflation will remain the primary concern. Inflation is only likely to return much later, once the current crisis has passed and Congress has to resort to bailing out Social Security and Medicare. For two to three years, possibly five, deflation rules.

As long as consumers are concerned about their jobs, savings, retirement, and living standard, they will not go back on a spending binge.

Uncertainty, fear, and concerns about the future will predominate for some time, allowing for almost unlimited money printing without causing inflation. Inflation returns once the velocity of turnover of money in the system increases.

In addition, boomers, the dominant population group, are aging, and aging people become naturally more risk averse as they grow older, especially after seeing their retirement accounts plummet as they have.

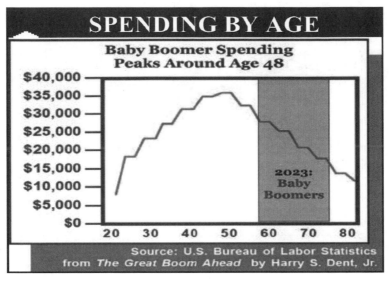

Chart 4-O

In Chart 4-O above you see the dilemma. By 2023 boomers will all be well past their peak spending years, certain to have a negative influence on the economy.

Mortgage Meltdown Goes Global

What started as a U.S.-based housing/mortgage problem soon spilled overseas. Great Britain, much like the U.S., also experienced a housing bubble and bust. Ireland hit the wall financially. Europe, for the most part, appears (believe it or not) in worse condition than we are here in the United States, at least as far as its major banks are concerned.

According to the EU Commission, potentially as much as 44 percent of EU banks' assets are *impaired*. Not only did European banks have their own domestic housing bubbles and busts to deal with, many of them also bought Wall Street's *securitized mortgage assets* from us here in the U.S. In addition, many loaned money to Eastern European countries who have since seen their economies crash. These loans of $32.7 billion are mostly denominated in either euros or Swiss francs and will be unrepayable without significant help from international agencies like the International Monetary Fund (IMF), as the currencies in these countries crashed with their economies.[11]

The Bank of England lowered interest rates to its member banks to the lowest levels in 315 years—the entire history of the British Fed.

Further compounding the concerns, by most measures the average European bank is far more highly leveraged than our U.S.-based counterparts. The average European bank is leveraged thirty-eight times the amount of their assets versus twenty-one times for the U.S. banks. Jiminy Christmas! These leverage levels are approximately where Bear Stearns and Lehman Brothers were before they failed.

Obviously, we don't know with precision where these bad, highly leveraged loans are hidden, but we certainly know that there's a lot of smoke. Hence, there's definitely a fire.

On top of seemingly everyone in the world speculating on risky real estate loans, consumer spending virtually ground to a halt in the fourth quarter of 2008. While at present things appear to be improving, nothing says that this is all over.

Look at Chart 4-P, which shows Japanese exports. The chart says it all.

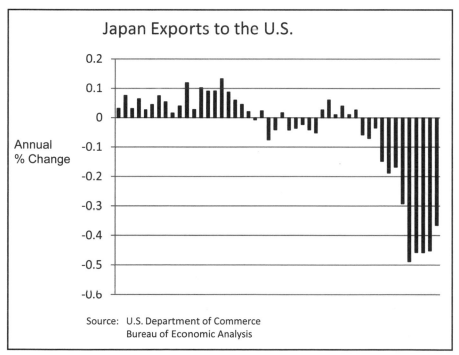

Prepared by Cornerstone Financial Services
Chart 4-P

While emerging Asia seems to be faring better than their more-developed counterparts, obviously they will be negatively affected as this growing global crisis unfolds. Emerging Asian banks largely avoided U.S. and European subprimes, plus their banks and debt ratios are much healthier than ours. Asia's problems stem from declining exports, as U.S. and European consumers cut back on spending, a trend destined to last for many years, as hyper-consumers turn into conservative savers and as boomers and their European counterparts move ever closer to retirement age with much less to show for their years of hard work than they'd anticipated.

In all, the crisis, while it appears contained at the moment, indeed became the financial equivalent of Chernobyl once the Treasury allowed (or forced) Lehman into bankruptcy. At that moment, deleveraging set in worldwide, and once a mass deleveraging sets in it is very difficult to stop.

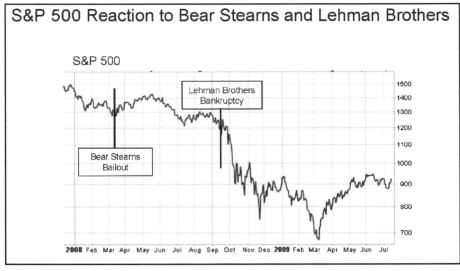

Source: Cornerstone Financial Services
Chart 4-Q

So, despite all these problems, central bankers appear determined to attempt to *inflate* away the problems. But there's no way that $4- or $5-trillion worth of a bailout/stimulus package can entirely offset the estimated $13 trillion of financial and real estate wealth wiped out for American consumers last year.

We hope their track record improves!

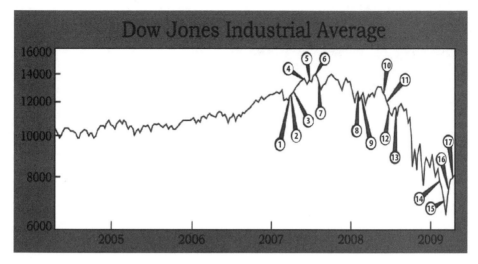

Source: Cornerstone Financial Services
Chart 4-R

Each of the numbers on Chart 4-R above link to the correlated number in the list below. Take a look at the responses of some authorities as this current crisis unfolded.

1. "The fallout in subprime mortgages is going to be painful to some lenders, but it is largely contained."—Treasury Secretary Henry Paulson on March 13, 2007[12]

2. "At this juncture...the impact on the broader economy and financial markets of the problems in the subprime markets seems likely to be contained."—Federal Reserve Chairman Ben Bernanke on March 28, 2007[13]

3. "I don't see (subprime mortgage market troubles) imposing a serious problem. I think it's going to be largely contained...All the signs I look at [show] the housing market is at or near the bottom."—Treasury Secretary Henry Paulson on April 20, 2007[14]

4. "Given the fundamental factors in place that should support the demand for housing, we believe the effect of the troubles in the subprime sector on the broader housing market will likely be limited."—Federal Reserve Chairman Ben Bernanke on May 17, 2007[15]

5. "This is far and away the strongest global economy I've seen in my business lifetime."—Treasury Secretary Henry Paulson on July 12, 2007[16]

6. "I don't think it [the subprime mess] poses any threat to the overall economy."—Treasury Secretary Henry Paulson on July 26, 2007[17]

7. "I see the underlying economy as being very healthy."—Treasury Secretary Henry Paulson on August 1, 2007[18]

8. "[The U.S. economy] is fundamentally strong, diverse and resilient."—Treasury Secretary Henry Paulson on February 14, 2008[19]

9. "I expect there will be some failures...I don't anticipate any serious problems of that sort [capital ratios] among the large internationally active banks that make up a very substantial part of our banking system."—Federal Reserve Chairman Ben Bernanke on February 28, 2008[20]

10. "The worst is likely to be behind us."—Treasury Secretary Henry Paulson on May 7, 2008[21]

11. "In my judgment, we are closer to the end of the market turmoil than the beginning."—Treasury Secretary Henry Paulson on May 16, 2008[22]

12. "The risk that the economy has entered a substantial downturn appears to have diminished over the past month or so."—Federal Reserve Chairman Ben Bernanke on June 9, 2008[23]

13. "Our banking system is a safe and a sound one...this is a very manageable situation...our regulators are focused on it."—Treasury Secretary Henry Paulson on July 20, 2008[24]

14. "We will have to try things we've never tried before. We will make mistakes. We will go through periods in which things get worse and progress is uneven or interrupted."—Treasury Secretary Timothy Geithner on February 10, 2009[25]

15. "We've put in place a comprehensive strategy designed to attack this crisis on all fronts. It's a strategy to create jobs, to help

responsible homeowners, to restart lending, and to grow our economy over the long-term. And we are beginning to see signs of progress."—President Barack Obama on March 24, 2009[26]

16. "The sense of a ball falling off a table, which is what the economy has felt like since the middle of last fall, I think we can be reasonably confident that that is going to end within the next few months, and we will no longer have that sense of free-fall."—National Economic Council Director Larry Summers on April 9, 2009[27]

17. "Recently we have seen tentative signs that the sharp decline in economic activity may be slowing."—Federal Reserve Chairman Ben Bernanke on April 14, 2009[28]

My final thought on these matters? In all, it looks to me as if the great financial storm of the twenty-first century is far from over. We are bracing for the big chill yet to come. In the remaining chapters, we will look closely at some of the concerns we need to address and then will shift our focus to providing solutions that you can incorporate into your own financial systems that will shelter you during this demographic winter and usher you into the spring of financial prosperity.

CHAPTER FIVE

BOOMERNOMICS: PENSIONS AND RETIREMENT ISSUES

T HERE ARE FOUR major long-term concerns facing America as a result of our current economic climate: consumer spending, pensions, Social Security, and Medicare. We established earlier that consumer spending drives the economy. Buying houses, cars, clothes, eating out, going to the mall—consumers fuel the economy, as people spend and circulate their money throughout the economy. The more money consumers spend, the faster the economy grows. (In the table below, you see a typical year for consumer spending.)

As you can see, direct spending (consumers buying houses, clothes, cars, going to the dry cleaners, buying groceries, etc.) made up 70.5 percent of the economy in 2008. All forms of government spending made up less than 20 percent of the total economy.

GROSS DOMESTIC PRODUCT, 2008[1]

GDP 2008	$14,264 (billions)	Percent
Personal Consumption	$10,057	70.5 percent
Business Spending	$1,993	13.9 percent
Net Exports	-$669	-4.6 percent
Gov't. Expenditures	$2,882	20.2 percent

However, consumers not only affect the economy with *direct* spending but also with business-to-business spending. (Not many homebuilders are buying table saws right now.) Business-to-business spending makes up another 10 percent or so of the economy once you net out imports and exports. Thus, if the consumer is not spending money, businesses won't spend money either. So consumer spending directly and indirectly really makes up just over 80 percent of the economy.

While the government does play a role, the best illustration I can use is that the government should play the role of referee, making sure the playing field is level and that all participants are playing by the rules.

No amount of government spending can fix the American economy if consumer spending breaks and the proverbial eight-hundred-pound economic gorilla goes away. The government can provide incentives to encourage or discourage the use of the free enterprise system and can use tax policies and regulations to encourage certain types of behavior. The government can have a big impact on the flow of economic traffic, just as a traffic cop can stop traffic on occasion or direct it, but even the government cannot fix the problems if the consumer stops spending altogether.

The only way to keep the economy going over the long run is to increase consumer spending. Tax cuts are beneficial because they put more discretionary income into the hands of consumers. This may seem contradictory to some who talk about increasing savings rates—savings and investments are both necessary—but the bottom line is that in the short run, the consumer is king.

Now let's take a little more in-depth look at the average family's income and spending. In Charts 5-A and 5-B, you see that the average family in the United States not only earns more money as they approach their late forties and early fifties, but they also spend more, because that is typically when most people have teenagers in the house. Once the kids are out of the house, the average income for a family tends to go down. (One spouse may work less because the family needs less earnings.) On average, both peak earnings and peak spending tend to occur between the ages of forty-five and fifty.

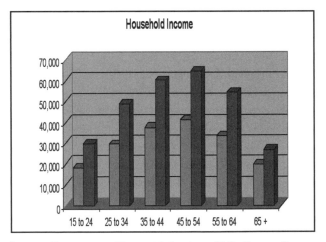

Source: Cornerstone Financial Services, U.S. Census Bureau

Chart 5-A

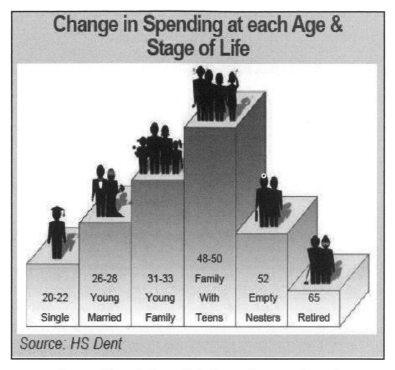

Source: Harry S. Dent, U.S. Census Data 1986–2006
Chart 5-B

Thus, as far as consumer spending goes, the most important factor for the growth of the economy is the number of consumers between the ages of forty-five and fifty. As people get older and their kids move out of the house, spending generally goes down. Most decide that they have not saved nearly enough for retirement, plus they've already bought most everything they need—houses, cars, appliances, and so forth. Some people will buck this trend and are exceptions to the rule, but the average family is going to downsize and *reduce* its spending after the kids are out of the house.

PENSIONS

A demographic winter will have a major impact on the retirement plans of Americans as well. Generally speaking, if you look at the bulk of the nation's pension assets and 401(k)s, the likelihood of those assets being funded properly in light of the coming demographic winter is not good. As a matter of fact, during the bear market of 2000 to 2003, the vast majority of American pensions showed up as woefully underfunded. Pension assumptions for financial needs were generated based upon the most recent returns during the boom years of the 1980s and 1990s, returns not likely to be seen again anytime soon.

If stocks, bonds, and other investments inside of those pensions are projected to yield a certain return over time and those projected returns are not achieved, then the amount of funding that these corporations will have to put into their pensions to keep them solvent will balloon.

S&P 500 Pension Status[2]	
86 percent	Percentage of companies in the S&P 500 index that have a pension plan and are currently *underfunded*. (Note: Most S&P 500 companies were woefully underfunded on their pensions *before* the fall 2008 meltdown.)
14 percent	Percentage of companies that are *fully funded as of August 9, 2008.*

For example, assume that you have projected the stock investments for a pension to grow at a 10 percent annual rate for the long run and have projected your bond return to be 4 percent. You also know approximately how many people will retire and when. So, based upon those assumptions you can make some extrapolations. This works out fine unless there is a *radical* difference in the rates of return that you are projecting versus the actual returns achieved. Most pensions assumed at least double-digit returns for their equity assets for the foreseeable future.

On the surface this looked reasonable, given the long-term history of stocks. However, keep in mind that there are significant periods of time when equities have underperformed for as long as fifteen to twenty years, times known as *secular bear markets*. For the years 1900 to 2000, the entire twentieth century, there were a total of fifty-six years when the stock market did not perform well. Now, look at the assumptions that have been made through a different set of lenses.

Many have read the Rich Dad, Poor Dad series. Robert Kiyosaki's "rich dad" father had extreme foresight that may prove prophetic. He saw that these challenges were coming for Americans as they got older and as people age and begin to cash in their financial assets at retirement. Let me quote Kiyosaki's book *Rich Dad's Prophecy*. He starts by questioning an underlying assumption of much of the financial services industry.

> You cannot question an assumption you do not know you have made.
> In business and investing, I have noticed many people lose and lose

badly because they did not know they had made certain assumptions. In other words, it was their unconscious assumptions that cost them dearly...assumptions they did not even realize they had made.

The reason I challenge this assumption is because it is the underlying assumption of much of the financial planning industry. Much but not all of the financial planning industry runs on the assumption that the stock market always goes up.[3]

He goes on to describe concerns about the market as boomers cash in financial assets:

The biggest problem will come from those employees who have diligently put money into their retirement account. It is those who have faithfully put money into retirement plans that will cause the biggest stock market crash in history.

The question is, what happens when millions of baby boomers are required to begin withdrawing money from the stock market? Will the stock market still go up by 10 percent, 20 percent, or 30 percent per year as it did in the 1990s? If you were born after 1946, and have a defined contribution pension plan, like a 401(k), filled with stocks and bonds and investments, for your sake, I hope the market keeps going up and never stops...but history is against that fantasy.

In other words, 75 million people buying anything will cause a boom. The reverse is also true. Seventy-five million people selling anything will cause a bust. It is the basic law of economics, *the law of supply and demand*.[4]

How will 76 million boomers sell their financial assets to 41 million baby busters (Gen X) without a huge reduction in price?

What if a corporation makes the assumption that it will earn an average of 10 percent a year on equities and ends up with actual losses instead? All of a sudden your corporate pension becomes grossly underfunded, and you have to change your projections to reflect the new reality that stocks are no longer generating 10 percent.

In this case, you would have to radically *ramp up* the amount of money that you are putting into the pension fund. As a result, this means that the earnings of the corporation will likely go *down*, as a higher percentage of corporate cash will be necessary to fund the pension. If the corporation has to fund *twice* as much, for example, toward its pension obligations than previously, then there is that much less that will go toward the bottom line for corporate profits. Thus, this will have a compounding or ripple effect upon the value of that stock. Corporate earnings will be lower due to the excess amounts that must be contributed to pensions, and that's likely to lower the value of stock as well. There is a domino effect here.

S&P 500 Health Status[5]	
1 percent	Percentage of companies that are *fully* funded
99 percent	Percentage of companies that are *underfunded*

Interestingly enough, in the longer term the biggest issue is going to be retiree medical obligations. How is it possible for a corporation to make it if they have more people who are currently retired than they do working for the company? This is part of the problem for General Motors (GM), as they have more retired workers receiving benefits than they do current workers. Obviously, this is unsustainable, and one of the reasons that General Motors's financial future is in severe jeopardy despite recent government bailouts.

They are not the only corporation in this predicament. What happens if we've entered a secular bear market lasting a decade or longer, as I believe we have? What happens if stocks, which had been projected to go up 10 percent per year ad infinitum, yield negative or no returns for a long period?

I am not implying that this is the end of the world or that the sky is falling. I am pointing out that if you look throughout history, you will find that there are significant periods of time when stocks have underperformed for long stretches. To assume that this will never happen again is folly. To assume that there will never be another secular bear market (I think we are in one now, as we will discuss in chapter 10) when history shows that these stretches have occurred during more than 50 percent of the last century indicates to me that it would be lunacy to assume there is not going to be another one soon.

Most people are like the frog in the kettle. You may remember the old story. If you throw a frog into a kettle of boiling water, he will immediately jump out. But, if you take a frog and throw it into a kettle of lukewarm water, the frog will enjoy his nice, comfortable swim. If you gradually turn the heat up so that he becomes acclimatized to the change, the frog will not jump out, and at some point he will boil to death.

In the same way, humans are creatures of habit. The newest school of economics, known as *behavioral economics*, has dubbed this phenomenon "recency." *Recency* simply means that as human beings we are hard-wired emotionally to put more emphasis on things that have happened to us recently than on things that are further away. This ensures that time heals all wounds.

Now, let me apply the phenomenon of recency to our economy today.

About thirty years ago, baby boomers entered the economy and began buying houses, cars, clothes, taking their kids to McDonalds, and going shopping and to the malls. The extreme boom engendered by this produced a wave of unprecedented prosperity. The stock market went up—and stayed up for nearly thirty continuous years (with occasional short and temporary bear markets). Each time, the market moved to a higher high, until all of a sudden, to quote economist and comedian Ben Stein's father, "When something is unsustainable, it tends to stop."

You can shoot an arrow into the air, but it will not continue to rise forever. At some point the flight of that arrow rolls over and goes back down. Historically, if you look at all of world history—all civilizations and economies, not just the United States—you will find that all booms are followed by busts. The bigger the boom, the bigger the bust.

We have seen an unprecedented wave of prosperity as baby boomers spent their way into oblivion, using plastic, home equity loans, whatever was necessary, driving this economy to ever-new heights. The gross domestic product of the U.S. economy in 1982 when boomers began moving into the economy en masse was less than $3 trillion. By 2007 the GDP was $14 trillion. The economy has increased by a factor of more than 400 percent in terms of the total output in goods and services over that period of time—unprecedented growth.

Now think about this as an investment advisor, financial planner, or pension manager. You may have been somewhat aware of what was going on in the world in the 1960s and '70s, but you probably weren't in a position of responsibility. All you have known for the bulk of your professional life is an ever-increasing stock market, increasing prosperity, and, from 1980 to 2008, a growing economy. All of your experience tells you that over time the market goes higher and higher, and the economy continues to grow up the side of every mountain, sustaining small dips, then moves on to a higher mountain. You are a victim of *recency*. Like the frog in the kettle, you are not thinking about the fact that, historically, every boom has led to a bust. These busts can be very short and painful, or they can last for extremely long periods, like we saw in the 1930s.

Like the frog in the kettle, you have come to believe, based both upon your own experiences and the slogan "The market always goes up in the long run," that you should just hold on for the long run. And, historically, the market *has* always gone up in the long run. But this is irrelevant to the facts. You can drown in a lake with an average depth of three feet if you step in the wrong hole, especially if you have fishing waders on and go straight to the bottom. The long-term rate of return for stocks over the past century is irrelevant— whether it is 10 percent or whatever number you want to use. You must realize that there are some very deep holes out there. Look at the hole that occurred between 1929 to 1933, the worst-case scenario and the worst investment crash we have seen in modern world history.

Does that mean you should throw this period of time out of your database just because it is the worst case? Can you guarantee me that another worst-case scenario will not take place? Obviously, you cannot. You now know about the extreme changes in the world today brought about by the boomers, changes that are affecting the economy and pensions, plus government issues with Social Security and Medicare. Other critical factors—such as oil prices that could go through the roof as a result of extremely unstable situations in the Middle East and what terrorists might try to do to this country at some time in the future—could greatly impact the economy.

What if a person needs income from his or her portfolio during a period of difficult times? Do fifty-five- or sixty-year-olds have the ability to withstand a fifteen- or twenty-year period of negative returns, such as those we've seen in past periods? Most, obviously, do not. If a person is very young and very determined, he or she might be able to endure a fifteen- to twenty-year secular bear market simply by adding money every year (dollar cost averaging). Yet, even this is no guarantee.

I believe we are facing the perfect economic *bust* during the next fifteen years or so. If this were only half true, would you choose to plan your finances as if the future would continue to look just like the recent past? Of course not. Just as you cannot drive your car while looking backward, so you must look forward economically. Unfortunately, few people seem to have the visionary foresight to look into the future economically.

It really does not take a rocket scientist to figure this out. As the greatest boom in world economic history—which occurred as 76 million baby boomer American citizens bought houses, cars, and clothes—fades into the sunset, a *radically different environment* will be created going forward than what we have seen in the recent past.

Almost everybody has projected past performance into the future. This is tantamount to not seeing the curve ahead in the road and going off the edge of the cliff. There is no way that the next twenty years will look anything remotely like the last twenty years. They are more likely to be the reverse of what has happened. History is limited in terms of how much it has recorded about demographic periods, but one thing we know for certain is that aging societies have not produced prosperity in the long run.

I am not being a pessimist, a Cassandra, or a doom-and-gloomer. I am asking you to be realistic about the economic future we will likely face over the next ten to fifteen years. If you are realistic about it, then you can find solutions for your own personal financial planning. Government and corporate leaders can work together on solutions to fix these problems in the future, and our country may ultimately go on to greater heights than ever before. But first we must address the current problems and use the *Good to Great* philosophy of being merciless in terms of looking at and dealing with our current set of problems while having unwavering faith about our long-term future.

SOCIAL SECURITY AND MEDICARE

> I say we scrap the current Social Security system and replace it with a system wherein you add your name to the bottom of the list, and then you send some money to the person at the top of the list, and then you...oh, wait, that is our current system.
>
> —DAVE BARRY[6]

Now consider for a moment the effects this will have on the economy as this most important age group, the baby boomers, move into their preretirement and retirement years. Aging boomers will put incredible stress on the social safety net of our country. Medicare is an enormous unfunded medical liability (some $85.9 trillion according to recent estimates, versus $14 trillion—the total U.S. annual income or GDP).[7] Social Security is an enormous unfunded pension. In my opinion, both are essentially Ponzi schemes that will ultimately force younger generations to be *overtaxed* in order to pay for benefits for the elderly. Wake up, America, there is no big savings account in Washington, D.C., with your name on it! Plus, Americans are living longer, with the average life expectancy from birth now age seventy-seven.[8]

There is an 80 percent chance that either one or both members of a sixty-five-year-old couple will survive to at least age eighty-two.[9]

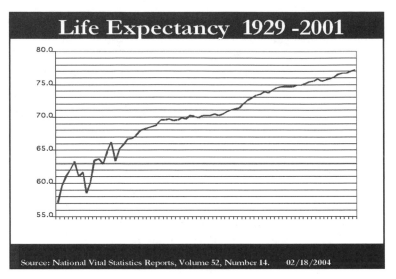

Chart 5-C

When Social Security was created, not only were Americans living shorter lives (the average lifespan was sixty-two years in 1933), but there were far fewer seniors and many, many more people paying into the system to support each retiree.

> This dramatic demographic change is certain to place enormous demands on our nation's resources—demands we almost surely will be unable to meet unless action is taken.
>
> —Alan Greenspan on Social Security[10]

We have known that this problem would arise for decades. Alan Greenspan was the head of a commission appointed by President Reagan back in the 1980s to address the stresses that they knew boomers would someday put on the system, stresses that, without reform, the system would be unable to handle.

The outcome of that study was that the government would essentially create a *sinking fund* to *overcollect* Social Security taxes while the boomers were working and put that money away for the proverbial rainy day. Later on, the government would tap those resources as boomers began to retire. It was obvious to all that there was no way on God's green Earth that the younger generations would have sufficient numbers to pay for the retirement needs of the baby boomers if Social Security remained a pure "pay as you go" system.[11] In theory, this was a great idea. In practice, with ever-pressing demands for reelection and political pressures, Congress has been unable to keep its hands out of the cookie jar. Essentially they have *borrowed* the money from the

Social Security and Medicare trust funds and *spent* it over the years. This is an accident waiting to happen. Congress essentially has two sets of books (or budgets), one called "on budget" items and another set for "off budget" items like Social Security and Medicare.

Looking to the pie charts, you can see clearly that over the last thirty years government spending has moved increasingly *away* from military spending and increasingly toward social spending on items like Medicare and Social Security.

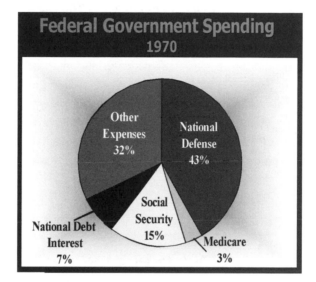

Source: Congressional Budget Office
Chart 5-D

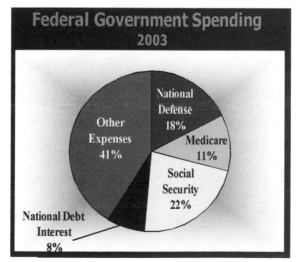

Source: Congressional Budget Office
Chart 5-E

Note that *despite* the Iraq/Afghanistan war, defense spending only made up 18 percent of all federal spending in 2003. As boomers age, it will put *enormous* pressure on the system, pushing Medicare and Social Security costs to simply unsustainable levels.

The problem with this is that not only do we spend more than we take in virtually every year (the government has only had a real balanced budget for a couple of years out of the last thirty), *but on top of that, we have just been through the greatest years of prosperity in our nation's history*!

We have seen the DJIA go from 777 on August 12, 1982, to 14,000 before peaking in 2007. Untold trillions were created in both the economy and the financial markets due to this unprecedented boom. *Yet, in spite of this incredible wave of prosperity and record tax receipts each and every cycle, the government has been unable to balance its budget for almost all of this time*!

Big government advocates always cite the same mantra for any problems: "We don't have enough money." Yet, record tax collections have passed through the government's hands over the past thirty years. Clearly it's not a case of too little money.

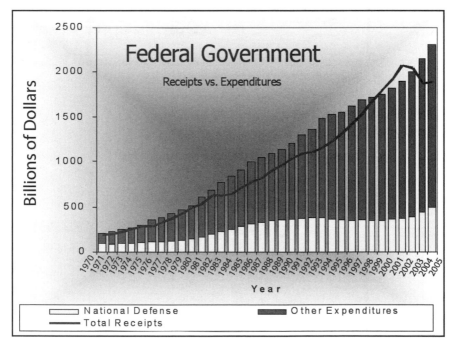

Chart 5-F[12]

Year	U.S. Government Revenue ($ billions)[13]
1970	192.8
1980	517.1
1990	1032.1
2000	2025.5
2008	2523.6

My greatest concern is that if the government has been unable to balance its budget during thirty years of phenomenal prosperity, what in the world is going to happen now that we have moved into a mega economic downturn, or demographic winter? What happens to these social safety nets, designed to pay for the boomers' retirement and medical needs as they age?

Federal debt grew to over $9 trillion deficits annually due to Congress overspending, despite the greatest economic boom in history. Now that the bust has begun, the debt is galloping ahead, rising to $11 trillion by June 2009 *before* boomers hit the Social Security and Medicare system en masse. Just how big will the numbers get as boomers tax the system? Fifteen trillion dollars? Twenty trillion dollars? Thirty trillion dollars? Who really knows?

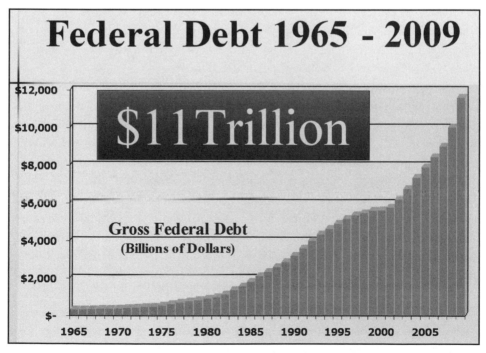

Chart 5-G[14]

Investor extraordinaire Jim Rogers has harsh words for the government's interventionist economic policy: "The federal government has increased its own debt by four, five, six times. We don't know much, because they took over Fannie Mae, AIG and the rest of them who had huge debts, which we are now responsible for."[15]

Without considering all of the loan guarantees, we've accumulated more than $11 trillion in debt due to government overspending during the greatest wave of prosperity in the history of the planet. What happens during the upcoming economic winter? These are sobering thoughts. Pete Peterson, billionaire author of the book *Grey Dawn* and former chairman of the Federal Reserve of New York and cofounder of the Blackstone Group, estimated as recently as 2004 that Social Security *by itself* was approximately a $10 trillion unfunded pension. Unfortunately, all of the money the government set aside to pay for the boomers' retirement/health needs has already been spent. The government's accounting would make Enron look good!

Estimates of actual government indebtedness, if you use the accrued method (when liabilities are incurred) versus cash accounting (when they're actually paid for), run as high as $56 trillion![16] This amounts to over four times our country's annual income or GDP and is still rising.

Peterson calculated that without reform, Social Security and Medicare taxes, which currently make up 15.8 percent of a corporation's payroll (7.65 percent FICA for the employee and 7.65 percent matching by employer), will rise to 31.9 percent by 2030 without major reform.

Social Security and Medicare were originally projected to run in the red by 2016. They are now projected to barely break even in 2010. Until that point, the Social Security and Medicare systems have been overfunded. Up until now, more taxes have been collected from the paychecks of working Americans than was needed to pay for current retirees in the Social Security and Medicare system.

While we have been booming, spending, investing, and saving over the past thirty years, Congress has essentially been spending, spending, spending, spending, and spending—often for unnecessary projects, political pork projects, and the like. Unable to keep its hands out of the retirement cookie jar, Congress has gorged on spending of all types, ultimately resorting to robbing Peter to pay Paul. The vaunted Social Security Trust Fund—which was designed to pay for boomers' retirement years—has already been spent and replaced with essentially a government IOU—a non-negotiable Treasury security.[17] Thus, the *current expenses* area of the government borrowed from the *retirement sector* of the government and owes it *all* of the money collected.

What happens when the bill comes due? What happens when boomers begin to retire and these resources are not there?

Soon, the trust *funds* will start to run in the red, with Social Security and Medicare running *annual deficits*, and over time these deficits become enormous.

MEDICARE

> Everything that's happened up until now in medicine is a prelude.
> What's really ahead is stunning. It's going to be…very expensive.
> —HEALTH TECHNOLOGY EXPERT WILLIAM SCHWARTZ[18]

In other words, based upon current assumptions, the government will soon be unable to collect enough in taxes from active workers to pay for the medical and retirement needs of boomers as they begin to retire in an enormous tsunami. At that point, the Social Security *Trust Fund* is supposed to kick in.

But the only way to pay for this will be for the government to pay the Social Security Trust Fund back. The only way the government can pay the Social Security Trust Fund back is through either the collection of additional taxes, deficit spending, or printing money. There is no free lunch. The money has long ago been spent. The only ways this can be remedied are to tax workers at progressively higher rates, to borrow even more money through deficit spending (which makes the national debt larger and increases our dependency upon foreigners to fund our debt), or by resorting to the printing press, which is highly inflationary. There is no painless way out.

> Too many people, living too many years and having saved far too little,
> will place increasing tax demands on smaller working generations.
> —KEN DYCHTWALD, *AGE WAVE*[19]

The vaunted government entitlement *safety net*—created in the 1930s to *prevent* another economic depression—will essentially need to be bailed out, because when push comes to shove, there will not be enough money available. This likelihood is very high. In almost all cases, we have seen the government bail out the system when things go bad through the use of artificially created money, otherwise known as fiat money (no gold or tangible asset backing).

Charles Blahous, President Bush's point man on Social Security, said, "Social security is not, nor has ever been, a savings program. Today's payroll taxes go to support today's retirees. Tomorrow's Social Security income—at least under current law—will be provided by taxing tomorrow's workers."[20]

As we said earlier, for the first few years after the wave of boomer spending has crested, this will have a deflationary impact (think California or Florida real estate) as boomers change their spending patterns. Yet, in the long run, I see little or no choice except for the government to resort to the printing press in order to help pay for all of these social programs and other obligations that the federal government has taken on. The government will not back out on these obligations. However, it also will no longer have the resources to pay for them as out-of-pocket expenses (*pay as you go*). My concern is that down the road this *could* ultimately lead to a *hyperinflationary* environment.

Thus, we have two giant tsunamis colliding. On the one hand, we have the boomers and the impact that they are going to have on the system as they retire, which is deflationary in the short run and ultimately inflationary if bailed out. On the other hand, we have developing markets like China and India using enormous natural resources, which is also *inflationary*. We'll discuss developing markets in more detail in a later chapter.

This is like two giant tidal waves crashing at sea. The deflationary impact of the boomers' spending cuts will affect the economy radically between 2009–2013 or so. The inflationary impact of developing countries and bailing out the social safety nets will start sometime after 2013, perhaps as late as 2020. This will definitely be an interesting period of time to live through! About the only thing that you can count on for sure is that the future is likely to look nothing like the recent past.

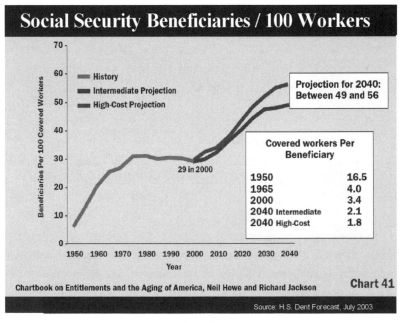

Chart 5-H

PART 2

PREPARING FOR THE SPRINGTIME

CHAPTER SIX

INFANTS, IMMIGRATION, ADOPTION—CREATING THE *NEXT* BOOM

W HAT WILL IT take to turn around the demographic winter? Are there solutions, or are we just headed for a demographic downhill slide into oblivion? What will turn things around?

One of the obvious solutions is to recognize the need to encourage infants, immigration, and adoption. Any demographer will tell you that the world's plunging birthrates, combined with people living longer, is a long-term recipe for disaster if unchecked.

You simply can't allow societies to move toward older and older populations and expect to have vibrant, growing economies. As we've demonstrated earlier, growth in an economy primarily occurs due to the number of people who are buying homes, cars, and other consumer items. So from birth to roughly age forty-five or fifty, families are growing the economy.

We will consider closely the contributions of Phillip Longman, journalist, economist, demographer, and author of *The Empty Cradle*, in this section.[1] Far from being a card-carrying conservative, Longman was trained on Malthus, Darwin, and the entire bevy of liberal ideals. He is a widower; has one child (adopted); and works for a progressive (i.e., liberal) think tank, The New America Foundation. By his own admission, he is not a person of faith. Yet, persuaded by social and economic trends, Longman has come to the conclusion that only by promoting both families and population will we create long-term growth and prosperity.

> A nation's gross domestic product is literally the sum of its labor force times the average output per worker. Thus, a decline in the number of workers implies a decline in an economy's growth potential. When the size of the workforce is falling, economic growth occurs, if at all, only through compensating increases in productivity.
>
> —PHILLIP LONGMAN, *THE EMPTY CRADLE*

When a nation has fewer and fewer children, combined with a much larger group of elders (due to advances in medicine), it creates a top-heavy society with an older population that is being supported by a smaller group of young people. You simply can't sustain that trend for long. Never in history has a country that has seen a major decline in birth rates due to a variety of factors, including those listed below, experienced long-term prosperity:

1. Birth control
2. Abortion
3. The sexual revolution
4. Changing moral norms
5. People waiting longer to get married
6. Cohabitation

The numbers of children in the world as a percentage of the population has declined sharply. People are waiting longer to get married and have kids, which skews the population curve toward an elderly society. And it's happening all over the world.

Global Demographics

Even though the world's population has grown from 3.7 billion to 6.7 billion since 1970, it has primarily been the result of people living longer, not having more children.[2]

> The reason the world has experienced a population explosion over the past century is not because human beings suddenly started breeding like rabbits, but because they finally stopped dying like flies...What's really driven up human numbers has been a health explosion.
> —Nicholas Eberstadt, PhD, Harvard University
> Henry Wendt Scholar in Political Economy
> The American Enterprise Institute[3]

What is the long-term solution to these problems? Look at the root cause of all our present economic issues—declining birth rates. For a society to break even in terms of population (not growing and not shrinking) requires a birth rate of 2.1 births per female.[4] If you have less than 2.1 babies per female, your society goes into reverse (i.e., more people will die than are born each year, and your society actually *shrinks*).

Having fewer children has, in fact, become a global trend, affecting both developed and developing countries. Yet developed countries are the ones headed for the biggest problems. Developing countries such as Mexico and countries in the Middle East and Africa are seeing rapidly declining numbers of children but are still well above the replacement rate. According to Nobel Prize–winning economist Gary Becker, PhD, University of Chicago, approximately seventy countries of the world are now below replacement rate.[5]

EUROPEAN DEATH SPIRAL

All over Europe countries are shrinking or near shrinking absent immigration. Shrinking societies historically are *not* prosperous over the long run. This reminds me of Proverbs 14:12 (NKJV): "There is a way that seems right to a man, but its end is the way of death." Without change, it seems much of Europe is headed for extinction.

> The European Commission, for example, projects that Europe's potential growth rate over the next fifty years will fall by 40 percent due to the shrinking size of the European workforce. With a shrinking labor supply, Europe's future economic growth will depend entirely on getting more out of each worker (many of them unskilled, recently arrived immigrants) even as it has to tax workers at higher and higher rates to pay for old-age pensions and health care.
> —PHILLIP LONGMAN, *THE EMPTY CRADLE*[6]

Italy, Russia, Greece, Spain, and France all have birth rates well below replacement rate. Parts of Eastern Europe are suffering actual population decline. Latvia's population dropped by 13 percent from 1989–2002, as once populated villages are becoming deserted. *All* of Eastern Europe is below replacement rate.[7]

Russia's birth decline has become so severe that Prime Minister Putin actually declared a national holiday for the sole, express purpose of procreation. Last year, as president, Mr. Putin declared 2008 the Year of the Family. On September 12, a holiday called Family Contact Day, he encouraged Russians to stay home and engage in marital intimacy in the hopes of producing children nine months later on Russia Day, June 12. The new holiday extends Russia's promotion of procreation, urging couples not only to have children but also to provide those children with two-parent, stable family lives.[8]

Countries in Europe, sensing that they may be headed for disaster if the trends don't change, are actually *paying couples to have children*. In Sweden, the government has created very generous social programs and benefits for child care (daycare, maternity leave, sick pay, etc.), yet this created only a small bounce in fertility in the 1980s, followed by another drop.[9] Sweden's birth rate in the year 2000 was 1.54, well below the replacement rate of 2.1 babies per woman.[10]

Germany, despite mandatory paid time off for maternity leave (part from employer, part from the state), a parental allowance (up to 14 weeks at a maximum of 1800 euros per month), and many other benefits, has still been unable to get its birth rate above 1.3 per female.[11]

2005 Fertility Rates by Country[12]

United States	2.11
Replacement Rate	2.10
New Zealand	2.01
Ireland	1.90
France	1.89
Australia	1.70
United Kingdom	1.60
Canada	1.48
EU Average	1.38
Germany	1.35
Japan	1.32
Italy	1.23
Russia	1.14

Once a nation's birth rate drops too far and the population falls way behind the curve, that nation enters a death spiral. Here the fertility rate falls so low that the nation never catches up, barring a completely miraculous rebound in fertility rates.

Italy, for example, with a 1.23 replacement rate, is set to see its population cut in half within thirty years or so. Not a recipe for long-term prosperity.[13]

All over Europe, governments are recognizing that their birth rates have fallen to such an extent that it threatens their civilization's long-term viability. Their native populations are shrinking, replaced only partially by immigrants, most of whom are Middle Eastern. Is America far behind?

Phillip Longman, researcher and demographer from the New America Foundation, explains it this way:

> Population growth is a major source of economic growth. More people create more demand for the products capitalists sell, and more supply of the labor capitalists buy. Once depopulation begins, new investment soon vanishes. Indeed, capitalism has never flourished except

when accompanied by population growth, and it is now languishing in those parts of the world (such as Japan, Europe, and the great Plains of the United States) where population has become stagnant...It is also true that nowhere in history have we had economic prosperity accompanied by depopulation.[14]

THE EFFECT ON SOCIAL SERVICES

As western societies move toward increasingly older populations, the question becomes: How can we possibly pay for social services, especially those designed to provide for the elderly?

Social Security and Medicare, as we've seen, are primarily pay-as-you go systems. Nothing has really been saved or put aside for boomers' medical retirement needs. Aging western societies will increasingly put pressure on the young to support their parents' and grandparents' generations.

When Social Security was created in the 1930s, more than thirty people paid taxes into the system to support one retiree. Presently, the ratio is just over three to one. Once boomers hit the system, it becomes even more tilted.

Chart 6-B restates this from a different perspective. In 1950 each worker supported 15 percent of one retiree (the first bar on the chart). Now each worker must support 33 percent of one retiree. *That's 120 percent more load per working individual.*[15]

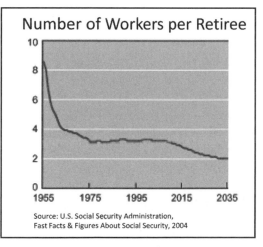

Chart 6-A[16]

Chart 6-A shows that in 1955, about eight workers shared the burden of supporting each retiree. In 1990 there were only four workers to carry each retiree—a 40 percent reduction. The load continues to increase dramatically. (Per the U.S. Treasury, in 2007 there were 3.3 workers per retiree.)[17]

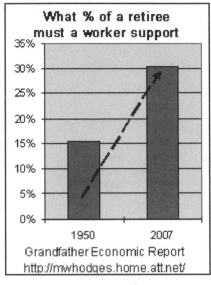

Chart 6-B[18]

Phillip Longman has stated:

> The financing and long-term political viability of social security systems throughout the world, for example, depend upon the assumption that each generation of taxpayers will be larger than the one that came before. Younger workers, finding that not only does the economy require them to have far higher levels of education than did their parents, but that they also must pay far higher payroll taxes, are less able to afford children, and so have fewer of them, causing a new cycle of population aging. If current projections prove true, the working population of the United States essentially will wind up paying one out of every five dollars it earns just to support retirees.[19]

Opportunity Costs

On a micro level, for the average family, having *fewer* babies appears to create more prosperity. For the average person to maintain the lifestyle he or she would prefer in terms of home size, car, clothing, vacations, and the like, having more kids makes supporting the desired lifestyle less affordable. Obviously, if you have a lot of kids, it costs much more to pay for living expenses.

My wife and I have no children of our own, but I adopted her two children from her first marriage back in the 1980s. (For those unable or unwilling to have children of their own, adoption is an awesome alternative. Adopting children, even from overseas countries, into stable, positive homes will not only ultimately create more producers and consumers here in the United States but also has the potential to radically impact and change those individuals for their betterment and the betterment of *their* children and grandchildren.) Based upon observations of many of our employees who have large families, I can vouch firsthand that it's a lot more difficult to raise a family with four kids than with just two. In the short term, each child is an economic burden. Maintaining a higher lifestyle is much easier to do with fewer children. But in my opinion, larger families are, in reality, a longer-term blessing.

While it might be easier for each individual family to maintain a higher lifestyle over the short run, over the longer run it's *counterproductive* to society as a whole. More children ultimately means more consumers and faster economic growth for the society as the kids grow up and become consumers and producers themselves. So, in the short run, it looks best to have small families. However, in the long run, at least for a society, it is counterproductive.

> Adam Smith, probably the greatest of all economists once wrote that prosperity is associated with growing populations and depression is associated with declining populations.
> —Nobel Prize–winning economist Gary Becker, PhD
> University of Chicago[20]

Longman believes that it is not hard to understand how most of us form the impression that overpopulation is one of the world's most pressing problems. Our day-to-day experiences and the impressions we gather from the media repeatedly suggest that population growth threatens whatever quality of life we enjoy. Sprawling suburban developments worsen traffic, drive up taxes, and diminish opportunities to enjoy nature. Televised images of third world famine, war, and environmental degradation prompt the private thought, "Why do these people have so many kids?"[21]

Keep in mind that much of our present-day thinking comes from an extension of the line of thought that started with Malthus, was then adopted by the humanists, and came to the public's attention in the 1970s with Ehrlich's *Population Bomb*. It is easy to believe that the world is overpopulated and resources are scarce when you live in an overcrowded urban area and people are literally living wall to wall.

What I'm about to say may seem radical at first because it so flies in the face of conventional wisdom. The entire world, so it seems (or at least the United States), is massively concerned about human overpopulation: famine in Africa equals overpopulation; pollution and greenhouse gases equal overpopulation; scarce resources equal obvious overpopulation.

But if you think that the world is overpopulated, think again. Here are some facts that you may not be aware of.

First, if you were to take every family in the United States and give them a half-acre of land, *all of the people in the United States could be contained inside the state of Texas*, with the entire rest of the country available for food production and manufacturing.

Second, in terms of the world's population, you could take the *entire population of the world*, give each family a half-acre of land, and contain them all inside the continental United States, leaving the entire rest of the world (more than 95 percent of the world's land mass) to provide the resources necessary for everyone to live on.

Urban sprawl and overcrowded cities make it easy to believe that the world is overpopulated; it truly creates a paradigm that is hard to break. But this paradigm fails to live up to inspection.

Longman asserts, "I think it's quite natural for people who live on a planet whose dimensions are fixed to have impressed upon their consciousness the idea that we live in a world with real limits. I can understand why the ordinary man on the street would be a little bit wary about grandiose population predictions after the last thing we heard from demographers was that we were on the throws [sic] of this population bomb."[22]

I'd challenge anyone who really believes the world is overpopulated to take one day to drive through Kansas, west Texas, or Montana. Better yet, drive from one end of the country to the other. Parts of the world, primarily the large cities, *are* overpopulated, but the world itself has plenty of space.

It's this *shortage, lack, scarcity* mentality that got us into this mess in the first place. It is basically the root cause of our economic problems. Due to a preoccupation with overcrowded cities, planetary limitations, and *limited or scarce resources*, we have hamstrung world population growth as well as economic growth. Population *control*, in the long run, is counterproductive. I'm reminded of one of the planks of the *Humanist Manifesto*: "No deity will save us; we must save ourselves."[23]

So, while in the short run it might appear better for society to have smaller families in order not to utilize too much of the world's resources, the problem is that in the long run it creates old societies.

New Technology Will Pave the Way

We have no way to know what new discoveries or technology will come about in the future to solve any resource problems we might encounter. In 2007 we experienced a shortage of oil, but given enough time and money it is likely that we will figure out ways to harness solar, wind, hydrogen, or perhaps even the ocean's tide, as well as find more fossil fuels. In time, other technological resources will appear to support the world's population. Nuclear energy, while unpopular, has obvious advantages as well.

Prior to the 1860s, the South could not possibly figure out how they could survive economically without slavery. However, once Eli Whitney created the cotton gin, it allowed for farming on a massive scale without enormous numbers of slaves.

> Between 1900 and 2000, human numbers almost quadrupled...over the past century...the inflation-adjusted, dollar-denominated international price of each of the major cereals—corn, wheat, and rice—fell by over 70 percent.
> —Nicholas Eberstadt, PhD, Harvard University[24]

It's the same with food supplies. Despite the fact that the world's population has ballooned during the past fifty years, food production has more than kept up with population.

According to Longman: "The name that historians gave to this phenomenon of rising production and consumption is, of course, the 'Industrial Revolution.' Exactly how and why it occurred is a matter of continuing debate. Certainly, the evolution of strong property rights was a factor, as was the development of new technologies, like the steam engine. Also required was a huge increase in the consumption of natural resources, and in pollution. But population growth was also key by providing for economies of scale and opportunities for specialization, as well as new incentives to innovate. At one turn of the cycle, rising population creates a spur to discovery of more efficient means of producing and distributing food, energy, and other scarce goods. At the next turn of the cycle, rising productivity allows the economy to provide for additional increases in population even as each person consumes more and more. Love this system or hate it, but acknowledge that it is the system that built the modern world. And acknowledge, too, that for better or worse, *population growth is still the prime driver of economic growth.*"[25]

Thus, rather than having a negative, pessimistic view of the world's future and holding tight to all available resources because there is no future, no hope, and no God, we should have an *optimistic* long-term view of the future that the resources or technology will be provided when we need them. We may not see how those solutions will be provided today, but we don't need to see them now. We have no idea what breakthroughs will develop over time to resolve these and future issues.

Long term, I am an optimist; however, we also have to deal with present realities. While it may appear to create more prosperity per family by having fewer children, in the long run the lesson that the world is about to learn is that if you don't have enough kids, you will not have enough consumers buying products or creating new jobs, and you will not have enough people paying into the social services systems to support the elderly. As a result, you could face long-term decline as a nation.

Longman helps us to put our realities in perspective by saying:

> The global decline in fertility rates, as profound and well established as the trend may be, is hard to spot simply by simply observing the fabric of ordinary life. Indeed, as I've noted, ordinary life gives most people the opposite impression. That's because, even in areas where birthrates are dramatically below the levels required to avoid population loss even in the near future, the absolute number of people is often still growing. Think of a train accelerating up a hill. If the engine stalls, the train will still move forward for a while, but its' [sic] loss of momentum implies that it will soon be moving backwards, and at even-greater speed. So it is when fertility rates shift from above to below replacement levels.
>
> When fertility falls below replacement levels, the population continues to increase for a while through sheer force of momentum. But this momentum is a dwindling legacy of a past effort when fertility rates were still above replacement levels. In the next generation, the pool of potential mothers will be smaller than before, and in the generations after that, the pool becomes smaller still. But then the momentum of population growth is lost, or more precisely, is working in the opposite direction with compounding force.[26]

Presently the United States is seeing this decline mostly offset due to immigration, primarily from Hispanics, but this factor is not sufficient to solve all of our economic problems. The question then becomes: What are the long-term solutions?

The first solution is to encourage families to have more babies or adopt! This will require changing our paradigm about families and society as a whole and will not occur easily or quickly. Yet, it must be done. While it may be a bit more painful economically in the short run to have more children to clothe, house, and feed, in the long run it creates much more prosperity for our society.

PATRIOTIC IMMIGRATION

A second solution is to *encourage* immigration to America. As we bring more people into this country, which is made up of immigrants, we will continue to grow our population. This, in turn, will create longer-term economic prosperity.

However, we must not follow the pattern of Western Europe. As we saw earlier, most European countries have very low birth rates and desperately need immigration. Yet, as people immigrate into European countries, by and large those immigrants are not *integrating* into their societies.

Western Europe is like a salad bowl. Each country has different racial and ethnic cultures, and each subculture largely retains its own unique characteristics and does not mesh or integrate fully into society at large. This ends up creating a *fragmented* society. Various factions will ultimately be vying for power, control, resources, and influence—not good for the fabric of a society.

America, on the other hand, is more like a soup bowl. Yes, you have potatoes, carrots, and beef—people who have immigrated from different cultures into the United States. Yet, historically this nation of immigrants has largely amalgamated as the people work and live together until society moves toward one harmonious flavor and texture. So, even though you have separate ingredients in the soup, we're more homogenized, which is much healthier for our society in the long run.

Currently, our greatest wave of immigration by far is coming from Latin America.[27]

Personally, I think it is a mistake for us to *encourage* Hispanics to speak their own language in public settings, such as schools and the workforce, and to retain a completely different subculture in ethnically isolated communities. While people should be proud of their heritage and culture (various cultures creates a colorful, interesting, and ultimately stronger society), we want them to *integrate* into the society as a whole.

We are all Americans, and we need to possess a loyalty to our country, even a newly adopted country, over loyalties to families, cities, states, and, ultimately, cultures. We should encourage immigrants to learn English in order to completely integrate. The school systems should be teaching English as the primary language. In the long run, this will create a stronger overall fabric for society. My ancestors had to learn English. Yours likely did, too.

As a side note, my own personal heritage and my last name of Tuma are Czechoslovakian. Yet, in my background and family tree I also have English, Irish, Dutch, German, and American Indian. Thus, I am a Heinz 57, a little bit of everything. In my view, this level of integration ultimately creates the strongest society possible. Each subgroup has its own strengths and struggles. Yet, the interweaving of these cultures forms a much stronger society, rather than allowing various subcultures to remain fragmented and potentially divisive.

So, the long-term solution to our problems, for America's sake, is not only to teach and adapt our social policies to encourage larger families as a whole, but also to encourage what Senator Lamar Alexander has termed *patriotic immigration*.[28]

All immigrants should become citizens if they become permanent residents. Give them a period to adapt and adjust, but all must ultimately help support the social service systems and infrastructures that have made this country great and are what attracted them to America in the first place.

> Although rising productivity is indeed a major source of economic growth, growth in the sheer number of workers and consumers is equally if not more important. Indeed, over the last three decades, population growth has accounted for between one half and two-thirds of all economic growth in all industrialized countries.
>
> —Phillip Longman[29]

There is no question in my mind that we will soon go through some even more challenging times due to the demographic winter and other issues that are taking place. There is also no question that America can become an even greater society over time, despite serious challenges now. The long-run future can be bright indeed.

America has led the world politically, economically, and militarily throughout the twentieth century. While we are going to see challenges to our society, there is no reason for the United States to follow the historical pattern of past great empires, such as the Roman Empire. We do not have to go into long-term decline. It is possible that we may go into decline, but it is not necessary. If we reform what needs reforming, change to adapt to the *new realities of the future*, and fix the root causes of our problems, America can become an even greater country and remain a leader, perhaps the world's great leader, throughout the twenty-first century.

CHAPTER SEVEN

GROWING YOUR WAY
INTO PROSPERITY

IN ADDITION TO looking at solutions from the standpoint of increasing our population, we should also look for business solutions that will continue to make America great. Above all, we must understand this does not involve the movement toward excess regulation and taxation. Most politicians, when pushed into a corner, will demand excess regulation in order to attempt to stop abuses and higher rates of taxation in order to pay for the social programs that they want to secure. For most of them, that's how they got elected in the first place, by promising the electorate the most goodies from the government.

As we have seen earlier, the government is limited in how much it can do. Yet, the government *can* be a very effective force for good. Think of the government as a lever. You can use a crowbar to move a two-ton boulder if you use it correctly at the right place and time. Government can provide extremely good leverage in either a positive or negative sense.

If you look at the history of tax policy and regulation, you will find that any time the government goes into a period of excessive, even obsessive focus on regulation, the economy generally goes into stagnation (like in the 1970s). Lately, after recent financial scandals and debacles, our government has begun implementing much more regulation and has begun to change the direction of the Reagan revolution.

Excessive regulation, as well as a well-meaning desire to keep the *crooks and idiots* from ripping-off the public, in the long run usually ends up hurting honest people far more than the crooks themselves. Overall, the damage to the system is often much higher due to zealous overregulation, adding massive bureaucracies with which the average business and consumer must deal.

Think of it as a race. For the United States to stay competitive economically, it must do everything it can to make our *Olympic business runners* the fastest in the world. Encourage our runners with good nutrition, training, the best facilities, and the best equipment. Do everything that we can do to make our economic runners the best.

This would not involve carrying another person. Have you ever seen an Olympic runner win a race while carrying another person on his back? Excessive regulation and taxation is the equivalent of trying to win the Olympic 400-meter relay with our anchor runner carrying another person.

Presently, government of all forms makes up nearly 20 percent of our country's annual production (gross domestic product).[1] Waste that is created due to excess regulation creates an environment in which it becomes increasingly difficult over time to do business and continue competing with the best in the world's marketplace.

The same is true about excessive taxation. The most likely thing that will happen during the coming demographic winter is that politicians will decide, "We need more tax revenue to pay for these social programs, and the answer is to raise tax rates." In the long run, this is *not* the right answer. Raising tax rates *suppresses* economic activity, thus giving you a smaller economic pie on which to pay taxes.

In fact, recent studies by Harvard University PhD Robert Barro and by highly regarded Italian economist Roberto Perotti both concluded independently of each other that every dollar spent by the federal government reduces private spending (consumer or corporate) by one dollar, with no net improvement to the GDP. Government spending will, however, increase the national debt, thus increasing the national debt without a net improvement in the economy.[2]

The answer should be *increasing the size of the pie*. By *lowering* tax rates and reducing excess regulation, you create *free enterprise zones* that will be more conducive to world-class business practices. Thus, you attract more businesses, as well as businessmen and women from all over the world. Creating an environment that is difficult to work in, for a particular locale, will tend to encourage people to move elsewhere. We are seeing this happen today in many states within the United States.

There are obvious exceptions to this, but generally speaking, intrastate migration is occurring within the United States. In general, the migration is moving *away* from the more highly regulated, higher cost-of-living states toward lower cost-of-living, lower-regulation states. Remember, more population translates into increased economic growth and prosperity.

TOP 10 OUTBOUND AND INBOUND STATES, 2003–2007[3]

Top 10 OUTBOUND States		Top 10 INBOUND States	
State	**5-Year Average**	**State**	**5-Year Average**
North Dakota	66.4 percent	North Carolina	62.0 percent
Michigan	63.3 percent	Nevada	61.7 percent
New Jersey	60.9 percent	Oregon	61.0 percent
Indiana	60.0 percent	South Carolina	59.8 percent
New York	59.5 percent	Idaho	59.3 percent
Illinois	58.5 percent	Alabama	58.3 percent
Pennsylvania	56.3 percent	Arizona	58.3 percent
Ohio	55.2 percent	Tennessee	55.3 percent
Wisconsin	54.6 percent	Delaware	55.2 percent
Massachusetts	54.5 percent	New Mexico	54.6 percent

With the exception of North Dakota, which has almost no residents (640,000) and a harsh climate, the other outbound states, generally speaking, are high-tax/regulation "blue" states. There are seven states that do not impose an income tax on individuals: Alaska, Florida, Nebraska, North Dakota, Texas, Washington, and Wyoming. Two additional states tax only dividend and interest income: New Hampshire and Tennessee. Looking at it purely from a tax perspective, between 1995 and 2007, the ten highest tax states lost 1.7 million people, while the ten lowest tax states gained 1.3 million. Population movement within the United States is also moving away from states with the highest tax burdens toward states with lower tax burdens. Migration means more people—hence, greater economic activity.

States such as New Jersey and California, because of excessive government policies, tax rates, and regulation, have pushed the cost of living and of doing business too high. Thus, many businesses are moving to different parts of the country so that they can better grow their companies. U.S. firms compete with foreign corporations, and if the foreigners can do it better and cheaper, they will take away our market share. In order to compete, many companies have been forced to relocate to other parts of the country that are friendlier to businesses, with fewer regulations, lower tax structures, and lower utility costs.

One example is Buck Knives. One of the world's leading manufacturers of hunting and fishing knives since 1902, this third-generation, family-owned business is legendary among hunters and outdoorsmen. Yet, due to rising costs (regulations, taxes, utilities, labor, etc.), Buck Knives found itself unable to stay ahead of its leading competitor and began steadily losing market share. After a long and exhaustive research, the CEO of Buck Knives, A. J. Buck, made the decision to move Buck's corporate headquarters from San Diego, California, to Post Falls, Idaho, in late 2004 and was able to reduce its costs by an estimated 30 percent.

Now that virtually every category of expense that Buck faces has been reduced drastically, the company is back on the upswing.[4] This will likely be an ongoing story over the next two decades as corporations move their headquarters to more favorable climates.

Hopefully, politicians will not respond to upcoming pressures by imposing big tax increases, which will suppress economic activity. (I am not holding my breath on this.) But the odds are high that those states that legislatively favor growing businesses and fostering climates that are business-friendly will continue to attract corporate ventures and new business.

A good example of unintentional consequences was a luxury tax passed in January 1991. Democratic leaders decided that they wanted to increase taxes on the *rich* in order to create a *more fair* sharing of the economic pie and as an attempt to raise government revenue, so they imposed a luxury tax on yachts and other expensive items.

The result: Did the rich get hurt? No, the rich decided to stop buying yachts. (People change behavior based upon incentives.) The people who got hurt were the yacht manufacturers and workers who lost their jobs when their companies went broke. This bill bankrupted several manufacturers and cost the jobs of the *average guys*—the people who the Democrats were trying to help in the first place. Not only that, but the business failures and lost wages actually created less tax revenue, the exact opposite of what was intended.[5] We call this *the law of unintended consequences*, and politicians are masters at it.

Our objective should not be to create more hurdles and difficulties for American businesses, but rather to free up the capitalist system to attract as much capital, labor, manpower, and brainpower to the United States as possible.

As has been the case in the past, we should make the U.S. the *best* free-enterprise zone in the world. We should make it a *very* attractive place to do business, more than ever before. If we do this, we will not be able to keep the people, manpower, knowledge, and capital *out* of the United States. Going backward into a policy of progressive taxation and regulation will be going the wrong direction. We would effectively be placing a person on the back of our sprinters. Please, Mr. Politician, don't do this.

SMALL BUSINESS SOLUTION

What other solutions are possible to fix the consumer spending problems? As we demonstrated earlier in the book, people tend to peak in spending when they have teenagers in their family. During the demographic winter (approximately between the years 2009 and 2023), if consumer spending becomes as big of a problem as we expect it will, this in turn will trigger a domino effect. First, it will affect the profitability of American corporations, which then affects their corporate earnings, the price of the company stock, and their 401(k) plans. This, in turn, affects both the ability of average Americans to retire, plus the value of their retirement accounts. Not a good situation. A chain reaction occurs, as one level of spending and problems spills over into another and another—and the string of dominos fall.

But is it possible to fix the consumer-spending problem? The answer again is *yes*, long term, but is not going to be obvious to most politicians, who by training are mostly lawyers with little or no economic training or background. Consumer-spending problems can only be solved by encouraging patriotic immigration—encouraging more and more businesses to come to the United States to set up shop—and *not* by discouraging businesses through excessive taxation and regulation, thus pushing more businesses offshore. We should encourage the proliferation of small business.

GREAT TRANSFORMATIONS

America, as well as the rest of the world, is currently going through a series of great transformations on four fronts. These four transformations were discussed in an excellent speech given by Herb Meyer, who was in the Reagan administration and received the Congressional Medal of Honor for being the first person to recognize and predict that the Soviet Union was about to collapse.

One of the transformations Meyer discusses is the "shifting demographics of western civilization," caused, according to Meyer, because "most countries in the Western world have stopped breeding"—a topic we've discussed extensively in previous chapters. Another transformation is the "restructuring of American business," as former developing countries become first-world, twenty-first century, Internet-age countries.[6] (Meyer's entire speech, which is outstanding, is included in Appendix A.)

In Meyer's example above, the fracturing of American business is positive, not a negative. It means that larger, centralized corporations are gradually being fractured into smaller and smaller subunits. New cottage industries are being formed. The technology available with Internet, cell phones, and the whole host of technology that we have today allows for smaller and smaller units of business. In the long run, these smaller units of business are usually more profitable per unit versus the great monolithic companies, which tend to become overly bureaucratic, structured, and regulated.

Larger, older companies find it more difficult to adapt and can become economic dinosaurs. So, the fracturing of American business into smaller and smaller subunits—smaller and smaller independent businesses—is a great part of the future of America. *Decentralization* is the byword for the hour.

We should do everything in our power in the political realm, using all of the leverage the government can provide—and that only the government can provide—through the use of the tax system (tax credits, depreciation, and things of this nature) to *encourage* the formation of small businesses. Indeed, economic studies time after time have conclusively proven that the vast majority (approximately 80 percent) of new job creation comes through small businesses. Yet, small business faces its own challenge for survival as well. And, as someone who has run a small business for almost thirty years, I know the challenges well.

These challenges are multiple, with the two largest being shortages of capital and expertise. But more and more, as the turnkey revolution continues changing American business, much of the technology and expertise needed can be purchased through outsourcing. This proliferation of outsourcing allows people access to goods and services they could not have had in the past.

For example, rather than hiring an accountant or bookkeeper to do my payroll, I use a Fortune 500 company that does the payroll for me much more competitively than I could pay someone by the hour to do it. The economies of scale available through the *specialization* that is occurring as American businesses fracture into smaller and smaller subunits is something we should encourage and that politicians of all parties should get behind.

If the Democrats truly want to help the little guy, this is the best way to do so. Encourage small business formation. Go into underdeveloped geographic zones or impoverished areas of the country, go into urban areas, and set up *free enterprise zones*. Use tax credits to create small businesses and help them thrive. The small businessmen in those areas will work to survive, prosper, and grow and will bring dignity, responsibility, and a productive work ethic to their communities.

Generally speaking, the higher the percentage of people who have owner-ship in our society (both of the use of the tools for production as well as labor), the more society will grow over the long run—and the more prosperity results. We should use the government to encourage responsible behavior and the use of free enterprise to tackle social problems, not allowing government dependency to attempt to solve them.

As most know, government dependency does not work in the long run. One of the primary roles of the government should be acting as referee, making sure that everybody is being treated fairly within the system, as well as encouraging the *growth* of the system from the small-business perspective.

What about solutions for Social Security and Medicare? In the short run, these are difficult topics. It has not been my intent in this book to put together *doom-and-gloom or Cassandra-type* projections based upon current trends. In the first place, straight-line projections based upon current trends over very long periods almost always go awry. Second, if you take the present Social Security and Medicare systems and structures and project them into the future without reform, the programs cannot be sustained.

Reform is going to *have* to take place in order for the systems to *survive*. Tackling the current prognosis on Social Security and Medicare can become extremely gloomy and depressing. Since there are a number of other books out there that have already taken on this topic, we will not tackle it here.

I am not necessarily part of the political process at this point. I am primarily trying to help individuals with their personal financial planning and investments. There are plenty of other people who are already working to do that, for example, Pete Peterson's group, The Concord Coalition. The bottom line is that there is great room for optimism and hope—but not without major reform. We will not get through the Social Security and Medicare mazes without some pain. Pain is inevitable, but as a long-term optimist, I know that pain can create great good.

Without the pain of the Revolutionary War, America would never have been born. Without the pain of Valley Forge, George Washington's army would never have been strong enough to defeat the British. Without the pain of the Civil War in the 1860s, slaves would never have been freed, and the beginnings of freedom from oppression for an entire culture in the United States would never have taken place.

Without the pain of the civil rights movement of the 1960s, it is unlikely that blacks in America would have achieved the economic independence that many have. Without the pain of World War I and World War II, freedom would not have survived. Had the Japanese and Hitler's Nazism conquered the world, human oppression would likely have gone to levels never before seen in world history. Through great personal and national sacrifice, these forces were defeated.

The pain of the cold war defeated the Soviet Union and resulted in freedom and prosperity for areas of the world where that never would have been possible. None of the "freedom revolution" that is taking place worldwide would have begun without America being the world's leader in establishing personal and economic freedom.

I am confident that although I believe we will see much pain over the next decade or so, we have the opportunity to create even greater levels of freedom and prosperity in the long run, if we will make the right choices during those periods of pain. These challenges have the ability to create great good if we will choose the right answers and avoid wrong ones.

I am continually drawn to a particular principle contained in what, in my opinion, is one of the best business books ever written, *Good to Great* by Jim Collins. In the book, he talks about several of the greatest corporate-growth stories in American history. Prior to that book, Collins and his cowriter had written another bestseller, *Built to Last,* a book about the enduring icons of American industry.[7] Collins was able to demonstrate what made these world-class companies great and enduring and what they did to maintain their status.

During a speaking engagement, Collins was challenged in a somewhat tongue-in-cheek way by the CEO of a corporation, who basically told him, "The information you are giving us is, of course, useless information."

This naturally took Collins back a bit, and he asked, "What do you mean by that?"

The CEO's response indicated that Collins had told the audience what those companies were like today but not how they got there. He hadn't told the listeners or readers how these companies went from being good, publicly traded companies to being great companies. This so sparked Collins's interest that he undertook a six-year-long study, entering Stanford Business School's MBA program, to discover how companies went from good to great.[8]

The criteria used for *Good to Great* were, first, a corporation had to be publicly traded (so as to allow Collins and his research team ready access to all of the data they needed). In addition, the corporation's stock had to outperform the S&P 500 by at least a three-to-one margin for a minimum of fifteen years, thus superseding any CEO's duration in office.

In a study of companies involving nearly fifty years' worth of data going back to the 1950s, Collins came up with only eleven companies that exhibited these characteristics. After isolating the test cases, he and the students at Stanford then studied what made these companies truly great—what made these companies go from good publicly traded companies to truly great publicly traded companies, some of the best the world has ever seen.

They attempted to boil it all down to the most common traits or characteristics. The Stockdale Paradox, one trait these companies shared that I outlined earlier, is *extremely* appropriate for the United States today: "Confront the most brutal facts of your current reality, while, at the same time, retain faith that you will prevail in the end, regardless of the difficulties."[9]

There is no question in my mind that during this demographic winter we will face great challenges. Will we have the intestinal fortitude to face up to those challenges? Will we have the guts to take these challenges head-on, instead of blaming someone else or trying to find a scapegoat? Will we look at the problems that we as a society have created through our own behavior, then look for solutions as to how to fix these problems? Will we refuse to allow ourselves to become overwhelmed with depression, but rather face the future, holding to absolute faith that we will ultimately prevail in the end? Will we conquer these challenges?

I am reminded of one story from my own state's heritage, that of the Alamo. Those of you familiar with the story know that 182 Texas settlers held off more than 5,000 of Santa Anna's best troops for thirteen days in an old Spanish mission that was jerry-rigged into a fort at the last moment. What is not widely understood is that all of the men knew they faced almost certain death yet chose to inflict as much damage as possible upon the enemy's troops before succumbing. And what damage they inflicted! Some 1,600 were dead and 500 wounded, almost ten-to-one, before the battle was over. All the men of the Alamo, including frontier legends Davy Crockett and Jim Bowie lost their lives.[10]

But the loss to the Mexican army was so severe, as the fort's commander, Colonel William Barret Travis, predicted, "The victory will cost the enemy so dear, that it will be worse for him than defeat."[11] Despite their defeat, the men of the Alamo so damaged the Mexican army's psyche that Sam Houston, some several weeks later, won the decisive Battle of San Jacinto for Texas's Independence, losing only 9 men versus the Mexican army's 630 in a battle lasting only eighteen minutes.[12]

I hate to say this, but I believe it will take this level of resolve, guts, and courage from many of the people in this country before America emerges from its crucible, but I believe that it will happen.

In order to do this, we are going to have to remember the lessons of history. As an unknown philosopher once said, "If we learn anything from history, it is the fact that man learns nothing from history." George Santayana wrote, "Those who cannot remember the past are condemned to repeat it."[13]

As Alexander Fraser Tytler has been credited with stating during the formation of American society, "A democracy cannot exist as a permanent form of government. It can only exist until the voters discover that they can vote themselves largesse [generous gifts] from the public treasury."[14] America is in the apex of this decision-making process as we speak, and over the next fifteen to twenty years will face this certain choice. Will we, out of our own ignorance and greed, decide to continue benefiting ourselves individually at the expense of society?

To do so would be counterproductive, short-term thinking in which pride, ego, and greed would create disastrous results. Will we as a society face up to the problems that we have created for ourselves? No one created these problems for us; we created them for ourselves. We bought into what, in my opinion, are falsehoods—such as that the world is overpopulated. I believe that it can be demonstrated without question that in the long run societies prosper as they have larger numbers of children, thereby growing both social systems and the economy, which benefits everyone in the long run. Will we indulge in pity-party, victimized, short-term, woe-is-me thinking, which leads us nowhere except into more pain? The challenge is ours!

CHAPTER EIGHT

GLOBALIZATION: THE FUTURE
THAT HAS YET TO BE WRITTEN

I F WE WANT to get a feel for the future, we must look farther down the road, beyond the current economic and demographic winter to the next economic springtime.

What forces and factors will likely produce the next economic boom? Sometime after 2020, increasing numbers of the children of the baby boomers in America, the so-called *echo boom* generation, will begin moving into their peak spending years. These are children born between 1977 and 1997, and by actual count they are a slightly larger generation than their boomer parents.[1] By 2020 or 2025, I expect America will have gone through quite a purging, yet could still face daunting problems related to old-age pensions and medical payments (Social Security, Medicare).

Nevertheless, once the debt purge is over, the situation should begin to improve as larger and larger numbers of consumers will be moving toward their peak spending years between 2020 and 2040. This creates the potential for another economic boom during this time, if America's economic infrastructure has not been dismantled through Socialism or *economic winter* issues and the enormous debts likely to be piled up by state and federal governments attempting to fix the system. So, boomer boom round two could start sometime around 2025. Improvements will hopefully start sooner than that.

GLOBAL TRADE

A major part of the future that has yet to be written revolves around the movement toward globalization in terms of world trade, *not* in terms of a world government, as discussed in chapter 1. Globalization is a unique story. Globalized free trade allows for *specialization*, allowing each country or region to use its strongest talents and resources to their best and highest use.

One of the miracles of the United States is that our founding fathers, in one fell swoop, created the world's largest *free trade zone*. Instead of Iowa putting a tariff (or tax) upon beef from Texas or Texas putting a tariff on corn produced in Iowa, each state can sell products to the other states. Each state, based upon its specific regional strength, can sell its products or services to others inside the United States without any trade barriers, intrastate taxes, or tariffs, as contrasted, for example, to Europe's long history prior to the establishment of the European Union in 1993.

One of the reasons that the United States, with only 5 percent of the world's population and less than 5 percent of the world's land mass, has been able to produce almost a third of the world's economy is because we have free intrastate trade. The problem is that we have policies that have become increasingly discouraging to businesses.

Protectionism is not good policy, and trade unions, while necessary earlier in the early twentieth century during the so-called Robber Baron Era (when greedy, powerful businessmen would use their economic wealth and power to dominate others), have in many ways become counterproductive.

If you can take a product and move it offshore where it can be manufactured more economically and efficiently, over the long run that means each economy is being allowed to work at its best and highest use. To try to prevent American corporations from moving wherever they have the best advantage is ultimately suicidal. It would mean that they could not effectively compete with other corporations worldwide in the production of goods or services.

I am not opposed to trade unions (I was a member of two different construction unions as I worked my way through college). But, I have seen unions become so inflexible in their objective of winning benefits for their workers that they ultimately bankrupt the company they work for or at least put the corporation into a position in which they are either not competitive with newer business models (contrast Southwest Airlines with its peers) or the only way they can survive and compete in the world marketplace is to move operations offshore. Talk about killing the goose that laid the golden egg.

This is what the movement toward offshoring and outsourcing is all about. Throughout the history of the world, the world has always focused on trade.

My good friend Barry Asmus, PhD, believes in the principle of mutual gains from voluntary exchange and is fond of saying:

> Mutual gain is the foundation of trade: parties agree to an exchange because they anticipate that it will improve their well-being. The motivation for market exchange is summed up in the statement, "If you do something good for me, I'll do something good for you."

Far too many people fear globalization, but only because they fear what they do not understand. Globalization might sound complicated, but its not. For example, do you hunt the forest for your food or build your own house or sew your own clothing? Of course not. Economically speaking, you buy food at a grocery store, live in a house built by a contractor, and wear clothing stitched by machines. All of these choices are faster, cheaper, smarter, and in your self-interest. The bottom line is that trade makes everyone wealthier.

You do your job in order to serve another who does their job to serve someone else. The needs of an entire society are met by the collective knowledge, skills and abilities hosted in the bodies, minds and spirits of all the members of that society. Trading knowledge, skills and abilities multiplies our choices. The result is a wealthier world. If a person can do something better than anyone else, we should in the name of prosperity, let them keep doing that job.

The Bureau of Economic Analysis data on 2500 multinational companies between 1991 and 2001 show that while employment in foreign affiliates rose by 2.8 million jobs, employment in U.S. parent firms rose even more—by some 5.5 million jobs. For every job outsourced, multinationals created nearly two jobs in the U.S.[2]

DEMOCRACY AND CAPITALISM

As you look at the last half of the twentieth century, you will see a strong pattern emerging.

Democracy and Capitalism Lead to Wealth Creation		
	1974	2001
Number of democratic nations	39	121
Percent of total nations that are democratic	27 percent	63 percent
Number of multinational companies (approx.)	7,000	40,000
Source: Calamos Investments Investment Insights: April 2005; U.S. Agency for International Development, "Global Trends in Democracy," 2002; Progressive Policy Institute, 2002 State New Index, June 2002		

As you can see, over the last century, more and more countries have moved *away* from Statism, Socialism, and Communism and have moved toward democracy and free enterprise. This should be no surprise, given that most of the *isms*—Communism, Socialism, Marxism, and Collectivism—failed miserably.

The primary reason for this is that they all lack one common element, self-interest.

Perhaps the greatest economist of all time, Adam Smith, wrote:

> It's not from the benevolence of the butcher, the brewer, or the baker that
> we expect our dinner, but from the regard of their own self-interest.[3]

No matter how hard you try, no matter how dedicated the devotees are to a collectivist economic system, they all ultimately fail without this one element. You cannot run a successful economic system over the long run without self-interest.

Let me tell you a very interesting story. It occurred during a crucial period during the founding of America. Shortly after the pilgrims landed, they recognized how woefully ill prepared they were for survival in the new world. During the first winter, due to malnutrition, poor planning, and lack of adaptation, almost half of the population died. The following winter they found that they did not have enough provisions for the winter, especially after another ship from the old world dropped off a new group of thirty-five additional settlers without bringing a single stock of equipment, supplies, or food. Due to the extreme conditions that arose, amazingly during that winter their rations were reduced to *five kernels of corn per day*! Five kernels!

After that horrendous winter of deprivation, when amazingly none died due to starvation, their leaders decided on a different course of action the following spring. Here's their story.

> It was April of 1623, time to get the year's corn planted. But as the Pilgrims went into the fields to till the ground and put in the seed, there was a listlessness about them that was more than just weakness from months of inadequate rations. They were well aware that they needed at least twice as great a yield as the first harvest and they did *not* want a repeat of the half hearted effort of the second summer (when they had been too busy building houses and planting gardens to give the common cornfields the attention they needed). So the principle men of the colony decided that there would be an additional planting. But for the second planting *individual lots would be parceled out*, with the understanding that the corn grown on these lots would be for the *planters' own private use*.
>
> Suddenly, new life seemed to infuse the Pilgrims:
>
> . . . it made all hands very industrious, so as much corn was planted than otherwise would have been by any means the Governor or any

other could use, and saved him a great deal of trouble and gave far better content. The women now went willingly into the field and took their little ones with them to set corn, which before would allege weakness and inability, whom to have compelled would have been thought great tyranny and oppression.[4]

An amazing transformation took place. Once incentives were changed, their economic outcomes staged a dramatic reversal, later allowing for bounty to fill their coffers.

Keep in mind these were rugged, dedicated people. During the first voyage to the new world, they'd endured sixty-six days at sea, most of it below deck due to extreme, stormy weather. One hundred and two horribly seasick men, women, and children were crammed in the hold of a tiny ship inside a space about the size of a tennis court!

After all they had endured thus far and having gone through back-to-back winters of near starvation and death, you'd expect that *if anyone* were highly motivated to farm, farm, farm, it would be these people. I don't know about you, but if I'd had to live on five kernels of corn a day all winter long, I think I'd be highly motivated.

Yet their version of *commune* farming failed miserably, despite repeated admonitions by leaders and ministers. These were hardy people, so dedicated to their cause that they'd ventured to a new world full of dangers, hostile inhabitants, and disease. They left behind homes and families for the great and dangerous unknown, all for their cause.

But their leaders couldn't seem even to get a proper farming venture launched. Not, at least, until they'd changed the incentives. Once the pilgrims were able to farm their own plots, bounty appeared, almost as if by magic. This *pilgrim* spirit and the values infused into the very fiber of the new-world settlers grew and later produced the seeds of a foundational document like none other in history.

Ultimately, these virtues became so ingrained within the fabric of our founding fathers that they became a part of our Constitution, the founding document of our nation.

> We hold these truths to be self-evident, that all men are created equal, that they are endowed by their Creator with certain unalienable Rights, that among these are Life, Liberty, and the pursuit of Happiness. That to secure these Rights, Governments are instituted among Men, deriving their just powers from the consent of the Governed, that whatever any Form of Government becomes destructive of these ends, it is the Right of the People to alter or abolish it.[5]

Now the question raised is: Isn't it obvious that more nations of the world are catching what we would view as the American spirit? More and more countries are catching on that collectivism, in whatever form, undermines individual incentive and produces *less* economically, despite all manner of well-intended ideals.

Increasingly, countries of the world have decided to copy what works, not what has failed. Despite our current economic challenges, capitalism has far and away produced more economic freedom and prosperity than any other system ever devised by man. That's because, in the long run, *freedom produces prosperity*!

> It is impossible to imagine people navigating shark infested waters in order to reach the shores of Castro's Cuba or risking amputation while crossing mine fields to enter Kim Il Sung's North Korea. No one has ever witnessed such lunacy. It is entrepreneurs and workers, not governments, that produce prosperity, and free societies. There are no exceptions and no subtle intellectual arguments to the contrary. When we compare South Korea [to North Korea], and West Germany to East Germany, we see identical culture whose wealth versus poverty gap is wide and attributed to a man-made line in the sand that separates a free people from an oppressed people.[6]

Freedom and Prosperity

When people are allowed to produce for their own self-interest, they are generally happier and more productive. To demonstrate this, economically more output is produced by the U.S. than any other nation in the world, by large measure.

More and more countries are turning toward the first principles that made America great. Despite present cascading moral values in America, we still lead the world in almost all categories.

"Land of the Free"[7]

5 percent of the world's population produces:
   70 percent of the world's Nobel Laureates
   90–100 percent of the most important inventions of the twentieth century
   Almost one-third of the world's GDP

Why does a country with less than 5 percent of the world's population produce most of the world's great inventions? It's been partly due to our morals, work ethic, and economic system, but also our *freedom*!

The purpose of this chapter is not to brag upon America or to present an egocentric perspective about the U.S. but to talk about economic freedom.

We want to know what makes a country and its people great and how we can spread our best ideals to other parts of the world.

As the world moves deeper into the twenty-first century, it is in everyone's best interest to work toward an economic system that produces the greatest good for all mankind. And that economic system is free enterprise.

WORLD POPULATIONS AND GLOBAL OUTPUT[8]

World Population in 2000		Global Output—2000 Share of GDP in U.S. Dollars	
Nation	Percentage	Nation	Percentage
United States	5 percent	United States	32 percent
Euro-area	5 percent	Euro-area	20 percent
Japan	2 percent	Japan	13 percent
China	21 percent	China	3 percent
India	17 percent	India	1 percent
Rest of the world	51 percent	Rest of the world	30 percent

Chart 8-A, prepared by the Heritage Foundation, underscores this. They rated more than 153 countries of the world and grouped them into five categories: free, mostly free, moderately free, mostly un-free, and repressed. Each country was graded upon a variety of measures, but they primarily looked at trade policy, cost of government, the degree of government intervention or regulation, and property rights. The results speak for themselves. As you can see from the study, far and away the "mostly free" countries produced the highest per capita income. There is a direct correlation. More freedom over the long run equals more prosperity.

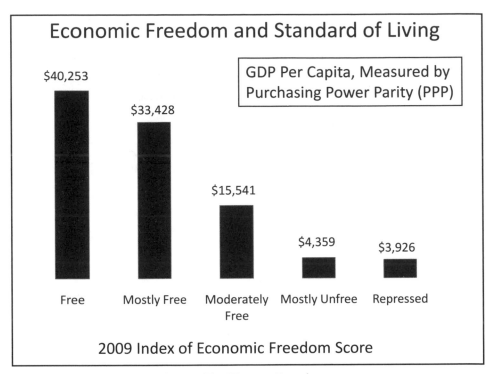

Economic Freedom and Standard of Living

GDP Per Capita, Measured by Purchasing Power Parity (PPP)

$40,253 — Free
$33,428 — Mostly Free
$15,541 — Moderately Free
$4,359 — Mostly Unfree
$3,926 — Repressed

2009 Index of Economic Freedom Score

Source: The Heritage Foundation
Chart 8-A[9]

Henry Weaver once wrote a book entitled *The Mainspring of Human Progress*, which sold more than one million copies.[10] In it he explained that human freedom, property rights, and rule of law (not tyrants) produce the greatest incentives for productivity and, indeed, progress.

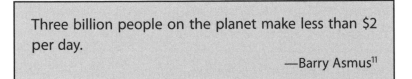

Three billion people on the planet make less than $2 per day.

—Barry Asmus[11]

GOVERNMENT AS REFEREE

As we stated earlier, I believe, as did the late Nobel Prize–winning economist Milton Friedman, that the best role for government is that of the referee. Too much control and intervention, whether well intended or not, stifles creativity, productivity, and wealth creation. Too little regulation (à la laissez-faire or libertarian extremes) allows for self-interest to go too far.

Greed, corruption, and power-mongering can affect both the corporate world and the world of government, because it's part of the downside to our human nature. But two wrongs don't make a right. Too little regulation—as we've seen with the subprime, Alt-A, and credit default swap mortgage meltdown—produced chaos, suffering, and loss in our whole society. But swinging the pendulum of change to the opposite extreme of big government is not the answer either.

FREE MARKET VIEW

A free market view includes:

- Pursuing maximum freedom and prosperity for citizens
- Government focus on economic liberty (not government control)
- Free trade
- Private property rights
- Proper incentives (taxes, etc.)
- Limited government
- Over time, living standards rise as knowledge, trade, and competition expand the pie.

As a free-market economist, I certainly favor free markets, but not chaotic, out-of-control, Wild West capitalism. It hurts everyone when any sector of our economy is allowed to run amok. By the same token, if government responds to the *too-little-regulation era* we've just been through by allowing the pendulum of change to swing to the extreme opposite, then it will create economic harm as well, likely through excessive taxation, regulation, and control. The best situation is a proper balance between too much and too little government, with the ideal in the middle.

Nevertheless, regardless of our current challenges in the U.S. and abroad over the next ten to fifteen years, the fact remains that more and more countries are moving toward economic freedom. Without question, more economic freedom produces more income per capita and higher living standards than any other single factor.

Critics might say that the median income levels in our society are influenced upward by the extremes. In other words, if you take Bill Gates and Warren Buffett—the wealthiest people in the world, who've accumulated billions or tens of billions—out of the equation, the same theory won't fly. Not true! Every society has someone at the top of the economic food chain. This is true even of oppressed societies. It's just that the entire economic pie grows larger and produces a lot more prosperity from which to eat in free countries.

> Free people are not equal—equal people are not free.
>
> —Barry Asmus[12]

Liberals tend to support the paradigm that economics is what is known as a "zero sum game"—in order for the poor to have more, you must take from those who have and give it to the underprivileged. Take from the rich, and give to the poor. This theory is faulty to an extreme. First of all, giving something to someone who hasn't earned it (I'm not talking about emergency situations but rather long-term dependency) works against human nature.

Remember the story about the pilgrims? Once the incentives changed, free enterprise blossomed and prosperity knew no bounds. Less privileged, more economically disadvantaged people need education, training, work ethics, and rewards to come up to the next level. A handout won't do. Give them a ladder to climb out. Don't give them handouts while they're in the pit or they'll likely stay there.

Taking from the rich to help the permanently needy doesn't work. It creates less incentive and productivity for those who have assets and work the hardest. We can't afford to have our most productive citizens de-motivated. In addition, it typically creates feelings of dependency, resentment, envy, and distrust for those on the receiving end.

Read these powerfully wise words from the Reverend William J. H. Boetcker:

> You cannot bring about prosperity by discouraging thrift. You cannot strengthen the weak by weakening the strong. You cannot help the poor by destroying the rich. You cannot lift the wage-earner by pulling down the wage-payer. You cannot keep out of trouble by spending more than your income. You cannot further the brotherhood of man by inciting class hatred.... You cannot build character and courage by taking away man's initiative and independence.... You cannot help men permanently by doing for them what they could and should do for themselves.[13]

Keep in mind that I'm greatly in favor of charitable giving. As a family, we have always been big givers. But, in the long run, confiscation through excessive taxation is counterproductive to both the confiscatee and the recipient.

The best way to produce freedom, prosperity, and quality of life—life, liberty, and the pursuit of happiness—is to pursue policies that grow the pie. The economic pie is not fixed; it is not constant. Despite setbacks, recessions, and the like, world GDP continues to grow, as evidenced by the following chart.

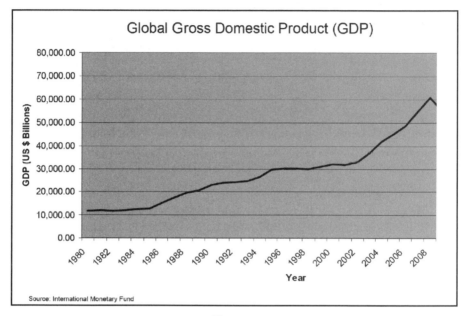

Chart 8-B

We don't live in a world of fixed economies, scarce resources, and limited opportunity. We live in a world endowed by its Creator with the ability to produce life, liberty, and abundance. These are available to all on the globe, if we allow freedom.

If we focus our efforts upon creating and fostering relationships and environments to encourage growth and productivity, if we create the right sets of incentives we can and will produce far more. Plus, we have the ability to help those less fortunate in the world move into a new era of prosperity that is available for all.

DEMOCRACY AND ASIA

In Chart 8-C you see the progress of various Asian countries in terms of per capita (per person) income, comparing them to the United States in 1964 and again in 2004.

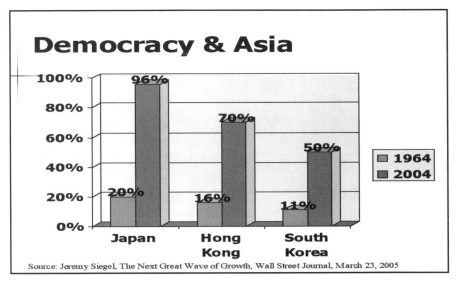

Chart 8-C

The progress is obvious. Those of us who put America first, as I am apt to do, need to realize that stronger competition from Asian or other countries does not make America weaker. Again, there is not a fixed economic pie; there is an unlimited economic pie.

As Asian countries expand and grow, they will provide competition to certain of our industries but opportunity to others. In fact, a recent Federal Reserve study indicated that the jobs being created through the benefits of globalization and outsourcing to other countries were, on average, better paying, better benefit jobs than those being lost.[14] A more prosperous Asia and world allows for the U.S. to receive greater rewards for trade and specialization in areas where we are strongest while allowing other countries rewards based upon their respective strengths. The global economic pie has *no limits*!

CHINA AND THE ASIAN MIRACLE

One of the leading stories of the early twenty-first century, if not *the* leading story, is the rise of emerging Asia, led by China. Following decades of economic and political repression under Mao Zedong, Deng Xiaoping made a decision to reverse the tide of China following years of economic devastation. Collectivism (Communism) failed miserably in China, as it has everywhere else in the world that it has been tried.

Deng, whose father was a prosperous landowner prior to the revolution, decided to begin incorporating free enterprise into the Chinese economy in an attempt to improve their results. The progress has been nothing less than stunning.

Rather than have me tell the story, I'd like to quote again from my good friend Dr. Barry Asmus, from his excellent book *Bulls Don't Blush, Bears Don't Die*.

Deng Xiaoping

Finally, in 1978, two years after Mao's death, Deng Xiaoping became the premier. The son of a prosperous landowner turned local government official; Deng went to Moscow for his college education. After Mao's 1949 victory and the establishment of the People's Republic of China, Deng labored with Mao as one of the senior leaders of the Communist party. During this time, Deng watched as Mao forced farmers into collective communes and exerted an iron grip over the population. Millions starved during the years of the great leap forward. Industrial production fell dramatically. Experienced managers were shuttled off to re-education centers until they could recite the sayings of the Chairman Mao philosophies word for word.[15]

Yes, Deng Xiaoping was a Communist. But watching the Cultural Revolution and the Great Leap Forward of the 1960s bring poverty and starvation to China, he was eyewitness to the failure of flawed economic policies. He was jailed for disagreeing with Mao's policy. After Mao's death, Deng was released from prison and returned to power.

> Don't expect to build the weak by pulling down the strong.
>
> —Calvin Coolidge[16]

In December 1978, the Third Plenum of the Eleventh Congress of the Chinese Communist Party assembled, and Deng made a break with the crimes of Mao. He said, "I can distribute poverty or I can distribute wealth."[17] Deng opted for wealth and began to privatize Chinese agriculture. The catalyst for his new policy was a drought and millions of peasants starving to death.

Beaten down, the Chinese refused to do the backbreaking work of farming unless they were promised a return to the old ways of pre-Communism. The old ways were dominated by privately held farms. When Deng granted thirty-year leases on land, he invoked a familiar Chinese proverb: "Give farmers a one hundred-year lease on a desert and they will turn it into a garden; but give them a one year lease on a garden and they will turn it into a desert."

A responsibility system was adopted, leases on land were approved, and material incentives were put in place. Deng had launched free enterprise. He allowed market process to work and establish property rights for the first time since 1949. As Deng instituted a wide range of economic freedoms, the results were spectacular.

Chinese farmers were allowed to sell most of what they grew. In 1978, less than 10 percent of the farm output was sold in the open market. By 2000 the share had gone to 90 percent. China's GDP grew at nearly 10 percent average annual rates. The income per person rose six times as fast as the world average, and nearly 20 percent of the population was raised out of subsistence-level living. Deng Xiaoping's privatization programs and market reforms produced the most rapid reduction of poverty the world has ever seen.

As the twenty-first century dawned, 125 million Chinese had been lifted out of poverty. Seventy percent of all the construction cranes in the world are now located in China. Real gross domestic product has expanded at an average of 9 percent a year for the last twenty years. Growth in foreign trade has averaged 15 percent annually since 1978. Each week, more than $1 billion of foreign direct investments flows into the country.

Following years of complete repression and backward economics, China's economy has become the growth story of the world.

SOME FACTS ON CHINA

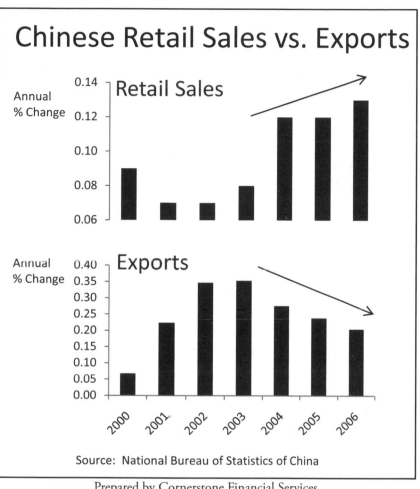

Chinese Retail Sales vs. Exports

Prepared by Cornerstone Financial Services
Chart 8-D

Despite a slow growth rate of exports for China in recent years (still growing at an amazing 15 percent per year), China has begun to develop its own middle class and is seeing retail sales inside their country boom, thus offsetting the decline in exports. This economic boom can be seen in the following areas:

1. *Consumer Spending* rose from $1.7 billion in 2000 to $2.7 billon in 2004. During this period, 11.7 million Visa cards were issued. Consumer spending in China is growing at the fastest rate in the world. Although China's 1.3 billion people cannot replace the

waning spending of baby boomers between 2010 and 2020, they will become a growing, dominant force for world economics.

2. *Incomes in China*—Fifteen million people in China are rated "affluent" with incomes of $4,500–9,999 or more per year. Affluence in China is totally different than the U.S. or Western Europe. Despite phenomenal growth, they are still years behind us in terms of affluence.

3. *Raw Materials*—In 2003, China used 37 percent of the world's cement, 27 percent of its steel, and 70 percent of the world's construction cranes. China has been consuming raw materials on a gargantuan level over the past decade. Energy will likely be the next big battle!

4. *Labor*—Although an estimated 10–13 million people are moving to urban areas per year, 60 percent of China's labor force is still rural (with an estimated 150 million excess rural laborers).

5. *Technology*—There are currently more Chinese Internet users than there are in the United States. China is the world's second-largest consumer of cell phones—3 million per month. China is increasingly moving toward becoming the world's largest consumer for technology.

6. *Education*—Most Ivy League schools have distance-learning programs in Asia, and Chinese students can get an Ivy League degree without leaving the continent. China has 300 million children under age 14—equal to the *entire* U.S. population.

7. *Capital Investment Boom*—No country in the history of the planet has embarked on a capital-spending boom like China, with more than 40 percent of the nation's economy (GDP) involved in building highways, roads, dams, electric plants, and airports. For example, China spent $4.2 billion on a high-speed railway from Beijing to Tibet; $25 billion on the Three Gorges Dam (the world's largest hydroelectric plant); and $35–$45 billion on the 2008 Olympics.

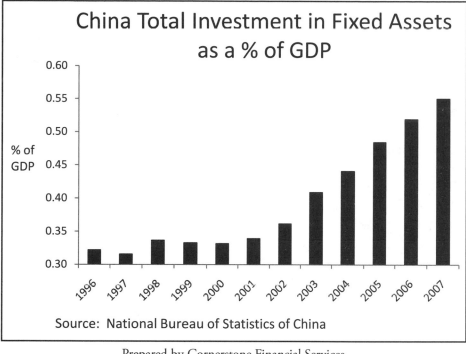

Prepared by Cornerstone Financial Services
Chart 8-E

8. *Automobiles*—GM sold more cars in China from January–April 2009 than it did in the U.S. *every month.* By 2010, China will own an estimated 56 million cars and SUVs.

9. *Energy*—In 2004, the U.S. consumed 24 percent of the world's energy, and China consumed 12.1 percent. China's energy needs will mushroom as the people continue increasing in their levels of affluence and development.[18]

China's unbelievable growth story will likely continue for decades. It is entirely possible, even likely, that by as early as the middle of the next decade, China will be the main source of new economic growth in the world, as the U.S. will still be in its demographic winter at that time. While, based upon current trends, it will take China years to catch up with America's income levels, it is still growing.

Thus, prosperity and growth for the next decade will revolve principally around the story of emerging Asia. Products, new materials, and goods needed for this awakening giant will create some of the world's greatest opportunities for growth.

India

After years of abject poverty and destitution, the world's second great economic miracle is now taking place in India. Once India was freed from British rule, India's leaders unfortunately modeled their economy after the Soviet Union, starting in the 1950s. Combined with a caste system that kept people in generational bondage and poverty, India became the world's poster child for destitution with, to quote Barry Asmus, "three-quarters of a billion people looking like an Auschwitz photo of gaunt cheeks, tired and taint skin, full-moon eyes, and bodies with more bone than flesh."[19] While half the Indian people today are still poor, living on a dollar per day, a change of leadership and economic systems is also creating miraculous growth in India, albeit about fifteen years behind China chronologically.

Quoting again from Barry's excellent book *Bulls Don't Blush, Bears Don't Die:*

> Finally in 1991, a breakthrough year in India occurred and a new reality emerged. A sweeping economic liberalization of India by the minority government of P.V. Narasimha Rao, opened the doors of the Indian economy. Tariff barriers were lifted, foreign aid was encouraged, licensing controls were abolished, the currency was stabilized, tax rates were lowered, and the government monopolies were broken. India's long decades of despair began to fade. Economic growth reached 7.5 percent per year by the mid 1990s, and inflation was reduced to just single digits. The previous finance minister and now Prime Minister, Manmohan Singh, rejected socialism and gave capitalism a first look. Entrepreneurial spirits, so long dormant under Indian Socialism, were finally unleashed by Singh's forward-looking policies.

> Of course, the world already knew about Indian competence. Anywhere Indians go in the world they are highly successful. Per capita family wealth in the Silicon Valley of California is higher among Indian families than any other ethnic group, including white Americans. Indians produce 70 percent of the wealth in Kenya. My wife and I visited the beautiful homes in Capetown [sic], South Africa, many owned by Indians. They are 10 or 20 thousand square foot mansions, with six car garages and private trolly railroads leading from the coastline up to their front doors. Indians are rich everywhere in the world, except India. That is about to change.

> India's emerging success in information technology is world renowned. Their electronics industry has been growing at high annual rates, and of all the global software companies, India has the majority

of those receiving the highest certification for quality leaders. In the 1990s, it was software, the early 21st century will have India dominating in the internet and IT services. As India now welcomes the end of Communism the relative decline of the nation-state, and the emerging single market world economy, the new revolution in telecommunications will play to India's strength.[20]

India's strengths include: engineering, computer science, software, the world's largest democracy, the youngest population of any major country, strong banking and legal systems, an entrepreneurial class, and free media.

The history of the world has always been about trade. It is a net positive when one society that is better at producing widgets trades with another country that is better at providing another service or product. Each society benefits as each uses the natural resources and talents that are more plentiful in its own society or culture to benefit others. Each culture has different skills and strengths in terms of work ethic and specialization.

GLOBALIZATION AND TECHNOLOGY

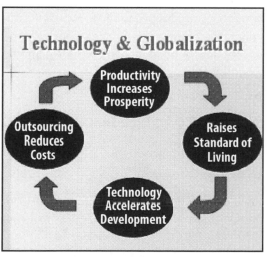

Source: Cornerstone Financial Services
Chart 8-F

Thomas Friedman, in his book *The World Is Flat*, notes that when access to freedom and opportunity are provided to people, their views on violence, terrorism, and wealth are changed. He tells the story of a young man growing up in India and shows how the country's changes have affected the people's thinking.

The story goes…When he got older, he asked his father one day why the Indian half of the family seemed to be doing better than the Pakistani half. His father said to him, "Son, when a Muslim grows up in India and he sees a man living in a big mansion high on a hill, he says, 'Father, one day, I will be that man.' And when a Muslim grows up in Pakistan and sees a man living in a big mansion high on a hill, he says, 'Father, one day I will kill that man.'" When you have a pathway to be the Man or the Woman, you tend to focus on the path and on achieving your dreams. When you have no pathway, you tend to focus on your wrath and on nursing your memories.[21]

Only twenty years ago, before the triple convergence, India was known as a country of snake charmers, poor people, and Mother Teresa. Today its image has been recalibrated. Now it is also seen as a country of brainy people and computer wizards.

Globalization plus technology will literally create a revolution worldwide over the next several decades. Only radical Islamic behavior or a return to the former ways of Communism and Socialism (which is more of a risk to the U.S. and the West than the Far East at this point) could slow this growth. China and India will not go backward. Once a civilization has begun to taste freedom, it does not return to bondage. Generally speaking, the more economic freedom they obtain now, the more political and human-rights freedoms they will obtain tomorrow.

Cycle of Liberty

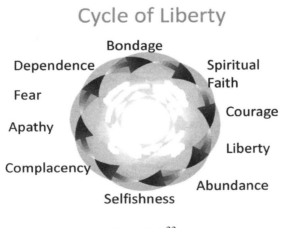

Chart 8-G[22]

Where do you suppose China and India are on the Cycle of Liberty? Somewhere between courage (remember Tiananmen Square?) and liberty, headed for abundance. Leaders come, leaders go; but man will always strive for freedom, liberty, and abundance, even if it means great personal risk and peril. China and India are moving toward abundance.

PART 3

HUNKERING DOWN FOR THE LONG WINTER

CHAPTER NINE

TRIAGE

T RIAGE IS A French word that indicates a process for sorting injured people into groups based on their need for immediate medical treatment. Triage is used in hospital emergency rooms, on battlefields, and at disaster sites when limited medical resources must be allocated. *Triage level one* is treating those likely to live regardless of care. *Level two* is giving treatment to those for whom immediate care will make a difference in their lives. *Level three* is treating those who are likely to die regardless of care. The caregiver determines the status of each patient according to the triage status.

In this section of the book, I want to apply the term *triage* to our present financial crisis. I firmly believe that it is critical to try and help as many people as possible as quickly as we can.

Remember this one thing: your money is *your responsibility*. It's not your adviser's (or broker's) responsibility. This is *your* responsibility as a steward of the money that God has entrusted to you. You must choose to do what is right with your own money.

A very important part of triage is resources. When you have limited resources, you have to decide where to allocate those resources. I have felt for a long time—really, since I entered this industry nearly thirty years ago—that there would be a day when America and the world would go through some incredibly difficult financial times. I have known from my own research that demographically everything pointed to the year 2010 for the economy to roll over, but I think we are now on the front edge of that storm, perhaps two years prematurely. The economic winter has just started, and I don't think it is going to be over anytime soon. Bounces will occur along the way, but the demographic winter has begun.

OUR FINANCIAL HURRICANE

It has been my purpose in this book to give you thorough information to help you understand how we got to the place where we are in our nation's—and the world's—economic climate. Throughout this book I have indicated that I believe we are in the beginning stages of a demographic winter—a Category 5 financial hurricane. Personally, I don't think there is any question about that. For me, that's the bottom line. It has been my intent to present ideas and solutions to help you survive this financial winter or hurricane. I don't want you to have to make fear-based, panic decisions. Those are usually bad decisions made irrationally and will not give you peace, because fear-based decisions fail to give you time to get a sense of direction. You don't have the ability to process properly when in panic or fear mode.

The same is true of greed. Operating out of greed is primarily what got us into this thing in the first place, as far as corporate America goes. You are unlikely to survive a demographic winter if your financial decisions are based on greed.

Before our nation fell into this economic crisis, we were living in a period of financial prosperity. If you borrowed money then, no doubt you leveraged up based upon an assumption of what your house would be worth or what your 401(k) would be worth several years into the future. Then suddenly we fell into a deflationary environment, which is where we are right now, and your assets were hit by deflation. The value of your home or of your 401(k) plummeted, along with the rest of America's assets. However, even though your assets deflated in value, your debts did not disappear. Your debt load can wipe you out, and obviously that is just what has happened to many people already during this current crisis.

In this book and continuing in this chapter, I want to give you a basic understanding of what is going on and why so that you have the power to know what to do next. The financial industry often quotes an old slogan that states, "The market always goes up in the long run." Let me use an analogy I mentioned briefly in the Introduction to clarify the fallibility of this position.

Let's say I'm the captain of a cruise ship and you are in the dining room eating shrimp cocktail, waiting for the next entrée. How safe would you feel if I suddenly got on the loudspeaker and announced, "Folks, I have some good news and some bad news. The bad news is that we have a storm headed our way. It is a *b-i-g* storm, as a matter of fact. It's a Category 5 hurricane. But the good news is that storms always blow over in the long run."

Would you feel pretty comfortable about the situation and think, "Oh, well, it is a Category 5 hurricane, but don't worry, storms blow over in the long run"? Would you want me to steer that cruise ship straight ahead, full speed ahead into the middle of the storm?

Or, would you rather hear me announce, "There is a big storm moving our way, but there is a port we can go into on the other side of the island in order to avoid most of the storm"? I don't know about you, but in my opinion, it is better to ride out the storm from the protection of a port on the other side of the island than to be totally exposed on the ocean.

The timing of last year's storm caught us off guard. This whole situation to me was very much like a gigantic Enron—not necessarily fraud, but we were facing hidden dangers. I don't believe the CEOs of the companies involved in this crisis really knew how much risk was being taken. It was a surprise, especially the timing.

To some degree this crisis is going to have to run its course. What we are dealing with here is the fact that this is not a temporary downturn. People are accustomed to experiencing short recessions. They take you backward for a year or two, then you recover fairly quickly over just a few years. We've outlined in chapters 3 and 4 that more mortgage problems are definitely on the way.

This is likely to be a very long downturn. Early on, Federal Reserve Chairman Ben Bernanke said, "Full recovery is likely to take more than two or three years."[1] Now he's sounding more optimistic, but I believe part of that is an attempt to reassure people so they don't panic and produce a self-fulfilling prophecy.

A pertinent question is: How deep is the hole? Throughout this book, I have pointed you to a principle from the book *Good to Great*, which states:

> You must never confuse faith that you will prevail in the end—which you can never afford to lose—with the discipline to confront the most brutal facts of your current reality, whatever they might be.
>
> —JAMES STOCKDALE[2]

Issues related to the housing market caused our economy to crash. The crisis essentially started in housing and moved to Wall Street, then to Main Street, and so forth. Until the housing market fully stabilizes, this economy is vulnerable.

Throughout the past twenty-five years, we have seen the typical bear markets, which are identified by a slight drop in the economy in which unemployment increases for a while, along with a downturn in the stock market. Normally, at that point the Fed stimulates the economy, lowers interest rates, and boosts the money supply—and everything goes back up again.

I do not believe our current economic crisis will be anything like the normal bear market we've seen over the past two decades. What's happening now is an unwinding of the buildup of debt that occurred over a thirty-year period of time. A deep economic cleansing of this type does not happen quickly and will likely take a long time to run its course.

Recently, an academic study was done to investigate the aftermath of a financial crisis of this magnitude. This study showed that an average adjustment for housing takes about six years to bottom out, which would be around 2012. During this time, unemployment is expected to rise at least 7 percent, which will put the nation in the 11- to 12-percent range before the crisis is over. The average bear market for stocks is three-and-a-half years, which could indicate that we are only about halfway through at this time. The study indicated that real gross domestic product would drop at least 9 percent.[3] In my opinion, we are nowhere near the end of the demographic winter. The economic drop could go a lot lower before finally bottoming.

Retail prices are still falling, the unemployment rate is rising, and household leverage is coming down as people are paying off debts and putting money into savings. Due to fear, most people are not borrowing more money, and the banks are not loaning anyway, due to balance sheets bloated with questionable assets. These are the symptoms of a *deflationary crisis*, and we haven't experienced one of those in seventy years in the United States.

In chapter 4 I gave you information on what has happened to global shipping and business. In early 2009, we saw a 94 percent decline in shipping costs. This is an enormous downturn, and it's unlikely to be over yet! The issue is that most of the economies of the world are either dropping or merely stabilizing at this point, and the things necessary to turn the world around have not yet occurred. World trade has bounced a little since then but is still far from healthy.

This started as a housing crisis, and then it became a credit crisis. Lines of credit dried up.

Also in chapter 4 I told you that Warren Buffett has referred to the enormous losses that have occurred in the S&P 500 index, due to the incredible leveraging of derivatives, by calling derivatives "financial weapons of mass destruction."[4] Some firms were leveraging as high as *thirty to sixty times their assets*.

So the bubble has now burst. What happens to a burst bubble? Once a bubble bursts it cannot be blown back up. An enormous debt bubble has been building up over a thirty-year period of time, and it's not possible to bring it back in one, two, or even three years. In the fourth quarter of 2007, the value of derivatives in just the five top banks totaled *more than ten times the entire U.S. economy*.[5] We have seen leverage used in an unprecedented fashion, which is why this crisis has been so difficult to resolve.

In response to all of the leverage blowing up, the Federal Reserve has printed enormous amounts of money! But the destruction of wealth has simultaneously occurred in both stocks, real estate, and commodities, which has not happened since the 1930s. Down the line, we will likely have to be concerned about inflation because of all of the bailouts and stimulus packages, but right now we are in the throes of an incredible deflationary crisis. We have only had two of these in the last hundred years—in the 1930s in the United States and in Japan in the 1990s.

It is as though the authorities are using a bicycle pump to try to pump up a life raft as a great white shark takes a bite out of the other end of the raft. Meanwhile, we are all dogpaddling in the middle of the ocean. It will be nearly impossible for our nation to pump out enough money fast enough to offset the amount of air that is leaking out from the shark attack. Wealth destruction has taken place at a much faster rate than the pumping up is occurring.

Deleveraging is what happens when people get too deeply in debt (or leveraged) and then the market moves against them. Examples would include margin loans, futures, or options. The problem happens when people lose many times more than they invested due to the leverage involved, as we discussed in chapter 3.

Deflation takes place when asset values fall across the board in the economy. Either the money supply or the asset values plummet, which then forces asset prices down even further.

So far, wealth destruction has occurred at a faster rate than things are getting bailed out due to deflation. I believe we have a two- to three-year period of intense deflation to fight, but it could last longer.

THE DEMOGRAPHIC AGING OF AMERICA

The demographics are not in our favor when it comes to the aging of America. I have been expecting this storm to come and have been telling people for nearly fifteen years that it would occur sometime close to when it hit. In my opinion, it occurred about two years prematurely. In the chapters you have already read, I've outlined for you why I believe that demographics are important, revealing the meaning of the old saying "Demographics are destiny."

In an earlier chapter, I described the consumer as the *800-pound gorilla*. Direct consumer spending comprises more than 70 percent of the economy.[6] This current crisis began with a housing bubble, which surfaced when consumers were unable to meet the payments on homes that were really too expensive for them to buy in the first place. Greed in the banking and mortgage industry allowed the housing market to get out of control by offering easy entrance into home buying.

But although it started as a housing bubble, and, in my opinion, could *and should* have been contained there, it spread to the credit markets. Again, instead of being contained there, just like a string of dominoes, all areas of the economy began to fall.

When Lehman Brothers failed, a worldwide panic set in—a nuclear reaction within the system. No one seemed able to definitively identify how many toxic assets were now falling to the bottom, and as institutions and banks took a plunge downward, investors wanted to know, "How bad are my losses going to be? Will the banking system survive?"

When a world economy has been built upon a pyramid of debt and suddenly the credit flows stop overnight, how do you do business? You can't very effectively.

As we have unveiled in this book, a study of demographics reveals that consumer spending drives the economy, and peak spending for the average family starts when adults reach their mid-forties. You have also learned that there are more people in the baby boomer generation than in any other generation in U.S. history. The enormous boom of baby boomers created an economic surge that has never been seen, literally, in the entire history of the planet.

Boomers created shortages everywhere. There was an enormous economic boom driven by seventy-six million people buying houses and cars, starting families, and moving all of the way up the chain. Unfortunately, they also learned to borrow money like mad—the plastic generation.

If you have been an investor, looked at the market over the last thirty years, and put money into your 401(k) or retirement plan since the boomers started making their way into the economy, you saw a particular type of bull market behavior. Now, since the onset of this economic crisis, we have entered what is called a *secular bear market*—meaning one of the grizzlies.

Some people don't know how to differentiate a bear market from a bull market. I want to give you an analogy about each that will help you. Think first about how a bear fights. It claws *down*. A bear market is a *down-trending* market, the kind you want to avoid. Now think about a bull in a fight; it gores upward with its horns. A bull market is an *up-trending* market, the kind of market we were experiencing as boomers created an economic surge.

The bear market we are currently experiencing is different than the normal black bear market that most of us are familiar with and financial advisors are accustomed to. (We will discuss this more in the next chapter.) The average black bear weighs 250 pounds. If you are camping at Yellowstone National Park and see a black bear in your camp, you want to bang on pots and pans and scream. You should yell, jump up and down, wave your arms, honk your horn, and fight back with everything you have! Generally speaking, the normal black bear will decide that this is too much trouble and leave you alone.

On the other hand, the grizzly bear is a different breed—and so is the secular bear market we are facing. The average grizzly male weighs six hundred pounds and can outrun a human. So, if you run into a grizzly bear, your best defense is to put your hands over your head, pull your knees up to your chest in the fetal position, and hope the bear doesn't like your taste. Grizzlies like to play with their prey before they eat them; if you fight back, the grizzly will think this is great fun, and you will be dead meat.

There are also different types of bear markets when it comes to stocks and different types of strategies for each. A secular bear market, which indicates more than a decade of effect, is the type that I believe we are in right now. This is the kind of bear you don't fight back against. What do I mean? In a normal black bear market, the market comes down and stocks go *on sale*. You put your money in when the market is declining and stocks are cheap, and then you hope that it comes back up in a short period of time—which it usually does. That is a great strategy for a black bear market.

But I don't believe we are in a black bear market. If you look at the pattern we are in, you can see clearly that we did not pass the old high. We'll look at this more carefully in chapter 10. The S&P hit 1,500 in 2000, then dropped a bunch over the next 3 years and went back up. But then it stopped at 1,500 again in 2007, failing to go to a higher high. (See Chart 2-F.) Remember, we discussed earlier in this book that people are accustomed to the market going down and then, when it goes back up, going back to a new, higher high. We've all heard, "The market always goes up in the long run!" And the market generally does go up in the very long run. But how long is the long run? How old are you now? Can you withstand a Category 5 hurricane if we are truly in a secular bear market?

If you look at the history of the market over long stretches, there are periods of time when it doesn't make sense to ride out the storm. The storm is just too severe. Even when the market rebounds, it is not likely to break the old high any time within the next few years. Now it is no longer going to new highs. Instead, with every market downturn, the market has broken through to new lows. In March 2009, we hit the lowest lows for the market going back twelve years.[7]

Now we are bouncing, and we are seeing a significant bounce that could take the market as high, possibly, as ten thousand or higher. It could potentially bounce even more, but we'd still be in a long-term grizzly bear market, as long as we stay below the old high for the market. Keep in mind that you have significant, even huge bounces within the context of a grizzly or secular bear. Bounces can last a year or two, or longer. But sooner or later, I believe we will likely see Phase 3 of this massive bear market.

Secular bear markets, like the one we're in now, have a way of exceeding what anyone expects on the downside, until seemingly all hope is lost and it appears to be the end of the world. In fact, bear markets usually go through three very distinct psychological or emotional phases, which could occur over a period of months or even years.

Phase 1 for bear markets is the *denial* phase. During this phase the bear is just waking up. In fact, there is usually great debate taking place as to whether this is really a bear market or just a pause in the bull market. Evidence appears to be and is, in fact, often contradictory.

Once *Phase 2* commences, all doubt about whether it's a bear market or not is over. By then we've entered what I refer to as the *deer in the headlights* phase. If you've ever encountered a deer while driving in the mountains at night, as I did once in Colorado, you'll know exactly what I mean. Once it is directly in the beam of the headlights, the deer freezes. Not sure which way to run, it *doesn't* run; it freezes right in front of the car, ensuring a collision and the death of the deer. Investors confronted with a mounting bear are usually equally panicked and freeze, not sure whether to hold on and try to ride it back up or bail out, thus preventing further losses. Unfortunately, the deer in the headlights phase is usually not the end.

Phase 3 of most major bear markets is what's known as the *capitulation* phase. In this phase, investors give up as the built-in instinct for survival kicks in. Capitulation phases normally mean that investors flee the market in enormous numbers as true panic behavior—"I quit," "I can't afford to lose it all," "My dreams have been dashed"—becomes prevalent.

After having been through and seen many bear markets during my almost thirty years in financial markets, it appears to me as if Phase 2 behavior (deer in the headlights) is all that we've seen so far. If and when a true Phase 3 capitulation starts, investors need to be advised on how to proceed and what their options are, which we'll detail in this chapter and the next.

We are presently under intense deflationary pressure. This is an animal most have never seen before! In a deflation, assets plunge and debts become fatal. In the 1930s, the market went down 90 percent.[8] The authorities did not handle it the way the authorities are handling our present crash, with bailouts and the printing press, so it's likely we'll see a different outcome this time. Nevertheless, I expect to be in the grip of this deflationary crisis for at least another two to three years.

Japan's deflation crisis was milder than the United States's in the 1930s. They stimulated their economy, continuing to push their money supply up. The fact that Japan was in deflation when the U.S. and the rest of the world were booming also kept them from a much worse situation.

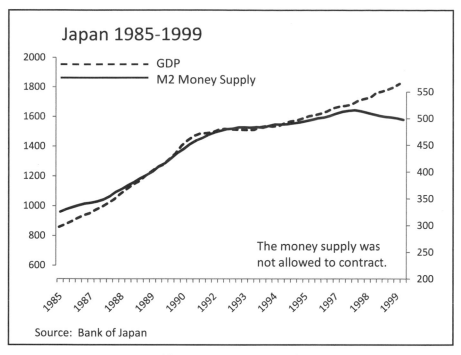

Prepared by Cornerstone Financial Services
Chart 9-A

Prepared by Cornerstone Financial Services with Super Charts by Omega Research
Chart 9-B

Despite Japanese authorities providing bailouts to prevent the money supply from contracting, they stayed in a prolonged deflationary bear market.

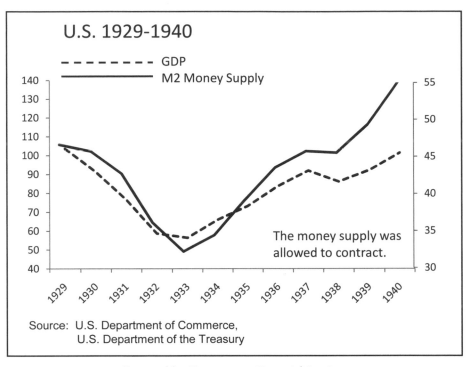

Prepared by Cornerstone Financial Services
Chart 9-C

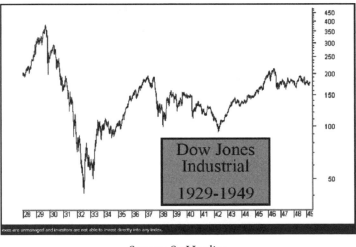

Source: Sy Harding
Chart 9-D

As you can see, in the United States in the 1930s, the government did not
bail out the banks. Thus, the country's money supply dropped substantially.

Almost one-third of the banks failed, contracting the nation's money supply by about one-third. Thus, retail prices fell by one-third (real estate and stocks fell much more), until ultimately FDR enacted the FDIC and stopped the bank panic. This is obviously the worst case of deflation we've seen. Since the authorities are handling this differently, I'd expect a somewhat different outcome, but deflation will, nevertheless, still be difficult to overcome.

I still believe that we are in the middle of the perfect storm. The national debt at the end of 2007 was up to $9 trillion and jumped to more than $11 trillion this year.[9] We could have a $3.5 trillion *annual* deficit within two or three years.[10] The national debt is going to run away from us over the next ten to fifteen years. We will still face deflating pressure for at least two to three years, but as the government keeps bailing, the national debt may rise to $20 or $30 trillion (which is where we are headed with Social Security and Medicare, without massive reform). At some point, possibly five to ten years from now, possibly sooner, we will need to become concerned about the U.S. dollar becoming worthless in the face of runaway inflation.

We are in a period of time when we have both extreme danger and extreme opportunity. Remember, change creates opportunity, and challenging times actually create the best opportunities! Wealth is not lost; it simply changes owners. It goes from the hands of the unprepared into the hands of the prepared. We want you to be on the prepared side, not on the side of the unprepared.

SEE THE CHALLENGE AS YOUR OPPORTUNITY

I am encouraging people to get involved, get prepared, and to grow and protect their capital. There will likely be people who suffer greatly in the next few years, and I believe that those of us who have resources are going to need to help others. Avoid becoming greedy or fearful in this time, and don't begin to hoard your resources. Continue to be generous and give. We need to *stockpile*, which is not the same as hoarding. *Hoarding* is fear-based and done for self-protection. Stockpiling enables you to provide for yourself and for others.

Remember, challenging times create the best opportunities. I believe helping people through difficult and challenging times is part of my calling in life, and I have been preparing for this for my entire career. When this economic crisis began in 2008 instead of 2010—the year I had thought it would start—it caught us off guard, not totally prepared. That's why I developed the concept of a financial triage—a plan to help people stop the bleeding, know what steps to take in the short run, and develop a strategy for weathering this financial storm and securing their futures. You need to know how to protect yourself, your family, and your financial futures. If you are able to do that, you will be able to help others.

Unfortunately, I believe many people are going to approach this crisis based upon their understanding of the black bear markets of the last thirty years. We need a better approach when facing this secular grizzly bear market!

When I first entered this industry in 1980, the Dow Jones Industrial Average had gone sideways for sixteen years. That was another period of secular bear market, but probably not as bad as the one we are in now. The Dow Jones Industrial Average hit 1,000 in 1966; fourteen years later in 1980 it was under 1,000; and in 1982 it finally bottomed. By then, nobody believed in buy and hold anymore. (See Chart 2-A in chapter 2, where we talked about stagflation.)

The generation of financial advisers who came after my peers and myself had been taught buy and hold in school, and that is all they have ever known. Up to now, it has worked throughout their professional careers. Although, generally speaking, the vast majority of people in the financial services industry want to help people, unfortunately most have only been taught how to be good on offense. During a long-term boom, this works, but in a bust—a deflationary environment like we are in now, a grizzly bear market—the strategies you use on the way up don't work once the balloon has burst.

Remember also that in this book my primary concern has been with giving financial information that will help you, the ordinary consumer. You are probably not the owner of a large institution or managing the pension fund for a large corporation. That would be similar to a *cruise ship*—unable to make a fast turn to get out of the market. Large corporations tend to be in the market *permanently*. They are big, long-term institutions, and they have long, long investment horizons.

But an individual is more like a speedboat or a WaveRunner. You are not big enough to capsize the whole market. You are small enough to do whatever you want. Peter Lynch, one of the best money managers of the last hundred years, has essentially said, "Your advantage as a small person is that you don't have to be a part of the herd or do what the rest of the herd is doing."[11] If the big institutions decided to get out of the market, they would create a self-fulfilling prophecy. They would crash the markets themselves. So they can't get out! Usually, they will encourage you to hold on because historically that is what has worked best most of the time. But, we are in a different period now, and we need a different strategy than what has worked over the last twenty or thirty years. Plus, as we said, the big institutions have very long time horizons. If you are fifty years old or above, your time horizons are much shorter. It may not be prudent to attempt to weather a fifteen- or twenty-year storm.

Ultimately everything points to the fact that we have not seen problems of this magnitude in seventy years. I don't know the future exactly or how bad this one is going to get, but so far we know the balloon has burst and is not likely to be reinflated. You have to decide how long your own long run really is, and this will vary from person to person. I do know that if I were in a position where I did not want to ride out the storm, especially if I were older, then I would try to get into a safe harbor until it could be determined how bad the storm is. You can always go back onto the water at a later date.

Additional Resource: Physical Preparation

Due to the strong likelihood that our cascading economic crisis will ultimately produce some measure of social upheaval, plus the fact that our enemies are unlikely to stay dormant, especially when we are undergoing challenges, prudence dictates some level of physical preparedness. Just how far each person or family takes the preparation will be something that needs to be discussed and prayed about individually. I've listed six steps we believe to be most crucial. For additional information or to go deeper in terms of physical preparation, please consult our Web site at www.cornerstonereport.com.

1. Water

Social upheaval/attack or physical calamity could produce disruptions to the water supply in your area. Consider buying thirty days' water supply in bottled water form for each member of your family, probably one gallon per person per day. One of our Web site sponsors, Berkey Water, provides one of the better and easier-to-use water filters around, which I'm told will purify almost any contaminant out of water supplies.[12] They have both countertop and portable units. I use them personally and have found they produce some of the best-tasting water around and are much less expensive in the long run than continuously buying purified bottled water. Units come in all sizes. Again, go to our Web site for more information.

2. Food supply

I recommend a thirty-day food supply for every family member. Canned foods may be best, as they require less preparation and no refrigeration. Electricity can go down for extended periods. Thus, camping stoves and/or propane grills should be stocked.

3. Medical supply

Everything from first aid to prescription drugs (a thirty-day supply) should be stocked for emergencies.

4. Ammunition

You might need ammunition, either for protection or for barter. Having a family defense plan in the event of social disruption is only prudent planning. Consider what your family would do in the event of a national emergency.

5. Miscellaneous

Major storms can knock out electricity for days. Solar-powered rechargeable battery units (see our Web site) could come in handy, as well as having a small portable generator. Extra clothing could be needed, depending upon climate and season.

The Defense Commissary Agency (DeCA) has prepared a "disaster preparedness shopping list," listing the most crucial items to have ready in the event of a disaster. Some of these items are things I have already recommended. I would highly recommend that you add these items to your disaster preparedness supplies:

- Water—At least 1 gallon daily per person for three to seven days

- Non-perishable foods—At least enough for three to seven days (canned meats, fruits and vegetables; pouched or canned juices; foods for infants and the elderly; dried fruits, nuts, raisins, granola, peanut butter; comfort foods like crackers, cereal, cookies, energy bars)

- Paper goods—Paper plates, paper towels, napkins, toilet paper

- Blankets and pillows

- Extra clothing—Seasonal clothing, rain gear, sturdy shoes

- First aid kit, medicines, prescription drugs

- Liquid bleach, hand soap, sanitizing spray

- Special diet foods

- Toiletries, hygiene items, moisture wipes

- Trash bags, resealable bags, plastic containers, plastic utensils

- Pet care items—Proper identification; immunization records; medications; ample supply of food and water; a carrier or cage; muzzle and leash

- Flashlight and batteries

- Candles and matches, stored in resealable, waterproof baggies
- Radio (battery operated)[13]

Is planning a lack of faith? Certainly not. Joseph stored grain for the upcoming famine in his time.[14] Proverbs says, "In the house of the wise are stores of choice food and oil" (Prov. 21:20).

Preparation should not come in a spirit of fear but as a result of wisdom.[15] Which of you, if you were told that a Category 5 hurricane was bearing down on your city, would not seek refuge elsewhere?

Stockpiling vs. Hoarding

Hoarding comes out of fear and self-preservation, and it is *not* the way we should go. Stockpiling, on the other hand, simply means storing extra in case it is needed for our own needs or for others. In the case of disasters, we should be willing to share and help others who may not be as fortunate or prepared as we were.

CHAPTER TEN

GRIZZLIES VS. BLACK BEARS

A s I've already indicated in an earlier chapter, there is a huge differ-ence between a normal bear market and the secular bear market I believe we are likely facing now.

Below you see charts of three secular or grizzly bears of the last century. In each case, if you were to buy and hold the stocks making up the Dow Jones Industrial Average, you would have either lost money or broken even over very long stretches of time. Again, these time periods are known as *secular* bear markets.

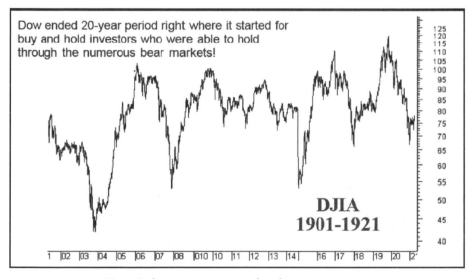

Dow ended 20-year period right where it started for buy and hold investors who were able to hold through the numerous bear markets!

DJIA
1901-1921

Note: Indexes are unmanaged and investors are not able to invest directly into any index.
Source: Sy Harding
Chart 10-A[1]

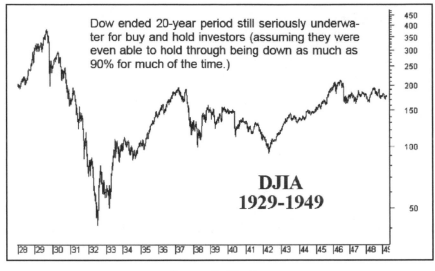

Source: Sy Harding
Chart 10-B[2]

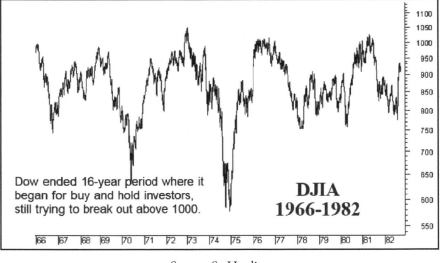

Source: Sy Harding
Chart 10-C[3]

During secular bears, the investing rules of engagement should be completely different. What worked well in the context of a secular bull market like the one we saw from 1982 to 1999 will not likely work well in a secular bear. Each environment is different.

Next take a look at the 1997–2009 timeframe, as depicted by the S&P 500 chart shown below. If you compare the pattern of the up-and-down movements, you'll see it certainly appears that we are in another secular bear period. Note the similar pattern to previous secular bears, shown in Charts 10-A through 10-C.

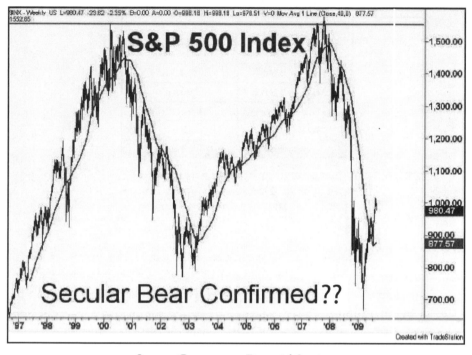

Source: Cornerstone Financial Services
Chart 10-D[4]

A way to envision the difference between a secular bull market and a secular bear market is this: Imagine a man with a yo-yo climbing a set of stairs. At each juncture, as he climbs level by level, despite the short-term ups and downs of the yo-yo, he is moving higher and higher over the long term—from the first floor to the second, third, and so on. A *secular* bull market is similar to what we saw from 1949 to 1966 or from 1982 to 1999.

A Century of Returns	
Years	**Returns***
1901 - 1921	—
1921 - 1929	25%
1929 - 1949	loss
1949 - 1966	14%
1966 - 1982	loss
1982 - 1999	14.8%
2000 - ?	??
* Approx. annual returns	

Note: Approximate returns are estimated
based upon the Dow Jones Industrial Average.
Source: Sy Harding
Chart 10-E[5]

Historically, there are very long-term periods where stocks and other financial assets outperform, typically followed by very long periods where stocks greatly underperform. A secular bear market (lasting a decade or more) can be devastating to an investor's portfolio.

A long sideways market like 1901–1921 or 1966–1982 creates an environment in which an investor's best-case scenario could be to break even over a fifteen- to twenty-year period, something most investors are unlikely to tolerate. Plus, that's assuming that they actually did manage to hold on for that entire period and did not get shaken out and sell out of their stocks during one of the big declines, which would've produced an even worse outcome.

However, a secular bear of the magnitude of the 1930s in the U.S. or the 1990s for Japan—the century's two previous examples of deflation, seen in chapter 9—would be devastating. My greatest concern is that the weight of the evidence indicates that we've currently entered another major secular bear market. In fact, if you realize that both the 1930s U.S. and the 1990s Japan crises were not only deflationary economic periods but were also periods in which each country's demography entered a winter, it should give us even more concern that our current period, which started out with extreme pain, is actually likely to continue creating pain over the next decade or so.

Based upon current data (which could change), I personally see virtually no chance that we have *not* entered a secular bear market. I see no chance that the next decade could produce a major rise like the 1980s or the 1990s. I personally see zero chance that buy-and-hold investors will enjoy the ride until after we've passed *through* the most difficult waters ahead, which we expect to last until at least some time around 2020 or so.

Thus, if this indeed is a secular bear market, as is my opinion, then you should consider adapting to a different type of strategy for the future. Change your paradigm.

BUY-AND-HOLD STRATEGIES

Buy-and-hold strategies tend to work best during secular bull markets similar to the ones we saw from 1982–1999. In theory, in a secular bull, every dip can become a buying opportunity. "Just keep adding," the old saying goes; "the rising tide lifts all boats." But buy and hold has historically not worked well in secular bears. In other words, as a philosophy, in my opinion, buy and hold works until it stops working. Historically, every generation has seen an extended period of time when buy and hold produced poor results. Buy and hold strategies during a financial bust could potentially lead to the poor house.

So, if buy and hold has failed miserably at these times, what other options are there? We call them *absolute return strategies*. Absolute return strategies are programs designed to make money in either up (bull) or down (bear) markets using tools available to professional traders. Obviously, those types of strategies are generally more expensive than buy-and-hold strategies but have the potential to make money in any market environment. Some of these strategies can be very aggressive, but not all.

Remember: Each investment product or service will have different fees and expenses, and those expenses and fees may differ from each brokerage or investment firm.

Generally speaking, most people should not attempt this on their own, as absolute return strategies can be challenging even to a professional, due to the fact that it can be extremely difficult to determine the appropriate time to change investments in response to a changing environment.

If you're an experienced trader, you may want to look up so-called bear funds, which are designed to make money in a bear market. Due to the sophisticated nature of these instruments, they may not be suitable for many investors. Special attention needs to be paid to numerous risk factors. Fees tend to be considerably higher in this category. There are no guarantees or assurances that any absolute return strategies will be successful. If you are not an experienced trader, consider hiring a professional for these strategies.

In all, it appears to me that this most challenging economic period is unlikely to end for at least a decade, sometime in the early to mid 2020s.

Obviously the market and economy can and do change very quickly. Thus, I cannot be specific on time periods or recommended strategies. For fine-tuning on both the changing economic landscapes and the market, go to our Web site and subscribe to our weekly newsletter (www.cornerstonereport.com).

FIRE AND ICE

The upcoming economic environment reminds me of an injury I had in high school. I was on the high school track team and severely sprained my left ankle just before the state track meet. As a discus thrower, your pivot foot is key; you can't throw without it. My coach decided to try a new remedy, not telling me ahead of time what it was. Now I call it the *fire and ice treatment*. Here's how it works.

First, heat the whirlpool as hot as it will go. Prepare an ice bucket or, in this case, an ice chest full of crushed ice and water; stir it until the water is freezing. Start by holding your foot in the hot, swirling water of the whirlpool for three minutes. Next, dunk your foot in the ice bucket for one minute. Repeat three times!

For a severe sprain, any change of temperature is excruciating! The coach had to literally hold my foot in the freezing water or it would have come out. But the good news is, it worked! A few days later I was able to throw with my ankle taped and just a little pain. But, I threw.

What I believe we're about to go through economically reminds me of the fire and ice routine, only in this case, the ice comes first. During the next decade-plus, I expect two distinctly different types of periods, which I refer to as "fire" and "ice." The ice period, which is likely to last at least two to three years or longer, is the deflationary period in which home prices fall, consumers cut back, and deleveraging takes place. During the ice phase, *cash is king*. Just earning a meager amount of interest is better than losing money in this environment. The objective here is to wait out the storm, then be able to buy when the real bargains are available. You may also want to look at absolute return strategies here as well. The main thing during the ice phase is not to lose all of your money. Making money is a secondary concern.

At present, our best estimate is that the deflationary ice phase will last until at least 2011 or 2012, possibly longer. There is simply no way of predicting in advance how long this will last. The only way is to monitor.

One thing we'll be watching for is the velocity of money. Once the velocity of money begins to turn around (we discussed this in chapter 4), then the massive amount of bailouts, printing press runs, and the like will likely come home to roost in inflationary terms, and the fire phase begins.

But as long as consumers are retrenching, cutting back, paying off debts, and worrying about their jobs, all this extra stimulus is not likely to produce inflation. As long as banks refuse to lend and consumers refuse to buy, you can pump money into the economy all day long and it will not likely produce inflation.

The situation with the economy and inflation reminds me of a time when we went on vacation in August and forgot to turn on the sprinkler system at home. Texas in August is hot and dry. You can imagine what the yard looked like two weeks later when we got back—dead, beige-colored grass.

Once we arrived back home, I turned on the sprinkler and just let it run for hours, eventually soaking the ground to the point of saturation with excess water running over the curbs and into the storm sewer. But no amount of watering could bring that grass back to life. The roots were still alive, but the grass stalks were dead. Not until we scalped the yard so the new growth could burst forth would that yard regrow green grass.

This is likely similar to the current inflation picture. Right now consumers, businesses, and banks have moved to very conservative buying, spending, and business practices. No matter how much liquidity the Fed puts in the system, inflation is not likely to return any time soon, because the second component of inflation—the velocity of money—is dormant. Like beige grass, consumers are in hibernation, not wanting to spend much while they save money and pay back debts. As long as deflation, housing, and unemployment remain concerns, we are unlikely to see the inflation rate move back up. Deflation rules as we unwind the burst bubble.

Inflation will likely return only once the turnover or velocity of money starts to accelerate again, which could be several years.

INVESTMENTS FOR THE ICE PHASE

Please keep in mind that nothing in this chapter should be considered a blanket recommendation. I could be wrong. Our purpose here is to provide readers with an understanding of certain financial tools that could fit into the scenarios we've outlined. Each category listed includes both good companies and poor companies, features, and benefits. Thus, buyer beware!

As we said, right now it appears that deflationary forces will rule for at least two to three years. During the ice or deflationary phase, the old saying is, "Cash is king." If deflation rules, one thing I think you're unlikely to want is a buy-and-hold stock market strategy. Buy and hold historically has performed miserably during this century's previous deflationary periods: the 1930s in the U.S. and Japan in the 1990s. For deflation, generally speaking, quality fixed-income or "safety"-type investments have historically held up well, plus accounts have the potential to make money if stocks decline. Some examples follow.

Fixed-income investments

Treasuries

Treasuries (direct debt obligations of the U.S. Treasury Department) at present are still considered the safest government paper in the world. Deflation produces falling prices for everything from houses to stocks. Your objective here is to keep your money, enabling you to buy when the *asset sale of the century* has bottomed out.

Treasuries will likely perform well until the deflation is over. My concern is that once the fire phase begins, assuming inflation kicks back in, Treasury investors could get hurt badly. In this present volatile and unprecedented environment, I wouldn't consider any kind of investment buy and hold, not even Treasuries.

The other concern is if foreigners bail out of our government debt. Presently, they are financing over half our national debt, as we discussed in chapter 5. If they ever decide they don't like our nation's long-term financial outlook (which could be a real concern given future Medicare and Social Security issues, on top of the current rate of growth of government debt) and start to flee the dollar, hyperinflation—the fire phase—could start quickly, because this would force the government to monetize our debt. (In other words, they would use the printing press to buy U.S. government debt by creating money out of thin air.)

Presently our government paper is top rated. But if foreigners flee en masse, the dollar will almost certainly plummet, creating economic chaos. (Note: China and other countries have recently been making serious noise about our long-term financial solvency. This is not an idle threat, but a real concern.)

For these reasons, you might want shorter-duration government paper. Longer-term debt will likely earn a lot more in a meltdown scenario but leave you wide open to inflation if it occurs later on. Holding longer-term paper for a year or two could work well, but watch out if and when the fire phase begins. Buying individual Treasuries directly typically incurs relatively low transaction casts, but the minimum investments are too high for many individual investors. Some bonds funds focus on Treasury securities, and investors should research their choices, as strategy and fees will vary considerably.

Certificates of deposit

Keep CDs under $250,000 per institution or registration to ensure government FDIC (insurance) protection. If the CD is at a bank, it is backed by the FDIC, which is backed by the U.S. government. Personally, I'd favor CDs at banks where the economy is strongest, but as long as you're under $250,000, hopefully it won't make much difference.

Money markets

Money markets come in two varieties—money-market accounts at banks and money-market mutual funds. For bank money markets, follow the same rules as for CDs, including FDIC protection up to $250,000. Money-market accounts normally pay less than CDs, especially in a falling-interest-rate environment like you normally see when the economy is in a recession (deflation). Once inflation returns, money-market interest rates usually rebound.

Money-market mutual funds come in several varieties, depending upon what the mutual fund invests in. Some invest in municipal bonds, some commercial paper (unsecured corporate IOUs), some in government securities or agencies. Obviously, the safest are the types that invest in government securities and/or agencies. Here, like bank money markets, interest rates are low because of liquidity (no time restraints; most provide check writing) and because interest rates are low during a recession. Again, when inflation returns, rates will rise. Fund fees in this category are typically low, but still merit close review, especially as returns in this area are currently very low as well. Of course, the risks of money market accounts or funds will depend on the underlying investments.

Fixed Annuities

Annuities come in a wide variety of types. While some fixed annuities have variable interest rates, the more popular ones in recent years have fixed interest rates for a specific period. Fixed annuities are guaranteed by the company that sponsors them; they are general obligations of the underlying insurance company. In addition, a majority of states have some sort of guaranty fund to further insure the annuity holder's account. (Check with your state's insurance department.) Fixed annuities are tax deferred, which could be a big plus if big government becomes even bigger government and looks for increasing ways to pluck the taxpaying goose. Stick with the highest-rated insurance companies during the ice phase. Of course, there is risk to guaranteed annuities to the extent that the insurer becomes insolvent or is unable to pay the principal or interest when due.

One source you may want to use is provided by www.TheStreet.com. They rate insurance companies A through F and have a pretty good track record at recognizing companies *before* they get into trouble. At our firm, we typically stick with A or B companies, which generally would comprise the top 15 percent or so of the industry, based on *The Street*'s criteria. No rating service is perfect or guaranteed, but their results have been good so far. You should regularly check the ratings, as they are subject to change. (Note: Any annuity guarantees are subject to the claims-paying ability of the insurer.)

Index annuities

Index annuities are fixed annuities that generally allow the policyholder some form of downside protection (can't lose principal) in exchange for lowered return in a bull market for stocks. Returns are linked to the stock market. For the ice phase, some of these may be helpful. However, I'd stay away from very long contracts with very large surrender charge periods.

Here the insurance company uses options in the stock market to create returns when the market goes up, while putting the vast majority into more secure investments. Historically, I've not been a fan of this type of annuity due to the very long periods of time that your money is tied up; plus a lot of them, early on, were filled with gimmicks and fine print. Due to recent changes, a handful merit consideration, although careful analysis of features and fees is still required. We use *The Street*'s rating service here also due to the fact these contracts are a form of fixed annuity and are general obligations of the underlying insurance companies. Company safety is of utmost importance. Again, the guarantee of the principal is subject to the solvency of the insurer. Check the ratings regularly, as they are subject to change. (Note: Any annuity guarantees are subject to the claims-paying ability of the insurer.)

Variable annuities

VAs are essentially tax-deferred vehicles containing investment choices known as sub-accounts, which can invest in almost any asset class. Most VAs are purchased in order to invest in the stock market, only on a tax-deferred basis.

In recent years, many VAs have added features to provide guaranteed income provisions in retirement available for an additional fee. While the subaccounts are owned by the investor and are not general obligations of the insurance company (thus, not likely at risk if the insurance company were to fail), the guaranteed benefits, like lifetime income benefits, are general obligations of the insurance company, and hence, are subject to the solvency of the insurance company. For this reason I'd stick with the highest-rated companies. Check the ratings regularly, as they are subject to change.

For VAs, I'm not recommending a buy-and-hold strategy for the sub-accounts any more than I'd recommend it for the stock market. Most have high-quality fixed-investment-type accounts available, plus the guaranteed income provision could prove beneficial, assuming that the insurance company survives the storm. Check the ratings regularly, as they are subject to change. (Note: Any annuity guarantees are subject to the claims-paying ability of the insurer.) Fees on variable annuities are generally higher than similar non-annuity investments.

Municipal bonds

Munis are issued by state or local governments and are tax free as far as federal income taxation goes. Historically, munis have a very good safety history, with only a small percentage of defaults—typically a better track record than corporate bonds. However, in the coming ice phase, considering that the average municipal government derives 72 percent of its revenue from property taxes and that most are significantly underfunded on pensions and health care benefits for their employees, the future could be quite different for munis in terms of safety. A careful decision should be made to determine the solvency or strength of the state or local government, therefore, its bonds, to determine the appropriate risks.

Many munis are insured, but the muni insurance companies could easily be overwhelmed, should major defaults occur, as I expect could happen during this demographic winter. As such, if too many defaults occur, the muni insurance company should not be relied upon.

Personally, I'd be cautious of states with huge real estate problems (California, Nevada, Florida, Arizona, and possibly Hawaii) and/or states with very high unemployment rates. States with lower unemployment, more dynamic economies, and those more connected to investments that could do well in the fire phase (like oil states, for example), might be a better source as municipal bonds tend to have longer durations, up to thirty years.

High-quality corporate bonds

Given recent issues with rating agencies giving subprime mortgage tranches AAA ratings, this one is harder to discern. High-quality corporates should hold up well during the ice phase, but I'd be cautious about default rates. Corporate bankruptcies could become severe if the ice phase intensifies. Companies that have overextended themselves on leverage will be in major trouble if consumer spending falls back as we expect over the decade. True, high-quality corporate paper may prove difficult to find for the average investor. Caution for the ice phase: due to the fact that the Fed and the government are bailing out so much of the crises, I'm concerned about tying up ice phase investments for very long periods. During the ice phase, there can be such substantial risks that even the most solvent-seeming corporations become distressed and their bonds subject to default. Should the fire phase start sooner (two to three years out), rather than later, I would lean toward shorter-term deflationary investments versus those lasting many years. For many investors, mutual funds are the most efficient way to access municipal and high-quality bonds. Strategies and fees can vary widely and should be carefully researched.

Investments for ice or fire

Absolute return strategies, as discussed on page 171, have the potential to perform well in either the fire or ice phase, as it is possible to make money in either bull or bear market deflationary or inflationary environments. Obviously, no guarantees can be made. As we stated before, those strategies are normally more expensive than typical buy-and-hold accounts. Some can be more aggressive, but not all.

FIRE PHASE INVESTMENTS

If we're correct in our belief that inflation will eventually return due to a combination of the printing press and bailouts (the ongoing deflationary bailout process, plus future problems in bailing out Social Security and Medicare), then inflationary investments could be of great value in future years.

Oil and gas

As we'll outline in the next chapter, we believe that energy problems worldwide could reach war-like proportions once the ice period has run its course. At present, energy consumption is down globally due to the recession. If the recession were to become a depression, this would further depress energy demand. However, this is unlikely to remain the case longer term.

Chinese and Indian consumers intend to move higher and higher up the economic ladder, and more and more will be buying cars. No matter what our concerns about carbon emissions, the growing Far East will become massive energy consumers in the next decades. Even in the recession, global supply and demand are not that far apart—plus we all know how precarious the Middle East is.

Longer term (over five to fifteen years or more), energy makes a lot of sense but could get very beat up in the ice phase if recessionary and secular bear market forces again prevail. No one knows with certainty the timing on these things, but it still looks like the ice/deflation phase has at least two to three years to run. I reserve the right to change my opinion later! That's one reason we publish a *weekly* newsletter. Oil and gas investments are, of course, subject to substantial fluctuation and can be high risk due to political instability as well as economic fluctuations. Such investments are subject to extremely high variability.

Metals

Precious metals will likely benefit in the fire phase. Historically, gold has been an excellent inflation hedge. Gold could also prove to hold up well in the ice phase if investors worldwide flee to gold for safety during a meltdown scenario.

Globally just a small percentage of portfolios moving into gold could have an outsized effect on the price. All the gold mined since the beginning of time only amounts to roughly $5 trillion, a tiny sum compared to all the amount of paper currencies worldwide. World GDP, for example, is more than $50 trillion per year. The Bank for International Settlements estimates global currency transactions to be $3.98 trillion every day.[6]

Silver, on the other hand, is primarily an inflation hedge but is also an industrial metal, whereas gold is primarily a monetary metal. I'm not too fond of silver for the ice phase, but gold has the potential to work well in either fire or ice. Silver will likely be a fire investment only.

Metals investments come in bullion, coins, and stocks. Bullion bars are usually too heavy and bulky for easy storage but can be placed in a safety deposit box. Coins may be the best choice for most consumers. But here you have to be careful, as this field is largely unregulated and has historically seen more than its share of shysters and con men. While there are certainly many honest and reputable dealers out there, there are also crooks and the unscrupulous, making this a potential minefield.

Coins come in various types: bullion-oriented coins (examples are U.S. American Eagle, Krugerrand, Canadian Maple Leaf), which sell for a premium above their bullion content, and numismatic or rare coins. The rare (or *numismatic*) coin market, in my opinion, should only be used by true specialists and professionals in that particular industry. It's very easy to get ripped off there. Plus, if true hyperinflation and/or social chaos hits, I don't think many people will care about the collectors' value of the coin.

Semi-numismatic coins, on the other hand, could come in useful. In 1933, Franklin Roosevelt passed a law forcing all Americans to sell their gold back to the U.S. government. Banks were collapsing right and left, and Roosevelt, I'm sure, was concerned more people would flee the banks for gold. But while the government did call in bullion gold and coins, it did not call in rare or semi-numismatic coins. The amount of money that can flow into rare or semi-rare coins is even more miniscule than bullion compared to all of the world's currencies, a small fraction of the amount of bullion available worldwide, which in itself is a tiny fraction of the world's currencies, stocks, real estate, or other forms of wealth. It's too small to count.

Semi-rare or rare coins must be graded, adding further complexity. It's highly unlikely—if push comes to shove—that the government will call in semi-numismatic coins. Semi-numismatic coins sell for a higher premium than bullion coins but are less likely to be subject to being called in by the government and are much less expensive than true rare coins. These investments are also subject to substantial fluctuation, not only based upon economic but also political and geopolitical events as well. Returns can be variable; large losses can occur if metals drop significantly.

Bullion ETFs

Over the last few years, several companies have created ETFs (exchange-traded funds) that hold precious metals and can be purchased just like stocks. In this case, someone else is storing the metal for you, allowing investors the ease of buying bullion-oriented investments, which should move up and down in proportion to the price of gold. (These are not mining stocks, which can move in a different direction from the price of gold to stock market concerns. See the next section.) These investments have similar risk to owning the metals themselves, although there are internal expenses and risk factors that investors should research.

Gold and silver mining stocks and funds

Gold and silver mining companies issue stocks, and these stocks can be purchased just like shares of IBM or Microsoft. In inflationary times, these stocks and/or funds have done very well, and they usually move up and down in relation to the price of gold. In fact, they often make more money than bullion-oriented investments during gold bull markets and, conversely, usually lose more during bear markets for gold.

However, at the end of the day they are still stocks that trade in the stock markets of the world. During the crash of 1987, gold went up from $450 per ounce to $500 per ounce as investors sought the safety of gold. Due to margin calls (when the market falls, margin loans get called as investors must either pay up more money or sell their investment due to leverage), gold stocks got hammered, some falling 50 percent or more a *couple of weeks* after the rest of the market fell due to liquidity problems.

At the end of the day, gold and silver mining stocks are still stocks and could be subject to stock market forces, despite what the precious metal price is doing. During the 2008 meltdown, they were hit hard as well but bounced back faster than most other stocks. They can be extremely volatile and extremely dependent on economic fluctuation, and as a specialized sector, funds in this area often carry higher fees.

Land

Potentially, one form of security could come in well-selected plots of land. Land historically holds up to inflation and is less likely to be taxed heavily, especially farmland. If conditions become less than desirable in the cities due to social upheaval or unrest, land prices could skyrocket, as more and more people decide to "get away from it all" and become more self-sufficient.

Land prices within one hundred miles or so of the major cities (long commuting distances) could prove best. In addition, with the incredible technology that we have today, more and more people are able to telecommute either full or part time. Land and housing within striking distance of the big cities, especially in areas of adequate or plentiful water supply, could prove very valuable. (Note: Water will be very important during this next decade; we expect land and water rights to become very big issues.) Land purchases are also subject to fluctuation and highly subject to regional and overall economic conditions.

In all, I believe we have to prepare for two types of environments: first, the continuing ice phase of the deflationary pressures as housing prices, foreclosures, and lending pressures rise between now and 2012 or so; later, the inflationary fire phase, which could become hyperinflation if/when government spending gets truly out of control.

We face challenging times for sure, but don't forget that challenging times create the best opportunities!

IMPORTANT DISCLOSURE INFORMATION

of a portfolio. There is no guarantee that an actively managed portfolio will produce greater returns or experience smaller losses than a portfolio that uses a buy and hold strategy. High turnover rates within a portfolio may increase transaction costs and taxable capital gains. Indexes are unmanaged and investors are not able to invest directly into any index.

Investors should be aware that there are risks inherent in all investments, such as fluctuations in investment principal. With any investment vehicle, past performance is not a guarantee of future results.

Material discussed herewith is meant for general illustration and/or informational purposes only. Please note that individual situations can vary. Therefore, the information should be relied upon only when coordinated with individual professional advice.

- The S&P 500 is an unmanaged index comprised of five hundred widely-held securities considered to be representative of the stock market in general.

- Sector investing may involve a greater degree of risk than investments with broader diversification.

- Investing in securities involves risk, including the loss of principal invested. Past performance is no guarantee of future results.

- Investments in real estate have various risks, including the possible lack of liquidity and devaluation based on adverse economic and regulatory changes. As a result, the values of real estate may fluctuate, resulting in the value at sale being more or less than the original price paid.

Global or international investing involves special risks, such as currency fluctuation, political instability, and different methods of accounting and different reporting requirements.

The price of commodities, such as gold, is subject to substantial price fluctuations of short periods of time and may be affected by unpredictable international monetary and political policies. The market for commodities is widely unregulated, and concentrated investing may lead to higher price volatility. In addition, investing in commodities often involves international investing in emerging markets, which involve significant risks.

All technical analysis and resulting conclusions and observations are based upon historical chart formations and patterns. Therefore, observations are a function of each analyst's interpretation of the charts—and also a function of mathematical probabilities. In effect, technical analysis is a study in probabilities. What happened x number of times in the past per a particular chart pattern does not mean it will always recur in the future. It logically follows that historical precedent does not guarantee future results.

CHAPTER ELEVEN

WEATHERING THE FINANCIAL STORM

HAVE YOU DEVELOPED a strategy to help your family cope with the economic crisis our world is facing today? In the previous two chapters in this section, I helped you to understand the root causes of this demographic financial winter we are facing and gave you some tools for improving your own situation financially, identifying areas where you need to strengthen the financial resources that keep you and your family secure.

In this chapter, you will learn to understand the root causes of many of your own financial difficulties and to develop some wise solutions that will help you and your loved ones better weather this financial storm. You will be able to apply these principles to our current economic crisis, but they will be useful for your future and even your children's futures, for an economy—whether individual, family, community, national, or world—runs in cycles. What you are learning today should be something you can apply to situations you will face anytime in the future as well.

As a veteran of the industry with nearly thirty years as a CERTIFIED FINANCIAL PLANNER™ professional, I certainly believe that personal financial planning is important.

SEVEN STEPS TO FINANCIAL FREEDOM

Let me give you some simple steps that you can take to assess your current financial situation and determine how to protect your family against financial crisis.[1] These are basic fundamentals that should apply to most families.

1. *Take Inventory*: If you have ever gotten lost while driving in a strange city, you now know the importance of finding out where you are in order to figure out how to get where you want to go. That is the first step to achieving financial freedom.

2. *Buy Adequate Life Insurance*: A good rule of thumb for a young
    family with children at home is to buy life insurance on the
    husband equal to ten times his earnings. This will give you a
    lump sum of money that can be invested to replace that income.

3. *Pay Off All Consumer Debts*: This includes credit cards and
    finance companies—anything beyond your automobile and
    home. These consumer debts are the worst form of debt since
    they primarily represent consumption and not investment, and
    they have the highest rate of interest. First cut out all unnec-
    essary spending, and then apply that freed-up money toward
    your smallest debt first. Each time you pay off a debt, take
    the monthly payment you had been making and use those
    additional funds exclusively for further debt reduction on your
    next-highest debt. It may take you several years to get out of
    debt, but this is definitely the best and quickest way to do it.
    Staying out of consumer debt will be one of the most critical
    things you can do to remain financially free in the future.

4. *Start an Emergency Reserve*: We advise that you set aside two
    to three months' living expenses—the bare-bones amount on
    which you could live—in an emergency reserve fund. This
    could be a bank account, an interest-bearing money market
    fund, or something similar. Ideally, we recommend that people
    build up at least three to six months' income in conservative,
    liquid accounts of some type.

5. *Begin a Long-Term Savings Plan*: Little by little, accumulate
    assets. We gave you some hints as to how to invest in the
    previous chapter.

6. *Pay Off Your Automobiles*: Financially, your best bet is to buy
    a reliable automobile and drive it as long as possible. Buy used
    cars, service them, and keep them as long as possible. The second
    alternative is to buy an inexpensive new car, service it well,
    changing the oil regularly, and keep it for a long, long time.

7. *Prepay on Your Home*: Prepaying on a home can save thou-
    sands and even hundreds of thousands of dollars, regardless
    of whether you have a fixed or variable mortgage. (For more

specific information on prepaying for your home—or on any of these seven steps—see my book *Smart Money*.)

Begin by looking closely at each of the seven steps to find creative ways to adapt in those areas for this current crisis, as they are arranged in order of priority. The first important need for your financial security is to cut back on spending in order to get rid of all consumer debt, starting with the most egregious debts first. Take the simple ideas we discussed, and strategize for the specific solutions you can create to eliminate your debt during this difficult economic season. Remember that *change creates opportunities, and challenging times create the best opportunities!*

Often the best way to learn is to study the example of someone who has done exactly what you are trying to do. There are people who are living debt free and prospering right now—right in the midst of a world gone financially amok. Look at the lives of some of these individuals and let their sound financial wisdom influence your financial practices and strategies.

A book that I strongly recommend is *The Millionaire Next Door*, written by Thomas Stanley and William Danko.[2] It is one of the most comprehensive studies on wealth ever done in the history in America. It isn't a flashy, get-rich-quick manual. It involves the slow process of becoming successful in your career or business, saving up your money instead of spending it, budgeting down to the last cent, investing carefully and prodigiously, seeking out good advice when necessary, and spending a tremendous amount of time on money matters.[3] Covering more than twenty years of study by two academic teams, this group set out to study millionaires and their habits and, furthermore, what made them millionaires to begin with. Of the five hundred millionaires interviewed, only 19 percent had received any income or wealth from a trust fund or estate, and fewer than 20 percent inherited more than 10 percent of their wealth. Take a look at some of the interesting factors this book uncovered about millionaires.

SEVEN FACTORS ABOUT MILLIONAIRES

1. They live well below their means.

2. They allocate their time, energy, and money efficiently, in ways conducive to building wealth.

3. They believe that financial independence is more important than displaying high social status.

4. Their parents did not provide economic outpatient care.

5. Their adult children are economically self-sufficient.

6. They are proficient in targeting market opportunities.

7. They chose the right occupation.[4]

What do most millionaires say they learned? "Think differently from the crowd."[5] One of the most important principles we can learn from that book is that most millionaires are frugal in how they spend their money. They believe in little or no personal debt. When they do go into debt, it is usually with the purpose of going into business, buying a house or property, or acquiring an education. Money is never spent frivolously.

Because these people typically were out of debt (most of them owned their own businesses, though not all), when there was a downturn in the economy or in their market, they weathered the storm and came out on the other side with a larger market share. In this case, difficult or challenging times surely proved to be an opportunity—a longer-term blessing!

This is the mentality that I recommend that you have going into the coming demographic winter. Don't look at this negatively, looking at the glass half empty. Look at this as an opportunity. Certainly, in our view there could be great devastation occurring to the wealth and the livelihoods of many people in the United States, primarily among those who are planning as if everything will continue without change and are not prepared. Those who lead high-consumptive lifestyles and those who are overleveraged (with large debts) will be the first to suffer.

Protect Your Capital

First, do your best to grow or at least protect your capital. Be aware of what is going on in the market and be ready if there is a point in time to get out of the market. Keep in mind that if we are in a secular (long-term) bear market, as I believe we are, there wil llikely be shorter-term, cyclical bounces along the way that could be spectacular. To know what to do you must stay current. See our Web site for our weekly newsletter to keep abreast of changes. You certainly want to be ready for the second phase of this crisis. Learn alternative strategies for managing your assets or hire someone who can assist. For the next few years, you may want to focus on preserving capital or possibly use *inverse strategies*, which I will explain below. The simplest approach to take in a deflationary environment is this: high-quality, fixed-income, and absolute-return strategies, as we discussed in the previous chapter. But keep in mind that the market will likely continue to have huge bounces from time to time.

If you feel, as I do, that our current economic situation is a potential Category

5 hurricane, you may not want to stay in the market on a buy-and-hold basis. (Buy and hold is a long-term investment strategy based on the view that in the long run, financial markets give a good rate of return despite periods of volatility or decline.)[6] Why? Because there are periods of time in history when buy and hold, in my opinion, has failed miserably, as we covered in the previous chapter. It certainly failed in the thirties and was horrible in the seventies.

I'm not necessarily advising you to get out of the market, as I have no way of knowing when you'll read this book or exactly what will be happening in the economy or market at that time. Plus, I can't give blanket recommendations anyway. For a better understanding of the current environment, check out our radio show and our Web site at www.cornerstonereport.com.

Inverse strategies, or *absolute return strategies*, aim to produce a positive absolute return regardless of the direction of financial markets.[7] Absolute return strategies are typically not strategies that people can easily learn on their own. If you have a 401(k), you likely do not even have access to these types of accounts. A more astute investor will know how to use an absolute return strategy that has the potential to make money when the market is going down.

Inverse strategies are difficult to pull off, and unless you are already an experienced and astute investor you should not try this on your own. If you do not know what an inverse strategy is—or understand how to use it—that is a good indication you probably should not attempt this strategy on your own. Hire someone to assist you.

I believe we have entered a secular bear phase that could last a long time. We don't know exactly what is coming or when, but the demographics and the number of people that have passed their peak spending period do not indicate another boom phase like this until at least 2023. That is a long time!

In my opinion, before we have another stock market boom, the demographics are going to have to turn around—and that is a long way off. Throughout this book we have been applying a principle from *Good to Great* that says, "You must never confuse faith that you will prevail in the end—which you can never afford to lose—with the discipline to confront the most brutal facts of your current reality, whatever they might be."[8]

That is why I have devoted this entire section of the book to triage. In this chapter we are looking at financial triage level two—developing wise solutions to weather this financial storm. We need to stop the bleeding. There may be a time when you want to get on the sidelines and see if this develops into a worse storm and, if it does, be ready with the solutions that are going to protect our financial futures.

Determine Your Exit Strategy

There is an old philosophy we use at Cornerstone: "Buy low and sell high." If the current storm becomes more pronounced, as we think it will, it might be more accurate to state, "Attempt to sell high and then later buy low."

Early in 2000, we warned people to get out of stocks entirely. Since that time, the regulations governing this industry have changed. Now I could not tell a person to get completely out of the stock market even if I wanted to. However, when we were telling everyone to get out in 2000, nearly everyone else was telling them to get rich quick with tech stocks or *dot-coms*. Close to 80 percent of the money that was flowing into the market in the first quarter of 2000 was directed into technology stocks. We were advising our clients and radio listeners to get out, which made us contrarians at that time. If you got out anywhere near the top of the NASDAQ, almost three years later, by October of 2002 many of the dot-com survivors—the companies that were going to make it after the bubble had crashed—*had a total market value that was less than their cash in the bank*. That was certainly a "buy low" opportunity at that point.[9]

The issue is, I don't believe that most people will enjoy attempting to ride this storm out long term on buy-and-hold basis. Most people are in denial right now; they don't want to go through the pain of loss, so they push it off. But we must face the future.

Supply and Demand

I am reminded of the bumper sticker that says, "I am spending my children's inheritance," seen frequently in places like sunny Florida. With the demographic storm taking huge chunks of capital out of the securities markets and out of the finances for most Americans, is there any likelihood that boomers, as they reach retirement age in mammoth proportions, might decide to use some of those assets for retirement income or for a more comfortable standard of living?

During a recent coaching session with a group of financial planners in San Diego, I asked them, "You work with clients every day; you do financial plans and work to help people accumulate financial assets. What do you think is the likelihood that the vast majority of those people would like to *spend* some of those assets in their retirement years?"

The answer was unanimous—*yes*, most of them will want to spend some of their assets. The vast majority of Americans will spend all or part of their financial assets as they retire. Given the upcoming environment, it's also entirely possible that many may decide not to retire. The vast majority of people are not content to simply to live on pensions and Social Security while passing on the vast majority of their assets to their heirs.

But what happens to the supply-and-demand balance for stocks, bonds, and other financial assets when the boomers begin spending their assets? This is not to say that there won't be investments that will go up in this kind of environment. In fact, the objective of our firm is to find assets that will prosper during tough times. Yet, those who continue to expect the same performance of the recent past in the near future are likely stepping into a gigantic hole.

> Assets such as stocks and bonds have no intrinsic value—you cannot eat your stock certificates. The only way their value can be realized is by selling them, and you can sell them only if there are enough willing buyers.
>
> —Jeremy Siegel, *The Future for Investors*[10]

When we consider those who reach the point of being ready to cash in their assets, we must remember that you cannot eat your stock or bond certificates! Assets can be turned into purchasing power *only if someone else is willing to give up his or her consumption so you can enjoy yours.*

Throughout history, when the younger generation reached middle age, they have had sufficient purchasing power to buy their parents' assets. But this time it is different. There are not nearly enough Generation Xers (the generation born in the late 1960s and 1970s) with sufficient wealth to absorb the boomers' substantial portfolio of stocks and bonds.

The looming problem of the boomer population is reminiscent of an old Wall Street story. A broker recommends that his client buy a small speculative stock with good earning prospects. The investor purchases the stock, accumulating thousands of shares at ever-rising prices. Patting himself on the back, he phones his broker, instructing him to sell all his shares. His broker snaps back, "Sell? Sell to whom? You're the only one who has been buying the stock!"

The words "Sell? Sell to whom?" might haunt the baby boomers over the next decade. Who are the buyers of the trillions of dollars of boomer assets? The generation that has swept politics, fashion, and the media in the last half of this century has produced an *age wave* that threatens to drown in their financial assets. The consequences could be disastrous not only for the boomers' retirement but also for the economic health of the entire population.[11]

It is *not* positive for the market that most of these people will begin to spend some of their assets at some point in time. Why is that? Who, pray tell, do you think is going to buy these assets? Remember, all markets work on supply and demand. How does a generation 76 million strong, the baby boomers, sell portions of their financial assets—their stocks and bonds—to a generation coming up behind them *that is only comprised of 41 million people* (the baby bust generation)? How can 76 million boomers sell their trophy homes to the next generation, which is almost half the size? As they spend (or sell) their financial assets, someone has to buy them. For every sale there has to be a buyer on the opposite end purchasing those assets.

The supply-and-demand numbers simply don't wash. They don't wash unless you somehow *hope* that foreigners, people who are not citizens of America, will continue to buy enough of America to bail out the boomers. Having most of America owned by non-American citizens is obviously not a good solution, either.

There has been and likely will continue to be a future boom in Asia that will play into the economics. But let me ask you this: If you were a foreign investor and could put your money anywhere in the world that you wanted, would you pick an American economy with a rapidly aging population, or would you pick the highest-performing growth areas of the world? Where would you put your money? Would you put it into an aging society with enormous entitlement (Social Security, Medicare) problems, or would you put it into areas of the world where growth is the most exciting? Hasn't China recently been complaining about our long-term financial picture and discussing alternatives to the U.S. dollar with other countries?[12]

We can learn from the experience of Japan's market when their society began to age after their demographics topped out in 1989. No foreigners rushed in to take financial assets off of the Japanese. We did not bail them out of their financial and demographic problems. No one wanted to catch a falling knife; no one knew where the bottom of the Japanese market would end up. Very few investors were attracted to buying into Japan once their bubble popped. There was no long-term solution—just a long time of pain before the Japanese market finally bottomed out.

There will be new products, new services, new companies, and new growth occurring in America as our businesses continue to innovate as well as fragment into smaller and smaller units. There will be opportunities, and there will be places to make money—without question. But, looking at the U.S. economy, the U.S. stock market, and U.S. financial assets as a whole, are they likely to be the most attractive to pull in mass numbers of buyers from foreign sources, or are they more likely to be putting their money into more dynamic growth areas of the world? The answer is fairly obvious. Most of these investors would prefer to put their money into the more dramatic growth areas.

The issue we face with the boomer age wave is not negativity; *the issue is reality*. In order to weather this financial storm, we must learn how to play the game in a way that wins instead of loses. Seek to develop wise solutions that will allow you to face your financial problems head-on, not wavering or hiding from them and certainly not sticking your head in the sand. The ostrich approach leaves you quite vulnerable to a swift kick in the pants. I don't recommend it.

WISE SOLUTIONS FOR SMALL BUSINESS

In economic downtimes individual consumers cut back to the bare necessities in their personal and family finances. As a small business owner or large corporate CEO, you will want to be in a businesses that will be somewhat resistant to recessionary (or worse) times. Consider whether or not your product, industry, or field is something that people can't live without and whether or not it fits an aging population or challenging times. As we head into the chill of this demographic winter, if you are a business owner, you will want to assess the value of your business to people in an economic downturn and develop solutions that will help you to weather the storm.

Some businesses will be resistant to the downturn; others will not. As a businessman or businesswoman you need to ask yourself, Am I trying to ride a dead horse, and do I need to change fields in order to adjust? Or should I persevere *through* the challenging times in order to gain more market share? The answer will be different for each individual and industry. Just keep in mind, it is likely to be *over a decade* before the next boom. That's a long time. Some technologies, service fields, and products could be completely different or obsolete within ten years.

You should go into the economic downturn looking forward to weathering whatever storm comes. Anticipate increasing your market share. Consider this upcoming time as a time of *great wealth transfer*. As we mentioned earlier in the book, the Great Depression of the 1930s was the worst economic period our country has ever seen and, indeed, the worst in the modern history of the world. The lesson learned from that chapter of our history is that it is possible to make enormous amounts of money during difficult times.

More millionaires were created per capita during the Great Depression than in any other time in U.S. history. This great wealth transfer will almost certainly take place in this financial storm, going from the hands of the unprepared to the hands of the prepared. Remember the football adage "Luck is what happens when preparation meets opportunity." I would encourage you to get prepared, because the opportunity is just about to knock on your door.

Prospering in a Hostile Economy

Some of the better opportunities America—and each person in America—will likely see in the longer-term future will come as we face increasing shortages of raw materials and energy sources. While in the short run deflationary forces during future years will doubtless keep commodity prices low, over the new few decades prices could explode. Similar to the shortages of the 1970s, which were brought on by the arrival of the baby boomer generation, the world, including America, will need to create new opportunities and sources for these assets as countries like China and India continue growing toward first-world status over the next ten to twenty years.

The world is not suffering from permanent deprivation, scarce, or limited resources. But there have been explosive demands for new raw materials and energy as the result of nearly one-third of mankind moving toward free enterprise. Deprivation caused by from Mao's Communist system and India's Socialism has finally given way to forward-thinking officials who have moved their countries and their respective populations into the twenty-first century, poised to become economic leaders within a few decades.

As the next decade or two progresses, there is a much greater likelihood that natural resources, especially oil, will become increasingly scarce, given current economic growth rates in China and India as they move from bicycles and public transportation to individually owned autos.

With a population of over 2.5 billion and booming economic growth, China and India are going to play an increasingly important role in global economic matters and energy markets.[13]

For many decades, no other country has been able to compete with the United States' huge domestic auto market, where 16 million to 17 million vehicles were sold each year. That is now changing, and while America's auto industry is reeling with financial devastation, the emerging markets of China and India have become large enough to support world-scale domestic manufacturing. India is still on the small side at about 2 million autos per year, but China—at 8 million vehicles and growing—is already half as large as the United States and is continuing to advance in size.[14] As noted in chapter 8, between January 2009 and April 2009, GM sold more cars in China than in the United States *each and every month*.

While the current ownership ratio of cars in China is very low as a percentage of their population, mass highway infrastructure has already been built, anticipating many more Chinese citizens driving cars. China's population and industrial output are mainly concentrated within the economically higher developed east coast, meaning that raw materials—especially coal—have to be transported from the far northwestern and northeastern provinces via railways or inland waterways. Not much attention has been paid to road conditions and access in many rural areas. However, China's national roads reached a total of 192,000,000 km in 2005 and a total of $240 billion was spent from 2000 until 2005. To further improve this situation, China planned to build another 180,000 km of rural highways in 2006, hoping to connect all administrative towns in China by highways at the end of 2010.[15]

The automotive industry in India is one of their largest industries and a key sector of the economy. India's Tata Motors recently produced a *$2,500 automobile*! While it is being rolled out on a limited basis (until 2010, only 3,000 cars a month are likely to be manufactured[16]), the Nano, as it's called, places auto ownership directly within the grasp of many Chinese and Indians based upon their incomes. The initial focus will be on the Indian market and its rising middle class, but the company plans to roll out a more expensive European version in 2011 with air bags and better emissions and safety ratings. It may also consider a model for the U.S. market.[17]

The old saying "You ain't seen nothing yet" likely holds true for India, China, and the rest of emerging Asia for the foreseeable future, as the bulk of the world's economic growth is likely to come from this region for at least the next decade. The U.S. and especially Europe are aging cultures. This creates great potential for profit by catching this mammoth wave, which could make the baby boomer wave look small in comparison before it's over.

Ultimately, if only a portion of the 2.5 billion people in India and China move into some semblance of middle class income within their respective countries, it will produce enormous growth. Since much of this growth revolves around creating and developing infrastructure, raw materials and energy, plus technology, will likely see the greatest gains.

ENERGY

Below you see a table showing the percentage of the world's energy that still comes from fossil fuels. Note that less than 10 percent comes from non-nuclear renewable sources.

2006 Energy Supply[18]	
Fossil	79 percent
Nuclear	11 percent
Renewable	10 percent

While I'm absolutely in favor of developing solar, wind, and other renewable resources, the fact remains that all renewable energy sources currently provide less than 10 percent of the world's energy supply, and those sources cannot possibly grow fast enough to keep up with burgeoning demand in Asia. You simply can't get there from here.

As China and India industrialize and move deeper into the twenty-first century, incredible demands will be placed upon raw materials and energy. Therefore, the best policy would be not only to encourage renewable sources of energy but also to radically accelerate the discovery of fossil fuels as well.

At the end of the day we will need all of the above in large quantities to support emerging Asia and the rest of the world. Holding an ideologically pure stance on ecology simply won't work and will likely produce more pain (again) in terms of very high costs for gasoline and potential fuel shortages.

You can worry all you want about global warming, but I can guarantee you that 2.5 billion Indians and Chinese care move about driving cars than melting icebergs. Right now, with energy usage down due to the global recession, is the best time to encourage energy development, not waiting until the next crisis. An "all of the above" energy policy is what we need.

Oil Rig Count[19]		
	Year	Count
Peak	1981	6,200
Bottom	1999	1,200
	2004	2,500

As you can see, the number of active drilling rigs worldwide peaked at 6,200 in 1981 and bottomed at only 1,200 in 1999. Given the very long lead times necessary to bring oil products online (as long as five years or more), it's no coincidence we experienced a mini energy shock in 2007 and early 2008. The energy supply got behind the curve compared to the great increases in global demand.

With Asia's energy needs starting to skyrocket and production growing only slowly, it was only a matter of time until demand caught up with supply. While the global recession has currently reduced demand, nothing has been done to fix the longer-term problem. Longer term, expect more problems with energy shortages unless a radical change occurs in current U.S. energy policy. In the following graph, the Energy Information Administration (EIA) estimated that with the average world growth in GDP at 3.8 percent, the world's energy needs will increase nearly 50 percent from 2003 until 2030. Given burgeoning demand for energy in China and India, these projections look way too conservative to me.

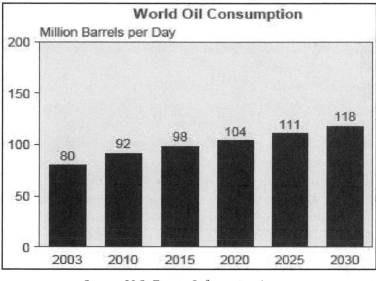

Source: U.S. Energy Information Agency
Chart 11-A

LOOK PAST THE VALLEY

While no one can be certain about the economic future, my belief is that we are going to have an extreme period of challenging times during the next ten to fifteen years. However, longer term, I see the potential for great optimism. As hordes of people come out of formerly repressed societies such as China and India and as undeveloped countries become developed countries, the world's potential for long-term prosperity is truly staggering.

I personally believe that America, as a nation, has a calling. Our founding fathers believed that the purpose of America was truly to be "a city on a hill," as articulated by John Winthrop as he pulled into Boston harbor in 1630.

> For we must consider that we shall be as a city upon a hill. The eyes of all people are upon us.
>
> —JOHN WINTHROP[20]

Somewhat like God's original plan for Israel of old, as the pilgrims came to the United States they received inspiration they believed to be from God, stating that this country was going to essentially show the rest of the world how to do it. And in many ways, we have. With just over 5 percent of the world's population, we produce approximately one-third of all the goods and services in the world. In terms of military might, the next twenty most-populated countries *combined* do not add up to the military might of the United States. While certainly this does not make us immune to terrorist attacks or impervious to all challenges, it does demonstrate that many, many of the things that our founding fathers set up in our society proved to be the best solutions yet created for man.

The problem is that we have gotten off the path and deviated from their ideals. While we certainly don't want to let our freedom become moral license, it is important for us to remember that there is a strong and definite correlation between freedom and prosperity. The freer a society, the more economically prosperous it will tend to be.

While we all have certain rights, we must also all yield those rights in certain instances for the betterment and common good of the country. Sometimes we must sacrifice our own personal freedoms for the betterment of society as a whole. This is one of the things that America has historically been good at. There is a moral underpinning to our society that was originally based, in part, upon the Ten Commandments of God and the Christian heritage of our forefathers.

As I look toward the future and look *past* the valley, I see the opportunity for incredible things happening to 6.5 to 7 billion people around the world if they emulate our best qualities and not our worst.

Truly, in terms of economic activity, foundational principles, freedoms, rule of law, property rights, and all the things that have made America great, America is a worthy example for other countries to emulate. I believe this can lead to an even greater level of overall prosperity, freedom, and enjoyment for the rest of the world. I consider America an *evangelist* to the rest of the world in terms of many of the right principles for financial prosperity. It has been America's destiny to shine as a "city on a hill," to model the way to "life, liberty, and the pursuit of happiness." It can continue to be if we will answer *the call*.

CHAPTER TWELVE

THE CALL

THE PURPOSE OF this book is not to be divisive, pitting individual against individual, culture against culture, liberal against conservative. Rather, my purpose is to unite all Americans against a common foe. The coming demographic winter has the potential—ready or not—to change everything within the United States.

Throughout the history of America and the world, major social change typically occurs in the midst of great crisis. Look at what occurred during the Great Depression. During the Great Depression, a socio-economic safety net was set up that regulated banking practices, reformed the stock market, protected workers' rights, and provided Social Security for retired individuals. These safety nets have had mixed results. In some cases, they have produced very good results in terms of benefits, as in the case of Social Security and Medicare. Other programs have helped to provide for the elderly, the widow, and the orphan, which I think is a positive thing and is encouraged biblically (Isaiah 58). But, by the same token, I think many other government programs instituted have proven to be counterproductive or even destructive at times.

Note that the *Humanist Manifesto I* was written in 1933, right at the bottom of the Great Depression. Part II was written in 1973, during the worst recession (up to that time) since the Great Depression. Crisis management allows or creates the opportunity for major power moves, for politicians to insert social agendas at a time of maximum pain, when it is less likely to be resisted and more likely to be accepted with open arms due to the crisis. Programs or agendas that would have been greatly resisted are easily passed during a time of major crisis.

As we are presently entering a major crisis, we must truly beware of what passes and exactly whose agenda becomes the rule of law for our future.

Certainly the Great Depression in America is not our only example. Historically, major changes have occurred whenever major economic crisis has hit. The French Revolution was induced by incredible deprivation, resulting in runaway inflation and social crisis. This led the French down the path to a dictator. Napoleon came to power after the French Revolution.

Germany also experienced this same phenomenon after World War I. Great Britain and her allies from World War I began the first of many of a string of unintended consequences by attempting to punish Germany with punitive damages for its actions in the war, with reparations and debt repayments. This actually made the situation much worse. Not only did this engender anger, hostility, and resentment among the German citizenry being punished, but it also led to the complete destruction of their economy with rampant hyperinflation.

This was one of the worst cases of inflation in world history. Prices changed by the moment. Workers at the factories would literally receive their pay three times a day, then run to the fence and stuff the money through to their spouses, who would then run to the store to spend it before it became worthless. Restaurants stopped putting prices on the menus because the cost of the meal went up even as you ate. Runaway inflation destroyed the German economy, leading to incredible anger and resentment against England and her allies and directly contributing to the rise of a dictator who spoke of world domination.

THE FOURTH TURNING

In 1997, prior to the dot-com bubble, 9/11, and the real estate bubble, two historians, Neil Howe and the late William Strauss, published a book based on the study of history titled *The Fourth Turning*. I am amazed at their insight—indeed prophetic in many ways. It reminds me of the saying: "If man learns anything from history, it's that man learns nothing from history."

In their book, Strauss and Howe make the case that modern history moves in ever-advancing but repetitive cycles ("turnings"), each one lasting about eighty years, the length of a long human life. Each cycle is composed of four different generations or turnings. These four generations propel us through the four stages of a cycle: the survival of a great crisis, followed by confident expansion of the new order, followed by rebellion against the established order, followed by total individualism and a crumbling of order. Society gradually unravels until the next great crisis is thrust upon it, which begins the cycle anew.

Strauss and Howe believe America has already passed through three critical cycles of turnings. In each case, during the crisis or Fourth Turning, the country has the potential either to literally fall apart and be destroyed, or to endure the period of suffering and come out the other side poised to become a greater nation in the next generation.

The last cycle—or Fourth Turning—occurred during the Depression and

World War II. Following that, the most recent set of turnings are produced below:

1. The First Turning was the *American High* of the Truman, Eisenhower, and Kennedy presidencies. As World War II wound down, no one predicted that America would soon become so confident and institutionally muscular yet so conformist and spiritually complacent. But that's what happened.

2. The Second Turning was the *Conscious Revolution*, stretching from the campus revolts of the mid-1960s to the tax revolts of the early 1980s. Before John Kennedy was assassinated, no one predicted that America was about to enter an era of personal liberation and cross a cultural divide that would separate anything thought or said after from anything thought or said before. But that's what happened.

3. The Third Turning has been the *Culture Wars*, an era that began with Reagan's 1980s "Morning in America" and is due to expire around the middle of the Oh-Oh decade, eight or ten years from now [2005]. Amid the glitz of the early Reagan years, no one predicted that the nation was entering an era of national drift and institutional decay. But that's where we are.[1]

Remember that *The Fourth Turning* was written in 1997, prior to any of the recent national crises we have already faced and certainly before the current global economic crisis we are facing right now. Without a doubt, crisis will unfold in America and the world in the days ahead. It has been my desire that in the pages of this book you will find information and principles that you can use to get prepared to face the future.

In *The Fourth Turning*, the authors describe the combination of these events as a catalyst:

> The catalyst will unfold according to a basic crisis dynamic that underlies all of these scenarios: An initial spark will trigger a chain reaction of unyielding response and further emergencies. The core elements of these scenarios (debt, civic decay, global disorder) will matter more than the details, which the catalyst will juxtapose and connect in some unknowable way. If foreign societies are also entering a Fourth Turning, this could accelerate the chain reaction.

At home and abroad, these events will reflect the tearing of the civic fabric at points of extreme vulnerability—problem areas where, during the unraveling, America will have neglected, denied, or delayed needed action. Anger at "mistakes we made" will translate into calls for action, regardless of the heightened public risk. It is unlikely that the catalyst will worsen into a full-fledged catastrophe, since the nation will probably find a way to avert the initial danger and stabilize the situation for a while. The local rebellions will probably be quelled, terrorists foiled, fiscal crisis averted, disease halted, or war forever cooled. Yet even if consequences are temporarily averted, America will have entered the Fourth Turning.[2]

The authors liken these turnings to the four seasons and say that the Fourth Turning, like nature's winter, will come. It cannot be averted. They further describe America's Fourth Turning (our demographic winter) like this:

Around the year 2005, a sudden spark will catalyze a crisis mood. Remnants of the old social order will disintegrate. Political and economic trust will implode. Real hardship will beset the land, with severe distress that could involve questions of class, race, nation, and empire. Yet this time of trouble will bring seeds of social rebirth. Americans will share a regret about recent mistakes—and a resolute new consensus about what to do. The very survival of the nation will feel at stake. Sometime before the year 2025, America will pass through a great gate in history, commensurate with the American Revolution, Civil War, and twin emergencies of the Great Depression and World War II.

The risk catastrophe will be very high. The nation will erupt into insurrection or civil violence, crack up geographically, or succumb to authoritarian rule. If there is a war, it is likely to be one of maximum risk and effort—in other words, a total war.... This time, America will enter a Fourth Turning with the means to inflict unimaginable horrors and perhaps, will confront adversaries who possess the same.[3]

Crisis and pain ultimately can create positive responses and positive results, but it also has the potential for devastating or negative results. It is our purpose to alert as many Americans as possible to the dangers that we are facing over the next fifteen years or so and to sound the alarm—so that we may take the proper steps and not head in the wrong direction during these times of social change.

IT'S TIME TO TAKE RESPONSIBILITY RESPONSIBLY

If we are to avoid the perils that are facing us in our demographic winter, we must stop playing the blame game. We must take responsibility—and do so responsibly. America has seemingly become a nation of victims, each person blaming someone else for his or her problems. This has to stop.

In *The Fourth Turning*, Strauss and Howe warn us of the consequences if we fail to act.

> Before long, America's old civic order will seem ruined beyond repair. People will feel like a magnet has passed over society's disk drive, blanking out the social contract, wiping out old deals, clearing the books of vast unpayable promises to which people had once felt entitled. The economy could reach a trough that may look to be the start of a depression. With American weakness newly exposed, foreign dangers could erupt.[4]

What are the problems we need to address? Where do we need to act? Let's take a brief look at some of America's pressing problems where powerful interventions are needed if our future is to be secured.

The federal debt

If you look at the history of the growth of the federal debt during the best of economic times, over the last thirty years the national debt has gone up during both Republican and Democratic administrations. No one has balanced the budget for long.

This problem isn't caused by a lack of money. So many times we hear, "If we just had more money, we could solve these problems." The problem is that most of the time we are just flailing away at the symptoms, never dealing with root causes, and more money never seems to solve anything.

The growth of federal tax revenues over the last thirty years has been enormous, as the baby boomer generation drove America into the most economically productive time in all of recorded history. Yet Congress still managed to outspend its income, spending money on whatever social programs or pork-barrel projects they desired.

According to our proposed federal budget for 2010, the federal debt will continue to rise through the coming years. The gross domestic product has risen by an average of 2.65 percent per year since 1980. The average household has seen its income rise by 4.32 percent per year.[5] The revenue the federal government has to spend has risen at an even higher rate than either of these two numbers—a 7.1 percent rate per year, *almost double the average household*.[6] The government has gotten bigger pay raises than most in the private sector. The fact is that the growth of government revenue has greatly surpassed the growth of the economy. This should not be.

Long-term federal spending should be tied in some form or fashion to the economic growth rate. When the economy is growing at more rapid rates and you need more money to spend on roads, infrastructure, and necessary items, then the money is available. During boom times, you should be able to generate surpluses, as boom times generate higher levels of capital gains and business and personal taxes. If the economy begins to go into a tailspin, you may incur deficits for a while, but you can't continue to spend more money than you take each and every year, as we've been doing.

The biggest problems occur due to the fact that once a federal program gets put on the books, it is rarely taken off. Even when a program has run its useful life, it tends to become a permanent part of the federal bureaucracy. If this doesn't change soon, we are all about to be victims of a runaway government. The issue is not a lack of resources for the government to spend; the issue is a lack of effective management of those resources and government waste. This will be coming at America from all sides.

Strauss and Howe discuss the climax of a crisis in *The Fourth Turning* by saying:

> Imagine some national (and probably global) volcanic eruption, initially flowing along channels of distress that were created during the unraveling era and further widened by the catalyst. Trying to foresee where the eruption will go once it bursts free of the channels of distress that were created during the unraveling era and further widened by the catalyst. Trying to foresee where the eruption will go once it bursts free of the channels is like trying to predict the exact fault line of an earthquake.[7]

I believe that we are moving toward a crisis in federal spending. I remember times in the 1980s when organizations like the National Taxpayers Union were decrying defense department purchases of $150 hammers and $1,100 stepladders. Yet, if you track the growth of the federal spending, you will certainly find that the vast majority of the growth in federal spending over the past thirty years has not occurred due to defense spending.

The percentage of the federal budget that was spent on defense in 1970 was 48 percent.[8] By the year 2005 (with a war going on in Iraq and Afghanistan), defense spending only comprised 24 percent of the overall spending of the government.[9] Liberals who would love to blame everything on defense are off track. Yes, defense spending has certainly contributed to the debt, but it is not the primary problem today.

Runaway social spending

The real issue is runaway social spending. We are now at a point in time where social spending for all forms of government benefits has taken on a life of its own. Remember, the baby boomers have not yet begun to retire en masse, which will tax the system like nothing we have ever seen. We are in an unfortunate situation in that during the best of economic times in the last thirty years—the greatest boom in history economically—we have continued to spend more than we take in as a federal government almost every year and have accumulated some $11 trillion in debt (by June 2009) to show for it. This amounts to more than $137,000 per man, woman, and child in America! According to the National Debt Clock Web site, USDebtClock.org, contingent liabilities amount to $58.9 trillion (including Social Security, Medicare, etc.), or more than $191,000 per person. *The Fourth Turning* says that one of the "molten ingredients of the climax" of the fourth turning point in a civilization is "economic distress, with public debt in default, entitlement trust funds in bankruptcy, mounting poverty and unemployment, trade wars, collapsing financial markets, and hyperinflation (or deflation)."[10] If we can't live within our own means during good times, how in the world can we expect to live within our own means during challenging times?

This has far-reaching and potentially devastating social implications if allowed to continue. Remember that I mentioned the runaway inflation that Germany experienced after World War I, which led to the rise of a dictator. The runaway inflation rates that occurred prior to and during the French Revolution led to the rise of a dictator. We cannot afford to allow our country to go this direction. Read again the quote by Alexander Fraser Tytler.

> A democracy is always temporary in nature; it simply cannot exist as a permanent form of government. A democracy will continue to exist up until the time that voters discover they can vote themselves generous gifts from the public treasury.
>
> From that moment on, the majority always votes for the candidates who promise the most benefits from the public treasury, with the result that every democracy will finally collapse due to loose fiscal policy, which is always followed by a dictatorship.[11]

As Americans—black, white, liberal, conservative, Hispanic, Asian, environmentalist, Republican, Democrat, whatever—it does not matter what your personal philosophy is; we must all realize that runaway government threatens our very existence as a republic and a democracy within the next twenty years. Massive reforms are needed, and they are needed now.

A Cry for Change

It is highly likely that those who rise to power during the next fifteen years will help set the course for America over the next fifty years. Remember that during social and economic upheaval, the general populace will cry out for change, as they have been already. They want someone to take control of the problems and fix them, which was evident in our recent elections.

But change that merely brings more of what is already making us sick—bigger government and more regulations—will not solve the crisis. The problems we are facing today were not caused by a lack of government. They were not caused by failure to spend enough money at any level of state, federal, or local government. We need a strong government, a strong defense, and strong social systems—but we don't need to be living beyond our means. It is only common sense that you cannot live beyond your means forever and get away with it. It eventually comes back to haunt you.

If a family lives beyond its means for an indefinite period of time, eventually the creditors will figure this out. That family will no longer be able to borrow enough money to continue to float. Sooner or later, it will start robbing Peter to pay Paul, borrowing money in order to pay the interest on previous debts. If the family members continue to live beyond their means long enough, creditors eventually will catch up to them, and they will have to file for bankruptcy.

A corporation operates the same way. If a corporation tries accounting shenanigans like Enron, eventually their excesses will catch up with them, and as soon as they face an economic downturn, they go under.

Not so with the federal government. It has an unlimited money supply, the ability to create money out of thin air, which can postpone insolvency for a long period of time yet and could lead to an inevitably larger crisis in the time of disaster.

Early in 2008, when Bear Stearns was in jeopardy, our whole financial system was threatened. Had they been allowed to fail, Bear Stearns would have taken down many other firms.[12] There could have been a string of domino-effect failings among commercial and investment banks. One default would lead to another and another and another. Obviously, if a firm goes bankrupt and can't pay its creditors, then others can't pay the people they owe, and so forth. You start the string of dominos.

This is precisely what happened in the 1930s. All the upheaval led to one company falling, then another, until eventually the system contracted so severely that one-third of the banks failed and the country's money supply shrank by a third. We experienced a *deflationary* depression. This is not a good idea.

There are times when it is helpful, even necessary, for the government to bail out institutions in order to prevent the failure of an entire system. This is what happened when the government bailed out AIG. However, if we are not careful we will soon reach a point at which there is not enough money to go around for all of the bailing.

In *The Fourth Turning*, Strauss and Howe highlight the issue of leadership with these words:

> Soon after the catalyst, a national election will produce a sweeping polit-
> ical realignment, as one faction or coalition capitalizes on a new public
> demand for decisive action. Republicans, Democrats, or perhaps a new
> party will decisively win the long partisan tug-of-war, ending the era of
> split government that had lasted through four decades of awakening and
> unraveling. The winners will now have the power to pursue the more
> potent, less incrementalist agenda about which they had long dreamed
> and against which their adversaries had darkly warned. This new regime
> will enthrone itself for the duration of the crisis. Regardless of its ideology,
> the new leadership will assert public authority and demand private sacri-
> fice. Where leaders had once been inclined to alleviate societal pressures,
> they will now aggravate them to command the nation's attention.[13]

WHO WILL PAY FOR THE BOOMERS?

As boomers begin retiring en masse, this will create an enormous negative cash flow upon the government. Social Security, Medicare, and other programs. When push comes to shove, how do you pay for it all?

What if foreign investors who have gotten wind of our issues decide that they no longer want to invest a lot of their money in U. S. government debt? In Chart 12-A you will see the approximate percentage of our national debt that is currently owned by foreigners. We are literally no longer in control of our own destiny. Foreigners could, at the snap of a finger, pull their money out of our government debt and send the U.S. economy into a tailspin. If they did this, the bond market would likely immediately crash and interest rates would spike, throwing us into a horrendous recession or worse.

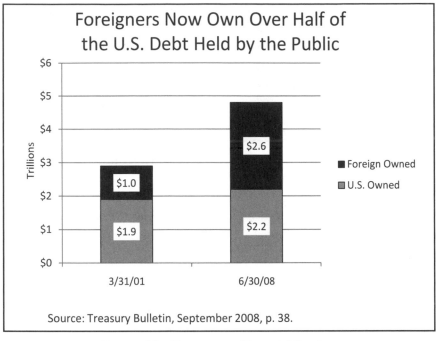

Foreigners Now Own Over Half of the U.S. Debt Held by the Public

Source: Treasury Bulletin, September 2008, p. 38.

Prepared by Cornerstone Financial Services
Chart 12-A

One of the shortcomings of our political system is that politicians face intense pressure to spend money on whatever the constituents are pushing them to address in order to get reelected. It is difficult for politicians in a political system in which they must run for reelection every two, four, or six years to focus on long-term economic problems that will take multiple years to fix, the benefits of which will not be seen for some time into the future, perhaps until after they're well out of office. This is one of the reasons that we have failed to remedy the Social Security and other entitlement problems up to this point.

Social Security is a political hot potato, referred to in Washington as "the Third Rail of American Politics." Talk about changing Social Security, and you are fried. (Imagine falling onto the tracks in a subway system and touching the middle or third rail, which is electrified—*fried!*)

Ready...Set...Apply

It's time to take action if you want a secure future for your family and yourself. This is a clarion call. If you love your country; if you love freedom; if you love the ability to work where you want to work, live where you want to live, travel; and if you value your lifestyle, not only for yourself but for your children and grandchildren—then you must take these issues seriously, *and the sooner the better.* As the crisis deepens, it will be much more difficult to navigate the ship. Any airline pilot can tell you the best plans are those that you make before the crisis, in preparation, not during the heat of the moment. So, what should we do?

Do not allow a runaway national debt

As a financial planner, we train people in the best ways to get out of debt. The best way to get out of debt is to first reduce your spending. By reducing the amount of money that you are spending, you create a surplus so that you can use that to pay your debts off. As a society we can do no different. Once the current deflationary crisis is over, we must rein in spending. The alternative is to inflate our way out of this, bankrupt our currency, and go through incredible social upheaval.

Once the baby boomers start retiring, we cannot just inflate our problems away, which would destroy our currency and threaten our very existence as a nation in its present form.

We need to make government lean and mean, cut back on unnecessary and harmful programs, and focus on making America as attractive of a location for business as we possibly can. This means *reducing* many present regulations that are pushing corporations to move from one state to another or to move offshore in order to escape a harsh and difficult environment. A hostile business environment pushes people to leave.

I am reminded of my studies as an undergraduate. If a professor had a reputation for being too difficult, guess what? People avoided his or her class like the plague. If you found out it was too difficult and the professor was unrealistic and too ideological in his or her viewpoint of things or in the way he or she taught the class, you would drop the class. These types of professors did not have big classes and were not popular teachers. The same analogy can be carried forward into a state-by-state analysis.

Encourage small business

Individual states in our country that create hostile environments for business will find more and more people and corporations fleeing the state, moving to a more hospitable state that gives them better tax policies and regulations. If we get into the type of environment in which the powers of government are making it increasingly difficult for people to stay in business and operate their businesses because of continuous government intervention, regulation, and difficult tax policies, people may leave and set up operations overseas.

The potential exists for individual states to enter a death spiral in which, because of adverse policies, more and more people flee the state to more hospitable areas.

A restaurant with bad service and bad food doesn't stay in business very long.

People are more attached to the places where they live and have grown up, so they are naturally resistant to moving. But, if you make them mad enough and make life miserable enough, they will move to a different locale. So, we must create the most attractive business environments that we can, with very favorable policies toward small businesses in particular, which is where the lion's share of all economic growth comes from. Over the past decade, small business net job creation fluctuated between 60 and 80 percent.

The more a state makes its policies business-friendly, the more people and corporations that state will attract. States that push *progressive* policies that continue to increase taxes and regulations will find, increasingly, that people are leaving that state, especially when more difficult times come.

Face the challenge and come back stronger

America is facing unprecedented challenges. The next fifteen to twenty-plus years have the potential to be some of the more challenging times in our country's history. Looking at the challenges we have faced as a country, we have been through some big ones. In each case, because the fabric of the country was good, because the principles that we were founded upon were based upon absolute truth, in each case our country came back and became stronger than it was before. My hope and prayer is that we will do the same this time.

I'm reminded of an old Yogi Berra story. Yogi was catching for the New York Yankees back during the 1950s, during one of their great World Series runs. Yogi had a funny way of phrasing his sentences. He'd say things like, "It's like déjà vu all over again," or, "When you come to a fork in the road, take it." He was always serious, never intending verbal faux pas. A few years later, Yogi's son Dale was a catcher in the minor leagues trying to make it with the Yankees. Reporters asked him if he was like his dad, to which he replied, "No, our similarities are different."[14]

Well, there are similarities between the current economic climate and that of the 1930s, but the similarities truly are different. The main difference is that today, unlike the 1930s, everything that goes wrong gets bailed out.

However, as a long-term optimist, I remain optimistic that God does have His hand upon America. I remain optimistic that when push comes to shove, eventually the right leaders will come to the fore and take the reins to bring positive reformation to our system rather than "fiddle while Rome burns." Will you be involved? Will you become proactive, and will you take a role in the preservation and reformation of our country? It must be reformed and changed from the inside out.

CONCLUSION

ARE YOU READY?

W E HAVE MOVED off the ancient paths and toward a destiny that many of us may not enjoy. *World government, socialistic programs,* and *control*—those are words that should strike fear in the hearts of our generation. Indeed, we stand to potentially lose all our fathers fought and died for. During the next fifteen years, the destiny of our nation may be determined.

In every generation, events occur that give our country the opportunity to choose to seek God or not. Our nation was founded by godly men and women seeking refuge from religious persecution who risked everything to establish a new world, a world established upon the benefits of freedom—freedom from tyranny, freedom of religion, freedom from religious and political persecution. Though the risks were high and the costs were grave, the price was paid, and a new self-governing experiment was launched that ultimately changed the world.

"If the Son gives you freedom, you are free" (John 8:36, CEV)! America, with its godly roots of education and government, while leading the world militarily and economically for the last century, has experienced the most freedom and economic prosperity in the world today. But America has strayed.

Are you prepared to apply the principles you have learned in this book to secure your future? We must do more than merely secure our financial future. Are you prepared to fight a battle to return this nation to our godly heritage? The choice is ours—invest our hearts, minds, and souls to secure a godly, prosperous future for our families and ourselves in America, or, like biblical Esau, sell our birthright and nation for a mess of pottage.

In James 1:5 we read, "If any of you lacks wisdom, he should ask God, who gives generously to all without finding fault, and it will be given to him." The bottom line is that He will give you wisdom liberally, but there are conditions. The conditions are:

1. You have to ask for wisdom in the first place.

2. You have to believe that God is willing to answer and that you are capable of understanding. (For those reading this book who

are not believers, I would quote the old TV commercial: "Try it; you'll like it!" I believe that God is a prayer-hearing and prayer-answering God.)

3. You must act upon the wisdom you receive.

There you have God's definition of *financial triage*! In this book, I can do nothing more than be a watchman. In Ezekiel 3:17, God told Ezekiel, "Ezekiel, son of man, I have appointed you to stand watch for the people of Israel. So listen to what I say, then warn them for me" (CEV). In Bible times, gatekeepers were positioned on the walls of Jerusalem above the gates to keep watch for enemies who were coming to attack the city. If the gatekeeper saw the enemy coming and he did not alert the city, then he failed to do his job. God says of those gatekeepers, "I will hold you accountable for his blood" (Ezek. 33:8). On the other hand, if the people were warned and they didn't listen, the responsibility was theirs; their blood was on their own heads.

I believe our nation has a calling from God. Our founding fathers believed that we were supposed to be a light to the world and a city on a hill. Freedom has produced incredible prosperity in unparalleled amounts for our country.

It took an enormous amount of research to expose and examine so many years of economic history in this book. We began by taking a look the Cycle of Liberty, showing how civilizations cycle through a life span from beginning to end. Where is America on this cycle? I believe that we are currently moving from fear to dependency and on toward bondage. I have wondered where America's leaders have been as inch by inch we have crept around through these cycles, moving slowly toward the end.

We are supposed to leave an inheritance for our children's children. This legacy does not consist just of money, but it is the economic, political, cultural, and spiritual freedom for generations to come.

Are you ready to join in the battle to secure your family's future? Are you alert to the times we are in? Are we a generation of true truth seekers, or are we "always learning but never able to acknowledge the truth" (2 Tim. 3:7)?

Are we givers or takers? If the laws change regarding taxation, will we still give to those in need even if we cannot *deduct* it?

Will we become a people who will *choose to live simply so that others can simply live*? Will we break out of a mentality of poverty and lack?

Will we tackle the seemingly unattainable? Will we believe God makes us creative and desires us to "be fruitful and multiply"? Will we risk it all for the sake of the next generation? Will we be a generation that writes *a new economic manifesto* over our lives and our children's lives?

Will we refuse dependency on government and all the *isms* that have been allowed to take root in our nation, or will we become a people of quitters and slaves?

There is an interesting story in the Bible that parallels where I believe we stand in America today. After the Israelites were let out of bondage in Babylon and were allowed to return to Jerusalem, they quickly rebuilt their homes. However, they failed to rebuild the house of the Lord—the temple. Through the prophet Haggai, God reprimanded the Israelites, saying:

> Now this is what the LORD Almighty says: "Give careful thought to
> your ways. You have planted much, but have harvested little. You eat,
> but never have enough. You drink, but never have your fill. You put
> on clothes, but are not warm. You earn wages, only to put them in
> a purse with holes in it...Give careful thought to your ways. Go up
> into the mountains and bring down timber and build the house, so
> that I may take pleasure in it and be honored," says the LORD. "You
> expected much, but see, it turned out to be little. What you brought
> home, I blew away. Why?...Because of my house, which remains a
> ruin, while each of you is busy with his own house. Therefore, because
> of you the heavens have withheld their dew and the earth its crops.
> I called for a drought on the fields and the mountains, on the grain,
> the new wine, the oil and whatever the ground produces, on men and
> cattle, and on the labor of your hands."
>
> —HAGGAI 1:5–11

America was founded on godly principles. But as we have moved slowly away from our foundation, we have moved through the cycles, closer and closer to bondage again. It's time for America to "give careful thought to your ways." Without the godly foundations that birthed America, it will not be possible to secure our future.

Will this generation of baby boomers heed the call to "give careful thought to your ways"? Will we apply powerful, godly principles and interventions to the current demographic winter that can propel us forward through the dark night into the beauty of springtime? Let's not leave a legacy of debt and dependency but a legacy of hope for the next generation.

It has been my desire in this book to do much more than describe the economic crisis that is facing our world. I want you to be able to develop a treatment plan that will eliminate the unhealthy symptoms from your personal finances. I want the principles in this book to empower you to deal with these symptoms to the point that you actually experience relief.

I believe that if you will consistently use the principles outlined in this book, you will discover:

- An understanding of the worldwide economic crisis and how it impacts you and your family;

- A clear vision of your financial goals for becoming a better steward of the assets God has entrusted to you;

- A step-by-step program that will allow you, over time, to build a better and more prosperous financial future for you and your loved ones; and

- True financial success—success reflected by heart attitudes, motives, and behavior, not by the quantity of money.

Some of us will be called to manage small assets, like the widow with the mite. Others may be called to manage large assets. Our success will be found in how well we manage what God has entrusted to us. Remember the words of Jesus in Matthew 7:24–27. He said the person who hears His words and puts them into practice is like the man who built his house on the rock. Even when storms came, the man's house was secure because it had a solid foundation. The foolish person who ignores His commandments is like the man who built his house on sand. When the winds came, it was blown away.

This demographic winter had a beginning—and it will have an end. The economy will repeatedly cycle up into springtime and summer, and cycle back down into fall and winter over the long run. But your financial prosperity does not need to rise and fall with every economic wave that rushes through the world. We've shown you how to assess your own financial situation and to determine what you need to do. We've shown you how to develop wise solutions to weather our current financial storm and those that come after it. And you can now apply the powerful interventions for our country that will give you and your loved ones a secure future.

You can have financial order in your household and in your business. If you are married, you and your spouse can work together in unity toward your goals and dreams. The principles of God remain the same, and He only desires for you to seek Him and to walk in His ways.

WHAT IN THE WORLD IS GOING ON?

A Global Intelligence Briefing for CEOs

By Herbert Meyer[1]

This is a paper presented in early 2007 (prior to the 2008 meltdown) by Herb Meyer—a very good summary of today's key trends and a perspective one seldom sees.

Meyer served during the Reagan administration as special assistant to the director of central intelligence and vice chairman of the CIA's National Intelligence Council. In these positions, he managed production of the U.S. National Intelligence Estimates and other top-secret projections for the president and his national security advisers. Meyer is widely credited with being the first senior U.S. government official to forecast the Soviet Union's collapse, for which he later was awarded the U.S. National Intelligence Distinguished Service Medal, the intelligence community's highest honor. Formerly an associate editor of *Fortune*, he is also the author of several books.

FOUR MAJOR TRANSFORMATIONS

Currently, there are four major transformations that are shaping political, economic, and world events. These transformations have profound implications for American business leaders and owners, our culture, and on our way of life.

1. The War in Iraq

There are three major monotheistic religions in the world: Christianity, Judaism, and Islam.

In the sixteenth century, Judaism and Christianity reconciled with the modern world. The rabbis, priests and scholars found a way to settle up and pave the way forward. Religion remained at the center of life, church and state became separate. Rule of law, the idea of economic liberty, individual rights, human rights—all these are defining points of modern Western civilization. These concepts started with the Greeks but didn't take off until the fifteenth and sixteenth century when Judaism and Christianity found a way to reconcile with the modern world. When that happened, it unleashed the scientific revolution and the greatest outpouring of art, literature, and music the world has ever known.

Islam, which developed in the seventh century, counts millions of Moslems

215

around the world who are normal people. However, there is a radical streak within Islam. When the radicals are in charge, Islam attacks Western civilization. Islam first attacked Western civilization in the seventh century, and later in the sixteenth and seventeenth centuries. By 1683, the Moslems (Turks from the Ottoman Empire) were literally at the gates of Vienna. It was in Vienna that the climatic battle between Islam and western civilization took place. The West won and went forward. Islam lost and went backward. Interestingly, the date of that battle was September 11. Since then, Islam has not found a way to reconcile with the modern world.

Today, terrorism is the third attack on Western civilization by radical Islam. To deal with terrorism, the U.S. is doing two things. First, units of our armed forces are in thirty countries around the world, hunting down terrorist groups and dealing with them. This gets very little publicity. Second we are taking military action in Afghanistan and Iraq.

These actions are covered relentlessly by the media. People can argue about whether the war in Iraq is right or wrong. However, the underlying strategy behind the war is to use our military to remove the radicals from power and give the moderates a chance. Our hope is that, over time, the moderates will find a way to bring Islam forward into the twenty-first century. That's what our involvement in Iraq and Afghanistan is all about.

The lesson of 9/11 is that we live in a world where a small number of people can kill a large number of people very quickly. They can use airplanes, bombs, anthrax, chemical weapons or dirty bombs. Even with a first-rate intelligence service (which the U.S. does not have), you can't stop every attack. That means our tolerance for political horseplay has dropped to zero. No longer will we play games with terrorists or weapons of mass destructions.

Most of the instability and horseplay is coming from the Middle East. That's why we have thought that if we could knock out the radicals and give the moderates a chance to hold power; they might find a way to reconcile Islam with the modern world. So when looking at Afghanistan or Iraq, it's important to look for any signs that they are modernizing.

For example: women being brought into the work force and colleges in Afghanistan is good. The Iraqis stumbling toward a constitution is good. People can argue about what the U.S. is doing and how we're doing it, but anything that suggests Islam is finding its way forward is good.

2. The Emergence of China

In the last twenty years, China has moved 250 million people from the farms and villages into the cities. Their plan is to move another 300 million in the next twenty years. When you put that many people into the cities, you have to find work for them. That's why China is addicted to manufacturing; they have to put all the relocated people to work. When we decide to manufacture something in the U.S., it's based on market needs and the opportunity to make a profit. In China, they make the decision because they want the jobs, which is a very different calculation.

While China is addicted to manufacturing, Americans are addicted to low prices. As a result, a unique kind of economic codependency has developed between the two countries. If we ever stop buying from China, they will explode politically. If China stops selling to us, our economy will take a huge hit because prices will jump. We are subsidizing their economic development; they are subsidizing our economic growth.

Because of their huge growth in manufacturing, China is hungry for raw materials, which drives prices up worldwide. China is also thirsty for oil, which is one reason oil is now at $100 a barrel. By 2020, China will produce more cars than the U.S. China is also buying its way into the oil infrastructure around the world. They are doing it in the open market and paying fair market prices, but millions of barrels of oil that would have gone to the U.S. are now going to China. China's quest to assure it has the oil it needs to fuel its economy is a major factor in world politics and economics.

We have our Navy fleets protecting the sea lines, specifically the ability to get the tankers through. It won't be long before the Chinese have an aircraft carrier sitting in the Persian Gulf as well. The question is, will their aircraft carrier be pointing in the same direction as ours or against us?

3. Shifting Demographics of Western Civilization

Most countries in the Western world have stopped breeding. For a civilization obsessed with sex, this is remarkable. Maintaining a steady population requires a birth rate of 2.1. In Western Europe, the birth rate currently stands at 1.5, or 30 percent below replacement. In thirty years there will be seventy- to eighty-million fewer Europeans than there are today. The current birth rate in Germany is 1.3. Italy and Spain are even lower at 1.2. At that rate, the working age population declines by 30 percent in twenty years, which has a huge impact on the economy. When you don't have young workers to replace the older ones, you have to import them.

The European countries are currently importing Moslems. Today, the Moslems comprise 10 percent of France and Germany, and the percentage is rising rapidly because they have higher birthrates. However, the Moslem populations are not being integrated into the cultures of their host countries, which is a political catastrophe. One reason Germany and France don't support the

Iraq war is they fear their Moslem populations will explode on them. By 2020, more than half of all births in the Netherlands will be non-European.

The huge design flaw in the postmodern secular state is that you need a traditional religious society birth rate to sustain it. The Europeans simply don't wish to have children, so they are dying. In Japan, the birthrate is 1.3. As a result, Japan will lose up to sixty million people over the next thirty years. Because Japan has a very different society than Europe, they refuse to import workers. Instead, they are just shutting down. Japan has already closed two thousand schools, and is closing them down at the rate of three hundred per year. Japan is also aging very rapidly. By 2020, one out of every five Japanese will be at least seventy years old. Nobody has any idea about how to run an economy with those demographics.

Europe and Japan, which comprise two of the world's major economic engines, aren't merely in recession—they're shutting down. This will have a huge impact on the world economy, and it is already beginning to happen. Why are the birthrates so low? There is a direct correlation between abandonment of traditional religious society and a drop in birth rate, and Christianity in Europe is becoming irrelevant.

The second reason is economic. When the birth rate drops below replacement, the population ages. With fewer working people to support more retired people, it puts a crushing tax burden on the smaller group of working age people. As a result, young people delay marriage and having a family. Once this trend starts, the downward spiral only gets worse. These countries have abandoned all the traditions they formerly held in regard to having families and raising children.

The U.S. birth rate is 2.0, just below replacement. We have an increase in population because of immigration. When broken down by ethnicity, the Anglo birth rate is 1.6 (same as France) while the Hispanic birth rate is 2.7. In the U.S., the baby boomers are starting to retire in massive numbers. This will push the elder dependency ratio from 19 to 38 over the next ten to fifteen years. This is not as bad as Europe, but still represents the same kind of trend.

Western civilization seems to have forgotten what every primitive society understands—you need kids to have a healthy society. Children are huge consumers. Then they grow up to become taxpayers. That's how a society works, but the postmodern secular state seems to have forgotten that. If U.S. birth rates of the past twenty to thirty years had been the same as post-World War II, there would be no Social Security or Medicare problems.

The world's most effective birth control device is money. As society creates a middle class and women move into the workforce, birth rates drop. Having large families is incompatible with middle class living.

The quickest way to drop the birth rate is through rapid economic development.

After World War II, the U.S. instituted a $600 tax credit per child. The idea was to enable mom and dad to have four children without being troubled by taxes. This led to a baby boom of twenty-two million kids, which was a huge consumer market. That turned into a huge tax base. However, to match that incentive in today's dollars would cost $12,000 per child.

China and India do not have declining populations. However, in both countries, there is a preference for boys over girls, and we now have the technology to know which is which before they are born. In China and India, families are aborting the girls. As a result, in each of these countries there are 70 million boys growing up who will never find wives.

When left alone, nature produces 103 boys for every 100 girls. In some provinces, however, the ratio is 128 boys to every 100 girls.

The birth rate in Russia is so low that by 2050 their population will be smaller than that of Yemen. Russia has one-sixth of the earth's land surface and much of its oil. You can't control that much area with such a small population. Immediately to the south, you have China with seventy million unmarried men who are a real potential nightmare scenario for Russia.

4. Restructuring of American Business

The fourth major transformation involves a fundamental restructuring of American business. Today's business environment is very complex and competitive. To succeed, you have to be the best, which means having the highest quality and lowest cost. Whatever your price point, you must have the best quality and lowest price. To be the best, you have to concentrate on one thing. You can't be all things to all people and be the best.

A generation ago, IBM used to make every part of their computer. Now Intel makes the chips, Microsoft makes the software, and someone else makes the modems, hard drives, monitors, etc. IBM even outsources their call center. Because IBM has all these companies supplying goods and services cheaper and better than they could do it themselves, they can make a better computer at a lower cost. This is called a fracturing of business. When one company can make a better product by relying on others to perform functions the business it used to do itself, it creates a complex pyramid of companies that serve and support each other.

This fracturing of American business is now in its second generation.

The companies who supply IBM are now doing the same thing—outsourcing many of their core services and production process. As a result, they can make cheaper, better products. Over time, this pyramid continues to get bigger and bigger. Just when you think it can't fracture again, it does.

Even very small businesses can have a large pyramid of corporate entities that perform many of its important functions. One aspect of this trend is that companies end up with fewer employees and more independent contractors.

This trend has also created two new words in business, integrator and complementor. At the top of the pyramid, IBM is the integrator. As you go down the pyramid, Microsoft, Intel and the other companies that support IBM are the complementors. However, each of the complementors is itself an integrator for the complementors underneath it.

This has several implications, the first of which is that we are now getting false readings on the economy. People who used to be employees are now independent contractors launching their own businesses. There are many people working whose work is not listed as a job. As a result, the economy is perking along better than the numbers are telling us.

Outsourcing also confused the numbers. Suppose a company like General Motors decides to outsource all its employee cafeteria functions to Marriott (which it did). It lays off hundreds of cafeteria workers, who then get hired right back by Marriott. The only thing that has changed is that these people work for Marriott rather than GM. Yet, the media headlines will scream that America has lost more manufacturing jobs. All that really happened is that these workers are now reclassified as service workers. So the old way of counting jobs contributes to false economic readings. As yet, we haven't figured out how to make the numbers catch up with the changing realities of the business world.

Another implication of this massive restructuring is that because companies are getting rid of units and people that used to work for them, the entity is smaller. As the companies get smaller and more efficient, revenues are going down but profits are going up. As a result, the old notion that revenues are up and we're doing great isn't always the case anymore. Companies are getting smaller but are becoming more efficient and profitable in the process.

IMPLICATIONS OF THE FOUR TRANSFORMATIONS

1. The War in Iraq

In some ways, the war is going very well. Afghanistan and Iraq have the beginnings of a modern government, which is a huge step forward. The Saudis are starting to talk about some good things, while Egypt and Lebanon are beginning to move in a good direction. A series of revolutions have taken place in countries like Ukraine and Georgia.

There will be more of these revolutions for an interesting reason. In every revolution, there comes a point where the dictator turns to the general and says, "Fire into the crowd." If the general fires into the crowd, it stops the revolution. If the general says "No," the revolution continues. Increasingly, the generals are saying "No" because their kids are in the crowd.

Thanks to TV and the Internet, the average eighteen-year old outside the U.S. is very savvy about what is going on in the world, especially in terms of popular culture. There is a huge global consciousness, and young people around the world want to be a part of it. It is increasingly apparent to them that the miserable government where they live is the only thing standing in their way. More and more, it is the well-educated kids, the children of the generals and the elite, who are leading the revolutions.

At the same time, not all is well with the war. The level of violence in Iraq is much worse and doesn't appear to be improving. It's possible that we're asking too much of Islam all at one time. We're trying to jolt them from the seventh century to the twenty-first century all at once, which may be further than they can go. They might make it and they might not. Nobody knows for sure. The point is, we don't know how the war will turn out. Anyone who says they know is just guessing.

The real place to watch is Iran. If they actually obtain nuclear weapons it will be a terrible situation. There are two ways to deal with it. The first is a military strike, which will be very difficult. The Iranians have dispersed their nuclear development facilities and put them underground. The U.S. has nuclear weapons that can go under the earth and take out those facilities, but we don't want to do that.

The other way is to separate the radical mullahs from the government, which is the most likely course of action. Seventy percent of the Iranian population is under 30. They are Moslem but not Arab. They are mostly pro-Western. Many experts think the U.S. should have dealt with Iran before going to war with Iraq. The problem isn't so much the weapons; it's the people who control them. If Iran has a moderate government, the weapons become less of a concern.

We don't know if we will win the war in Iraq. We could lose or win. What we're looking for is any indicator that Islam is moving into the twenty-first century and stabilizing.

2. China

It may be that pushing five hundred million people from farms and villages into cities is too much too soon. Although it gets almost no publicity, China is experiencing hundreds of demonstrations around the country, which is unprecedented. These are not students in Tiananmen Square. These are average citizens who are angry with the government for building chemical plants and polluting the water they drink and the air they breathe.

The Chinese are a smart and industrious people. They may be able to pull it off and become a very successful economic and military superpower. If so, we will have to learn to live with it. If they want to share the responsibility of keeping the world's oil lanes open, that's a good thing.

They currently have eight new nuclear electric power generators under way and forty-five on the books to build. Soon, they will leave the U.S. way behind in their ability to generate nuclear power.

What can go wrong with China? For one, you can't move 550 million people into the cities without major problems. Two, China really wants Taiwan, not so much for economic reasons—they just want it. The Chinese know that their system of communism can't survive much longer in the twenty-first century. The last thing they want to do before they morph into some sort of more capitalistic government is to take over Taiwan.

We may wake up one morning and find they have launched an attack on Taiwan. If so, it will be a mess, both economically and militarily. The U.S. has committed to the military defense of Taiwan. If China attacks Taiwan, will we really go to war against them? If the Chinese generals believe the answer is no, they may attack. If we don't defend Taiwan, every treaty the U.S. has will be worthless. Hopefully, China won't do anything stupid.

3. Demographics

Europe and Japan are dying because their populations are aging and shrinking. These trends can be reversed if the young people start breeding. However, the birth rates in these areas are so low it will take two generations to turn things around. No economic model exists that permits fifty years to turn things around. Some countries are beginning to offer incentives for people to have bigger families. For example, Italy is offering tax breaks for having children. However, it's a lifestyle issue versus a tiny amount of money. Europeans aren't willing to give up their comfortable lifestyles in order to have more children. In general, everyone in Europe just wants it to last a while longer.

Europeans have a real talent for living. They don't want to work very hard. The average European worker gets four hundred more hours of vacation time per year than Americans. They don't want to work and they don't want to make any of the changes needed to revive their economies.

The summer after 9/11, France lost fifteen thousand people in a heat wave. In August, the country basically shuts down when everyone goes on vacation. That year, a severe heat wave struck and fifteen thousand elderly people living in nursing homes and hospitals died. Their children didn't even leave the beaches to come back and take care of the bodies. Institutions had to scramble to find enough refrigeration units to hold the bodies until people came to claim them. This loss of life was five times bigger than 9/11 in America, yet it didn't trigger any change in French society.

When birth rates are so low, it creates a tremendous tax burden on the young. Under those circumstances, keeping mom and dad alive is not an attractive option. That's why euthanasia is becoming so popular in most European countries. The only country that doesn't permit (and even encourage) euthanasia is Germany, because of all the baggage from World War II. The European economy is beginning to fracture. Countries like Italy are starting to talk about pulling out of the European Union because it is killing them. When things get bad economically in Europe, they tend to get very nasty politically. The canary in the mine is anti-Semitism. When it goes up, it means trouble is coming. Current levels of anti-Semitism are higher than ever. Germany won't launch another war, but Europe will likely get shabbier, more dangerous and less pleasant to live in.

Japan has a birth rate of 1.3 and has no intention of bringing in immigrants. By 2020, one out of every five Japanese will be seventy years old. Property values in Japan have dropped every year for the past fourteen years. The country is simply shutting down. In the U.S. we also have an aging population. Boomers are starting to retire at a massive rate. These retirements will have several major impacts:

1. Possible massive selloff of large four-bedroom houses and a movement to condos.

2. An enormous drain on the treasury. Boomers vote, and they want their benefits, even if it means putting a crushing tax burden on their kids to get them. Social Security will be a huge problem. As this generation ages, it will start to drain the system. We are the only country in the world where there are no age limits on medical procedures.

3. An enormous drain on the health care system. This will also increase the tax burden on the young, which will cause them to delay marriage and having families, which will drive down the birth rate even further.

4. Although scary, these demographics also present enormous opportunities for products and services tailored to aging populations. There will be tremendous demand for caring for

older people, especially those who don't need nursing homes but need some level of care. Some people will have a business where they take care of three or four people in their homes. The demand for that type of service and for products to physically care for aging people will be huge.

Make sure the demographics of your business are attuned to where the action is. For example, you don't want to be a baby food company in Europe or Japan.

Demographics are much underrated as an indicator of where the opportunities are. Businesses need customers. Go where the customers are.

4. Restructuring of American Business

The restructuring of American business means we are coming to the end of the age of the employer and employee. With all this fracturing of businesses into different and smaller units, employers can't guarantee jobs anymore because they don't know what their companies will look like next year. Everyone is on their way to becoming an independent contractor.

The new workforce contract will be: Show up at my office five days a week and do what I want you to do, but you handle your own insurance, benefits, health care and everything else. Husbands and wives are becoming economic units. They take different jobs and work different shifts depending on where they are in their careers and families. They make tradeoffs to put together a compensation package to take care of the family.

This used to happen only with highly educated professionals with high incomes. Now it is happening at the level of the factory floor worker.

Couples at all levels are designing their compensation packages based on their individual needs. The only way this can work is if everything is portable and flexible, which requires a huge shift in the American economy.

The U.S is in the process of building the world's first twenty-first century model economy. The only other countries doing this are U.K. and Australia. The model is fast, flexible, highly productive and unstable in that it is always fracturing and re-fracturing. This will increase the economic gap between the U.S. and everybody else, especially Europe and Japan.

At the same time, the military gap is increasing. Other than China, we are the only country that is continuing to put money into their military. Plus, we are the only military getting on-the-ground military experience through our war in Iraq. We know which high-tech weapons are working and which ones aren't. There is almost no one who can take us on economically or militarily.

There has never been a superpower in this position before. On the one hand, this makes the U.S. a magnet for bright and ambitious people. It also makes us a target.

We are becoming one of the last holdouts of the traditional Judeo-Christian culture. There is no better place in the world to be in business and raise children. The U.S. is by far the best place to have an idea, form a business and put it into the marketplace.

We take it for granted, but it isn't as available in other countries of the world. Ultimately, it's an issue of culture. The only people who can hurt us are ourselves, by losing our culture. If we give up our Judeo-Christian culture, we become just like the Europeans.

The culture war is the whole ballgame. If we lose it, there isn't another America to pull us out.

NOTES

INTRODUCTION

1. Harry S. Dent, *The Great Boom Ahead* (New York: Hyperion Books, 1993).

CHAPTER ONE
PARADIGM SHIFT IN REAL TIME

1. "Humanist Manifesto I," *American Humanist Association*, accessed at http://www.americanhumanist.org/Who_We_Are/About_Humanism/Humanist_Manifesto_I, on July 14, 2009.

2. "Humanist Manifesto II," *American Humanist Association*, accessed at http://www.americanhumanist.org/who_we_are/about_humanism/Humanist_Manifesto_II, on July 14, 2009.

3. "America, the Beautiful" words by Katharine Lee Bates. Public domain.

4. For more information about the 2009 Barna Group poll, see http://www.barna.org/barna-update/article/12-faithspirituality/260-most-american-christians-do-not-believe-that-satan-or-the-holy-spirit-exis, accessed July 14, 2009.

5. "Fannie and Freddie's refi plans differ," *HSH Associates Financial News Blog*, accessed at http://www.blogcatalog.com/blog/hsh-associates-financial-news-blog/d611e1a948ca1087f889625398d40114, on July 14, 2009.

6. Alexander Fraser Tyler [Tytler], "Cycle of Democracy (1770)," *Famous Quotes*, accessed at http://www.famousquotessite.com/famous-quotes-6934-alexander-fraser-tyler-cycle-of-democracy-1770.html, on July 14, 2009.

7. "What Is the Tytler Cycle?" *Project Liberty*, August 22, 2008, accessed at http://projectlibertyutah.blogspot.com/2008/08/what-is-tytler-cycle-where-is-united.html, on August 6, 2009.

8. Benjamin Franklin, at the close of the Constitutional Convention of 1787, accessed at http://www.bartleby.com/73/1593.html, on July 14, 2009.

9. Jim Collins, *Good to Great* (New York: HarperCollins, 2001).

CHAPTER TWO
FALLACIES THAT RULE THE WORLD

1. "Thomas Robert Malthus," *Biographies*, accessed at http://www.blupete.com/Literature/Biographies/Philosophy/Malthus.htm, on July 13, 2009.

2. This paragraph was adapted from Phillip Longman, *The Empty Cradle* (New York: Basic Books, 2004), 133.

3. David Morris, "Ethanol and Land Use Changes," *Policy Brief*, February 2008, accessed at http://www.bioenergywiki.net/images/1/10/Morris_Ethanol-and-Land-Use.pdf, on August 5, 2009.

4. "Biofuel Crops That Require Destroying Native Ecosystems Worsens Global Warming, *Science Daily*, February 11, 2008, accessed at http://www.sciencedaily .com/releases/2008/02/080207140809.htm, on August 5, 2009.

5. Michael B. McElroy, "The Ethanol Illusion," *Harvard Magazine*, November–December 2006, accessed at http://harvardmagazine.com/2006/11/the-ethanol -illusion.html, on July 27, 2009.

6. Roberta F. Mann and Mona L. Hymel, "Moonshine to Motorfuel: Tax Incentives for Fuel Ethanol," accessed at http://www.law.duke.edu/shell/cite.pl?19+Duke +Envtl.+L.+&+Pol'y+F.+43, on August 5, 2009.

7. Mark Steyn, "Chickenfeedhawks: Global Warm-Mongering," *Greenie Watch*, accessed at http://antigreen.blogspot.com/2008_05_01_archive.html, on July 14, 2009.

8. "Moving Millions Rebuild a Nation," *China Daily*, October 2, 2004, accessed at http://www.china.org.cn/english/China/108570.htm, on July 14, 2009.

9. "Meeting the Needs of a Hungry World," *Center for Global Food Issues*, April 29, 2005, accessed at http://www.cgfi.org/tag/hungrey-world/, on July 14, 2009.

10. "Should We All Be Vegetarians?" *Time* magazine, July 15, 2002, accessed at http://www.whatisaids.com/timevegetarians.htm, on July 14, 2009.

11. Joel K. Bourne Jr., "The Global Food Crisis, " *National Geographic,* June 2009, accessed at http://ngm.nationalgeographic.com/2009/06/cheap-food/bourne -text/1, on July 14, 2009.

12. For more information about The Club of Rome, see http://www.clubofrome .org/eng/home/, accessed on July 13, 2009.

13. "The U.S. Economy at the Beginning and End of the 20th Century," *Joint Economic Committee of the United States Congress*, December 1999, accessed at http://usinfo.org/enus/economy/overview/docs/century.pdf, on July 14, 2009.

14. Paul Ehrlich, *Population Bomb* (New York: Ballantine Books, rev. 1971).

15. David Cork, *The Pig in the Python* (Toronto: Stoddart Books, 1996).

16. "The U.S. Population Is Aging," *Urban Institute*, accessed at http://www .urban.org/retirement_policy/agingpopulation.cfm, on July 14, 2009.

17. Francis Bator, "LBJ and the Vietnam/Great Society Connection," *American Academy of Arts and Sciences*, 2007, accessed at http://www.amacad.org/ publications/BatorWeb.pdf, on July 14, 2009.

18. Information in this paragraph was obtained from a 2002 CNBC Broadcast.

19. Information in this table was obtained from The Heritage Foundation.

20. "Timeline: The Pill," *PBS Home Programs*, accessed at http://www.pbs.org/ wgbh/amex/pill/timeline/timeline2.html, on July 14, 2009.

21. "Legalized Abortion," *Political Base*, accessed at http://www.politicalbase .com/issues/legalized-abortion/1/, on July 14, 2009.

22. Milton Friedman, "Famous Quotes by Milton Friedman," *Book of Famous Quotes*, accessed at http://www.famous-quotes.com/author.php?aid=2647, on July 29, 2009.

23. Robert Barro and Xavier Sala-i-Martin, *Economic Growth* (Cambridge, MA: The MIT Press, 2003).

24. "State of the Social Security and Medicare Programs," Actuarial Publications, *Social Security Online,* accessed at http://www.ssa.gov/OACT/TRSUM/index .html, on July 15, 2009; see also Bruce Schobel, "Social Security Income and Outgo," *American Academy of Actuaries,* accessed at http://www.acsw.us/spring06/ 06%20Schobel%20-%20Future%20of%20SS.pdf, on July 15, 2009.

25. Bill Gross, "'Bon' or 'Non' Appétit?" Investment Outlook, *PIMCO,* accessed at http://www.pimco.com/LeftNav/Featured+Market+Commentary/IO/2009/ Investment+Outlook+July+2009+Gross+Appetit.htm, on July 24, 2009.

26. For more information about the decade of deflation in Japan during the late '80s and early '90s, see Gary Saxonhouse, *Japan's Lost Decade* (Hoboken, NJ: Wiley-Blackwell, 2004).

27. William Overholt, "Asia's Continuing Crisis," p. 5, accessed at http://www .phy.duke.edu/~myhan/overholt.pdf, on July 15, 2009.

28. "Nikkei 225 Hit All-Time High of 38,957.00 on December 29th, 1989," *Dave Manuel,* accessed at http://www.davemanuel.com/2009/04/16/20-years-later-and-the -nikkei-225-still-hasnt-recovered-or-come-even-close-to-recovering/, on July 15, 2009.

29. Chart 2-F may be accessed at http://www2.standardandpoors.com/spf/xls/ index/S500EPSEST.XLS.

30. "Global Income Per Capita," *World Bank Development Indicators,* accessed at http://web.worldbank.org/WBSITE/EXTERNAL/DATASTATISTICS/ 0,,contentMDK:21298138~pagePK:64133150~piPK:64133175 ~theSitePK:239419,00.html, on July 15, 2009.

31. "How to Become a Millionaire During the Depression," *Money Management Solutions,* June 11, 2008, accessed at http://moneymgmtsolutions.com/blog/debt -consolidation/how-to-become-a-millionaire-during-the-depression/, on July 15, 2009.

32. "Thomas Robert Malthus," *Wikipedia, the free encyclopedia,* accessed at http://en.wikipedia.org/wiki/Thomas_Robert_Malthus, on August 7, 2009.

33. "The Population Bomb," *Wikipedia, the free encyclopedia,* accessed at http:// en.wikipedia.org/wiki/The_Population_Bomb, on August 6, 2009.

34. "Club of Rome," *Wikipedia, the free encyclopedia,* accessed at http:// en.wikipedia.org/wiki/Club_of_Rome, on August 6, 2009.

Chapter Three
Bubble, Bubble, Toil, and Trouble

1. Thomas Jefferson, *The Works of Thomas Jefferson,* Federal Edition, 12 vols. (New York and London, G.P. Putnam's Sons, 1904–1905).

2. Hester Capital Management, L.L.C., *Capital Chronicle,* October 24, 2008, accessed at http://www.capital-chronicle.com/, on July 15, 2009.

3. "Glut: 5.1 Million Homes for Sale," *Los Angeles Times,* accessed at http:// latimesblogs.latimes.com/laland/2007/09/glut-51-million.html, on July 15, 2009.

4. Information from this table was obtained from Harry S. Dent.

5. Martin J. Pring, *Investment Psychology Explained* (Hoboken, NJ: Wiley, 1995).

6. Gibbons Burke, "How to Tell a Market by Its Covers," All Business, April 1, 1993, accessed at http://www.allbusiness.com/specialty-businesses/367410-1.html, on August 6, 2009.

7. Richard Greenberg and Chris Hansen, *The Hansen Files*, MSNBC, March 22, 2009, accessed at http://www.msnbc.msn.com/id/29827248/ns/dateline_nbc-the_hansen_files_with_chris_hansen/, on July 15, 2009.

8. Michael Lewis, "The End of Wall Street's Boom," *Condé Nast Portfolio*, December 2008, accessed at http://www.portfolio.com/news-markets/national-news/portfolio/2008/11/11/The-End-of-Wall-Streets-Boom, on July 13, 2009.

9. "An Overview of the Housing Crisis and Why There Is More Pain to Come," T2 Partners LLC, *Scribd*, accessed at http://www.scribd.com/doc/17131576/The-Housing-Crisis-By-T2-Partners, on July 15, 2009.

10. Ibid.

11. "An Overview of the Housing/Credit Crisis and Why There Is More Pain to Come," *T2 Partners, LLC*, April 3, 2009, accessed at http://www.scribd.com/doc/14166113/T2-Partners-Presentation-on-the-Mortgage-Crisis4309-3, on August 7, 2009.

12. Martin Pring, *Investment Psychology Explained*.

13. Information in this table was obtained from T2 Partners LLC.

14. Charles MacKay, *Extraordinary Popular Delusions and the Madness of Crowds* (NP: Wilder Publications, 2009.

Chapter Four
Bracing for the Big Chill

1. *Gary Shilling Insight*, July 2009.

2. "An Overview of the Housing Crisis and Why There Is More Pain to Come," T2 Partners LLC.

3. Ibid.

4. Ibid.

5. Carmen M. Reinhart and Kenneth S. Rogoff, "The Aftermath of Financial Crises," December 19, 2008, accessed at http://www.economics.harvard.edu/files/faculty/51_Aftermath.pdf, on July 21, 2009.

6. Federal Reserve Flow of Funds Accounts of the United States, IMF Global Financial Security Report, October 2008, Goldman Sachs Global Economics Paper No. 177, FDIC Quarterly Banking Profile, OFHEO, S&P Leverage Commentary and Data, T2 Partners estimates.

7. Information in this table was obtained from T2 Partners LLC.

8. Chart 4-J may be accessed at www.chartoftheday.com.

9. Kimberly Amadeo, "Savings and Loans Crisis," *About.com: US Economy*, accessed at http://useconomy.about.com/od/grossdomesticproduct/p/89_Bank_Crisis.htm, on July 16, 2009.

10. This information was obtained from Cornerstone Financial Services.

11. Harry S. Dent, July 2009.

12. From an interview on CNBC, cited by Gabriel Madway, "Paulson: Subprime mortgage fallout 'largely contained'," *Market Watch*, March 13, 2007, accessed at http://www.marketwatch.com/story/paulson-subprime-mortgage-fallout-largely -contained, on July 16, 2009.

13. From a speech given to Congress, cited by Jeannine Aversa, "Bernanke says no recession in sight," *The Seattle Times*, March 28, 2007, accessed at http:// seattletimes.nwsource.com/html/businesstechnology/2003639710_webbernanke28 .html, on July 16, 2009.

14. In a speech to The Committee of 100 in New York, cited in "Subprime woes likely contained: Treasury's Paulson," *Reuters*, April 20, 2007, accessed at http://www.reuters.com/article/gc06/idUSWBT00686520070420, on July 16, 2009; and in Wanfeng Zhou, "Paulson urges China to make yuan more flexible," *Market Watch*, April 20, 2007, accessed at http://www.marketwatch.com/story/ treasurys-paulson-urges-china-to-make-yuan-more-flexible, on July 16, 2009.

15. From a speech before the Federal Reserve Bank of Chicago, cited in Evelyn M. Rusli, "Bernanke Believes Housing Mess Contained," May 17, 2007, *Forbes.com*, accessed at http://www.forbes.com/2007/05/17/bernanke-subprime-speech-markets -equity-cx_er_0516markets02.html, on July 16, 2009.

16. From a conversation with President George W. Bush, cited in Marc Gunther, "Paulson to the rescue," *CNN Money*, September 16, 2007, accessed at http:// money.cnn.com/2008/09/13/news/newsmakers/gunther_paulson.fortune/index2 .htm, on July 16, 2009.

17. From an interview in Washington, cited in Kevin Carmichael and Peter Cook, "Paulson says subprime rout doesn't threaten economy," *Bloomberg.com*, July 26, 2007, accessed at http://www.bloomberg.com/apps/news?pid=20601087&sid=aM y9XODlJOnc&refer=home, on July 16, 2009.

18. From the transcript of Secretary Paulson's Press Roundtable in Beijing, China, on August 1, 2007, *Press Room, U.S. Department of the Treasury*, accessed at http://www.treas.gov/press/releases/hp525.htm, on July 16, 2009.

19. From comments presented before the Senate Banking Committee about the economy, cited in Chris Isidore, "Paulson, Bernanke: Slow Growth Ahead," *CNN Money.com*, February 14, 2008, accessed at http://money.cnn.com/2008/02/14/ news/economy/bernanke_paulson/index.htm, on July 16, 2009.

20. From comments presented to the Senate Banking Committee, cited in Alistair Bull, "US Banks Should Seek More Capital—Bernanke," *Reuters*, February 28, 2008, accessed at http://www.reuters.com/article/bankingFinancial/ idUSN2857366320080228, on July 16, 2009.

21. From an interview published in the *Wall Street Journal* on May 7, 2008, cited in "Paulson says worst of financial crisis is over," *Thomson Financial News, Forbes.com*, accessed at http://www.forbes.com/feeds/afx/2008/05/07/afx4978703 .html, on July 16, 2009.

22. From a speech to business executives in Washington, cited in "Markets Calmer, says Treasury Secretary," *CBSNews.com*, May 16, 2008, accessed at http:// www.cbsnews.com/stories/2008/05/16/business/main4103698.shtml?source=RSSattr =Business_4103698, on July 16, 2009.

23. From remarks to the Boston Federal Reserve's 52nd annual economic conference in Massachusetts, cited in Craig Torres and Scott Lanman, "Bernanke Says Risk of 'Substantial Downturn' Has Diminished," *Bloomberg.com*, June 9, 2008, accessed at http://www.bloomberg.com/apps/news?pid=20601087&sid=aH6u3wsqw MFM&refer=worldwide, on July 16, 2009.

24. From an interview on *Face the Nation* on CBS, July 20, 2008, cited in "Paulson: U.S. Banking System Fundamentally Sound," *Reuters*, accessed at http:// www.cnbc.com/id/25764545/, on July 16, 2009.

25. "Excerpts from Geithner's speech on bank plan," *Reuters*, February 10,2009, accessed at http://www.reuters.com/article/ousiv/idUSTRE5194C920090210?sp =true, on July 16, 2009.

26. From a transcript of President Obama's news conference on March 24, 2009, accessed at http://www.nytimes.com/2009/03/24/us/politics/24text-obama.html, on July 16, 2009.

27. From remarks to the Economic Club of Washington, cited in Corbett B. Daly and David Lawder, "Summers says economic 'free-fall' to end soon," *Reuters*, April 10, 2009, accessed at http://www.reuters.com/article/ousiv/ idUSTRE53859920090409, on July 16, 2009.

28. From an address to students and faculty of Morehouse College in Atlanta, cited in Ben Rooney, "Bernanke sees 'signs' decline is easing," *CNNMoney.com*, April 14, 2009, accessed at http://money.cnn.com/2009/04/14/news/economy/ Bernanke/index.htm, on July 16, 2009.

CHAPTER FIVE
BOOMERNOMICS: PENSIONS AND RETIREMENT ISSUES

1. Information in this table was obtained from National Economic Accounts.

2. Harry S. Dent Demographic School, August 9, 2008.

3. Robert T. Kiyosaki and Sharon Lechter, *Rich Dad's Prophecy* (Boston, MA: Business Plus, 2004, originally Warner Books, 2002), 23, 55, 70.

4. Ibid.

5. Standard & Poor's, Harry S. Dent Demographic School, August 9, 2008.

6. Dave Barry, *Miami Herald* Syndicated Columnist, September 24, 2000.

7. Pamela Villarreal, "Social Security and Medicare Projections: 2008," *National Center for Policy Analysis*, April 30, 2008, accessed at http://www.ncpa.org/pub/ba616, on July 17, 2009.).

8. "Expectation of Life at Birth, 1970 to 2005, and Projections, 2010 to 2020," *U.S. Census Bureau*, accessed at http://www.census.gov/compendia/statab/tables/09s0100.pdf, on July 17, 2009.

9. "Live Long and Prosper," Rollins Capital Management, *The Educated Investor*, accessed at http://www.rollinscapital.com/downloads/Live_Long.pdf, on July 17, 2009.

10. Alan Greenspan, testimony before the House Budget Committee, February 25, 2004.

11. "National Commission on Social Security Reform (aka The Greenspan Commission)," *Social Security History Online*, accessed at http://www.ssa.gov/history/greenspn.html, on July 17, 2009.

12. Chart 5-F may be accessed at www.bea.gov/bea/da/nipaweb/TableView.asp?SelectedTable=85&FirstYear=20028&LastYear=2004&Freq=Qtr.

13. Information in this table was obtained from CBO.gov.

14. Chart 5-G may be accessed at http://www.whitehouse.gov/amb/budget/fy2008/pdf/hist.pdf.

15. Jim Rogers interview with *MoneyNews*, cited at Dan Weil, "Rogers: America Bordering on Communism," July 15, 2009, accessed at http://moneynews.newsmax.com/streettalk/jim_rogers/2009/07/15/235777.html, on July 24, 2009.

16. George Will, "The Recidivist Congress," *Real Clear Politics*, February 1, 2009, accessed at http://www.realclearpolitics.com/articles/2009/02/the_recidivist_congress.html, on July 24, 2009.

17. Don Luskin, "Social Security: There Is No Trust Fund, Only IOU's," *Capitalism Magazine*, April 11, 2005, accessed at http://www.capmag.com/article.asp?ID=4190, on July 17, 2009.

18. Peter Peterson, *Gray Dawn* (New York: Three Rivers Press, 2000).

19. Ken Dychtwald and Joe Flower, *Age Wave* (New York: Bantam, 1990).

20. Charles Balhous, originally appearing in the *Wall Street Journal*, June 10, 2004; also cited in "Social Security This Week," *Social Security Choice*, June 11, 2004, accessed at http://www.socialsecurity.org/sstw/sstw06-11-04.pdf, on July 17, 2009.

CHAPTER SIX
INFANTS, IMMIGRATION, ADOPTION—CREATING THE *NEXT* BOOM

1. Phillip Longman, *The Empty Cradle* (New York: Basic Books, 2004).

2. "Current World Population," *About.com: Geography*, accessed at http://geography.about.com/od/obtainpopulationdata/a/worldpopulation.htm, on July 17, 2009.

3. *Demographic Winter: The Decline of the Human Family*, directed by Rick Stout and Steven Smoot, produced by Barry McLerren (SRB Documentary, LLC, 2009).

4. "Replacement Level Fertility and Population Growth," *PubMed NCBI*, accessed at http://www.ncbi.nlm.nih.gov/pubmed/7834459, on July 17, 2009.

5. Gary S. Becker, "Missing Children of the World," *WSJ Opinion Archives*, September 3, 2006, accessed at http://www.opinionjournal.com/extra/?id=110008892, on July 17, 2009.

6. Phillip Longman, *The Empty Cradle*.

7. The statistics in this paragraph are taken from *Demographic Winter: The Decline of the Human Family*.

8. Harry S. Dent, "HS Dent Monthly Economic Forecast," *HS Dent*, August 8, 2008, accessed at http://www.hsdent.com/economicforecast/?gclid=CMrD6Mn E3ZsCFUdM5QodP1iS_A, on July 17, 2009.

9. Britta Hoem and Jan Hoem, "Sweden's Family Policies and Roller Coaster Fertility," accessed at http://www.ipss.go.jp/syoushika/bunken/data/pdf/16896401.pdf, on July 17, 2009.

10. "Total Fertility Rate: Sweden 1970–2007," August 6, 2008, accessed at http://micpohling.wordpress.com/2008/08/06/total-fertility-rate-sweden-1970-2007/, on July 17, 2009.

11. "German Women Take the Rap for Declining Birth Rate," *DW-World.de*, April 25, 2006, accessed at http://www.dw-world.de/dw/article/0,,1980293,00.html, on July 17, 2009.

12. Mark Steyn, *America Alone* (Washington, D.C.: Regnery Publishing, 2008).

13. Ibid.

14. Phillip Longman, *The Empty Cradle*.

15. Ibid.

16. U.S. Social Security Administration, "Facts and Figures About Security, 2004."

17. Ibid.

18. Ibid.

19. Phillip Longman, *The Empty Cradle*.

20. *Demographic Winter: The Decline of the Human Family*.

21. Phillip Longman, *The Empty Cradle*.

22. Ibid.

23. "Humanist Manifesto II," *American Humanist Association*.

24. Nicholas Eberstadt, "Too Many People?" *International Policy Network*, accessed at http://www.sdnetwork.net/files/pdf/Too%20Many%20People_%20web.pdf, on August 4, 2009.

25. Phillip Longman, *The Empty Cradle*.

26. Ibid.

27. "Foreign-Born Population in the U.S.: 1850–1930, 1960–1990, 2004," *InfoPlease: Society and Culture*, accessed at http://www.infoplease.com/ipa/A0778579.html, on July 20, 2009.

28. Newt Gingrich, *Winning the Future* (New York: Regnery Publishing, 2006), 91.

29. Phillip Longman, *The Empty Cradle*.

CHAPTER SEVEN
GROWING YOUR WAY INTO PROSPERITY

1. "A 125-Year Picture of the Federal Government's Share of the Economy, 1950 to 2075," *Congressional Budget Office*, accessed at http://www.cbo.gov/doc.cfm? index=3521&type=0, on July 20, 2009.

2. Hoisington Investment Management Company, *Quarterly Review and Outlook*, Second Quarter 2009.

3. Harry S. Dent, "The Right Tool for Predicting and Capitalizing on Today's Market Opportunities," *HS Dent Economic Forecast*, August 8, 2008, accessed at http://www.hsdent.com/economicforecast/?gclid=CMTtkaS55JsCFU1M5QodHg ObAw, on July 20, 2009.

4. Dennis Nishi, "How Buck Knives Decided to Move HQ," *Wall Street Journal*, July 14, 2009, accessed at http://bx.businessweek.com/employee-relocation/view?url=http%3A%2F%2Fonline.wsj.com%2Farticle%2FSB124760533703141285 .html%3Fmod%3Ddist_smartbrief, on July 20, 2009.

5. Kim Web, "Luxury Tax Rides Off Into the Sunset," *Kiplinger Report*, November 15, 2002, accessed at http://www.highbeam.com/doc/1G1-123379236 .html, on July 20, 2009.

6. Herb Meyer, "What in the World Is Going On? A Global Intelligence Briefing for CEOs," accessed at http://www.nnseek.com/e/uk.local.manchester/herb_meyer_ at_the_world_economic_forum_in_davos_sw_118690975m.html, on July 24, 2009.

7. Jim Collins and Jerry Porras, *Built to Last* (New York: HarperCollins, 2004).

8. Jim Collins, *Good to Great*, Introduction.

9. Ibid., 86.

10. There are numerous accounts of the Battle of the Alamo available online. One account may be seen at http://www.destination360.com/north-america/us/ texas/the-alamo, on July 20, 2009.

11. William Barret Travis, "To the President of the Convention, March 3, 1836," *William Barret Travis—Alamo Letters*, accessed at http://www.ntanet.net/travis. html, on July 20, 2009.

12. Kennedy Hickman, "Texas Revolution: Battle of San Jacinto," *About.com: Military History*, accessed at http://militaryhistory.about.com/od/battleswars1800s/ p/sanjacinto.htm, on July 20, 2009.

13. George Santayana, "The Life of Reason, Volume 1 (1905)," *The Quotations Page*, accessed at http://www.quotationspage.com/quote/2042.html, on August 4, 2009.

14. Alexander Fraser Tyler [Tytler], "Cycle of Democracy (1770)."

Chapter Eight
Globalization: The Future That Has Yet to Be Written

1. Mark L. Arch, "The Echo Boom Generation: A Growing Force in American Society," *The Futurist*, September 1, 2000, accessed at http://www.allbusiness.com/professional-scientific/scientific-research/621952-1.html, on July 20, 2009.

2. Barry Asmus, *Bulls Don't Blush, Bears Don't Die* (Marietta, GA: AmeriPress, 2006), 55.

3. Adam Smith, with Introduction by Alan B. Krueger, *The Wealth of Nations* (New York: Bantam Books, 2003).

4. Italics added. Peter Marshall and David Manuel, *The Light and the Glory* (Grand Rapids, MI: Fleming H. Revell, Co., 1977), 141.

5. "The Declaration of Independence of the Thirteen Colonies," *School of Law, Indiana University*, accessed at http://www.law.indiana.edu/uslawdocs/declaration.html, on July 20, 2009.

6. Barry Asmus, *Bulls Don't Blush, Bears Don't Die.*

7. Ibid.

8. Ibid.

9. 2009 Index of Economic Freedom (Washington D.C.: The Heritage Foundation and Dow Jones & Company, Inc. 2009), at http://heritage.org/index; International Monetary Fund, World Economic Outlook database, April 2007, at http://www.imf.org/external/pubs/ft/weo/2008/01/weodata/index.aspx.

10. Henry Weaver, *The Mainspring of Human Progress* (New York: The Foundation for Economic Education, 1965).

11. Barry Asmus, *Bulls Don't Blush, Bears Don't Die.*

12. Ibid.

13. William J. H. Boetcker, "Facsimile Documents," *Illinois Historic Preservation Agency*, accessed at http://www.state.il.us/HPA/facsimiles.htm on August 4, 2009.

14. Ben Bernanke, "Embracing the Challenge of Free Trade: Competing and Prospering in a Global Economy," from a presentation at the Montana Economic Development Summit 2007, May 1, 2007, accessed at http://www.federalreserve.gov/newsevents/speech/bernanke20070501a.htm, on July 20, 2009.]]

15. Barry Asmus, *Bulls Don't Blush, Bears Don't Die.*

16. Calvin Coolidge, *The Quotations Page,* accessed at http://www.quotationspage.com/quote/34545.html on August 4, 2009.

17. Barry Asmus, *Bulls Don't Blush, Bears Don't Die.*

18. BCA Research, January 2007; *Wall Street Journal,* October 17, 2005; The Bank Credit Analyst, July 2006.

19. Barry Asmus, *Bulls Don't Blush, Bears Don't Die.*

20. Ibid.

21. Thomas Friedman, *The World Is Flat* (New York: Farrar, Strauss, and Giroux, 2006).

22. "What Is the Tytler Cycle?" *Project Liberty*.

CHAPTER NINE
TRIAGE

1. Ben Bernanke, cited in "Bernanke sees possible end to recession in 2009," *USA Today*, February 25, 2009, accessed at http://www.usatoday.com/money/economy/2009-02-24-bernanke-economy_N.htm, on July 21, 2009.

2. James Stockdale, cited in Jim Collins, *Good to Great*.

3. Carmen M. Reinhart and Kenneth S. Rogoff, "The Aftermath of Financial Crises."

4. Warren Buffett, quoted in "Buffett warns on investment 'time bomb'," *BBC News*, March 4, 2003, accessed at http://news.bbc.co.uk/2/hi/business/2817995.stm, on July 31, 2009.

5. "OCC's Quarterly Report on Bank Trading and Derivatives Activities Fourth Quarter 2007," *Comptroller of the Currency, Administrator of National Banks*, accessed at http://www.occ.treas.gov/ftp/release/2008-36a.pdf, on July 29, 2009.

6. "Facts on Policy: Consumer Spending," Hoover Institution, *Stanford University*, December 19, 2006, accessed at http://www.hoover.org/research/factsonpolicy/facts/4931661.html, on July 29, 2009.

7. Alexandra Twin, "Stocks at 12-year lows," *CNN Money*, March 3, 2009, accessed at http://money.cnn.com/2009/03/03/markets/markets_newyork/index.htm, on July 22, 2009.

8. "2008 Stock Market Crash Analysis for Testing Times," *Online Stock Trading Guide*, Harold Bierman, "The 1929 Stock Market Crash," *EH.net*, accessed at http://eh.net/encyclopedia/article/Bierman.Crash, on July 22, 2009.

9. Kimberly Armadeo, "The US National Debt and How It Got So Big," *About .com: US Economy*, accessed at http://useconomy.about.com/od/fiscalpolicy/p/US_Debt.htm, on July 22, 2009.

10. "Federal Government Debt Report," *Grandfather Economic Report Series*, accessed at http://home.att.net/~mwhodges/debt.htm, on July 22, 2009.

11. Peter Lynch and John Rothschild, *One Up on Wall Street* (New York: Simon and Schuster, 2000).

12. You can find more information about Berkey water filters at http://www.berkeyfilters.com.

13. "Disaster Preparedness Shopping List," *Defense Commissary Agency*, accessed at http://www.commissaries.com/documents/disaster_preparednessshoppinglist.pdf http://www.commissaries.com/documents/disaster_preparednessshoppinglist.pdf, on August 3, 2009.

14. See Genesis 41:46–49.

15. See 2 Timothy 1:7.

CHAPTER TEN
GRIZZLIES VS. BLACK BEARS

1. *Sy Harding's Street Smart Report*, www.StreetSmartReport.com, accessed on August 6, 2009.

2. Ibid.

3. Ibid.

4. Prepared by Cornerstone Financial Services, created with TradeStation.

5. *Sy Harding's Street Smart Report*, www.StreetSmartReport.com, accessed on August 6, 2009.

6. "Forex Market," accessed at www.autocurrency trading.com/forex_market.aspx on August 18, 2009.

CHAPTER ELEVEN
WEATHERING THE FINANCIAL STORM

1. Adapted from Jerry and Ramona Tuma, *Smart Money* (Dallas, TX: Cornerstone Financial Services, rev. 2003, 1994), 187–209.

2. Thomas J. Stanley and William D. Danko, *The Millionaire Next Door* (New York: Pocket Books, 1999).

3. Adapted from the summary for Thomas J. Stanley and William D. Danko, *The Millionaire Next Door* (New York: Pocket Books, 1999), accessed at http://www.bizsum.com/articles/art_the-millionaire-next-door.php, on July 22, 2009.

4. Thomas J. Stanley and William D. Danko, *The Millionaire Next Door*, 3–4.

5. Thomas J. Stanley, PhD, *The Millionaire Mind* (Riverside, NJ: Andrews McMeel Publishing, 2001).

6. "Buy and Hold," *Wikipedia, the Free Encyclopedia*, accessed at http://en.wikipedia.org/wiki/Buy_and_hold, on July 22, 2009.

7. "Absolute Return Investing," *Absolute Investment Advisors*, accessed at http://www.absoluteadvisers.com/ari.htm, on July 22, 2009.

8. James Stockdale, cited in Jim Collins, *Good to Great*.

9. Christian Tondo, "Effects of the dot-com crash on pensions in industrialized countries," accessed at http://www.watsonwyatt.com/pubs/directions/media/2009_EU_12059_Directions_04_dot-com_web.pdf, on July 22, 2009.

10. Jeremy Siegel, *The Future for Investors*.

11. Jeremy Siegel, *Stocks for the Long Run* (Columbus, OH: McGraw-Hill, 3rd edition 2002).

12. "Reserve Currency: China Says Move Beyond the US Dollar, Calls for a New Super-Sovereign Currency," *Economy Watch*, June 29, 2009, accessed at http://www.economywatch.com/economy-business-and-finance-news/reserve-currency-china-says-move-beyond-the-US-dollar-calls-for-new-super-sovereign-currency-06-29.html, on July 29, 2009.

13. "Growing Energy Demand in India and China," *Energy Business Reports*, October 2007, accessed at http://www.rcscarchandmarkets.com/reports/563478, on July 23, 2009.

14. Martin Hutchinson, "Auto Industry Moves to India and China," *Money Morning*, accessed at http://www.moneymorning.com/2008/01/14/auto-industry -moves-to-india-and-china/, on July 23, 2009.

15. "Infrastructure in China," *Electronic Product News*, accessed at http://www .epn-online.com/page/37042/infrastructure-in-china.html, on July 23, 2009.

16. "Tata Nano geared up for grand launch," *InfiBeam*, accessed at http://news .infibeam.com/blog/news/2009/02/25/tata_nano_geared_up_for_grand_launch .html, on July 23, 2009.

17. Mark Magnier, "India's Tata Motors unveils the world's cheapest car," *Los Angeles Times*, March 24, 2009, accessed at http://articles.latimes.com/2009/ mar/24/world/fg-india-car24, on July 23, 2009.

18. Information in this table was obtained from U.S. Energy Information Agency.

19. Ibid.

20. Governor John Winthrop, "A Model of Christian Charity," accessed at http:// religiousfreedom.lib.virginia.edu/sacred/charity.html, on July 22, 2009.

CHAPTER TWELVE
THE CALL

1. William Strauss and Neil Howe, *The Fourth Turning* (New York: Broadway, 1997), 5–6.

2. Ibid., 272–274.

3. Ibid., 6.

4. Ibid., 275–276.

5. "The Perfect Economic Storm," accessed at http://finance.baylor.edu/ financialcrisis/docs/The%20Perfect%20Economic%20Storm.pdf, on July 23, 2009.

6. Grover Norquist, "We Can't Keep Spending Like This," *National Review Online*, July 12, 2006, accessed at http://article.nationalreview.com/?q=NzFjOTE5N ?F.?NjF5MzUxN2IxNGFjYjE4ODUzN2VlZGQ=, on July 23, 2009.

7. William Strauss and Neil Howe, *The Fourth Turning*, 277–278.

8. "United States Federal State and Local Government Spending, Fiscal Year 1970 in $ Billion," *USGovernmentSpending.com*, accessed at http://www .usgovernmentspending.com/year1970_0.html, on July 23, 2009.

9. "United States Federal State and Local Government Spending, Fiscal Year 2005 in $ Billion," *USGovernmentSpending.com*, accessed at http://www .usgovernmentspending.com/year2005_0.html, on July 23, 2009.

10. William Strauss and Neil Howe, *The Fourth Turning*, 277.

11. Alexander Fraser Tyler [Tytler], "Cycle of Democracy (1770)."

12. David Ellis and Tami Luhby, "JP Morgan scoops up troubled Bear," *CNNMoney.com*, March 17, 2008, accessed at http://money.cnn.com/2008/03/16/news/companies/jpmorgan_bear_stearns/index.htm, on July 23, 2009.

13. William Strauss and Neil Howe, *The Fourth Turning*, 275.

14. "Yogi Berra Sayings," *RetroGalaxy.com*, accessed at http://www.retrogalaxy.com/sports/yogi-berra.asp, on July 23, 2009.

APPENDIX A

1. This excerpt is from a speech by Herb Meyer, "What in the World Is Going On? A Global Intelligence Briefing for CEOs."

INDEX

EDUCATION

A graduate of the University of Texas at Arlington (BBA, 1979), Jerry studied under one of the nation's top economic forecasters, a disciple of Nobel Prize–winning economist Milton Friedman, and is currently completing his master's with the College for Financial Planning in Denver, Colorado.

AUTHOR

Jerry has authored his own monthly newsletter, *The Cornerstone Report*, since 1984, and contributes to numerous nationwide publications. Jerry and his wife, Ramona, wrote their first book, *Smart Money*, which looks at your temperament and how it affects your financial behavior.

RADIO, TELEVISION, CONFERENCES

A nationally acclaimed speaker on the economy and investment markets, Jerry is a frequent guest of both local and national radio and television shows, and a regular speaker at investment conferences. Jerry has done daily and weekly radio programs discussing financial topics, investments, and the economy since 1981, and currently hosts the nationally syndicated financial show *Smart Money*.

CONTACT INFORMATION

To contact Jerry about possible
speaking engagements, or to inquire
about a consultation:

14901 Quorum Dr. Suite 785
Dallas, Texas 75254
Phone: 800-327-4285
Fax: 972-241-9541
Email: info@emailcfs.com
CornerstoneReport.com

Jerry E. Tuma, CFP™
A Certified Financial Planner™
professional, Jerry Tuma is presi-
dent and founder of Cornerstone
Financial Services, Inc., a Regis-
tered Investment Advisor. Jerry
is a Registered Principal with
Cambridge Legacy Securities,
LLC., member FINRA/SIPC &
MSRB registered.